Women, Power,
and Economic Change
The Nandi of Kenya

Women, Power, and Economic Change

The Nandi of Kenya

REGINA SMITH OBOLER

STANFORD UNIVERSITY PRESS 1985
STANFORD, CALIFORNIA

Stanford University Press, Stanford, California

© 1985 by the Board of Trustees of the
Leland Stanford Junior University

Printed in the United States of America

CIP data appear at the end of the book

Photographs courtesy of Leon Oboler

For the Nandi people, and for Leon

Preface

WHEN I began intensive reading of ethnography as a graduate student of anthropology, I noticed, as many others have, the surprisingly small extent to which women emerge as social actors in most ethnographic accounts. It seemed to me that this was particularly true of writings about East Africa. Thus, when I arrived in Kenya in 1976 to do fieldwork for my doctoral dissertation in anthropology, one of my goals was to help fill this gap. I chose to do fieldwork specifically among the Nandi for several reasons. First, published descriptions of the Nandi seemed to me especially deficient in the area of gender. Second, I was interested in the impact of socioeconomic change on sex roles, and Nandi was said to be an area in which agricultural change and the penetration of the cash economy were particularly marked. Third, I was interested in examining the institution of woman-woman marriage among other aspects of gender roles, and I knew that it had traditionally been practiced in Nandi; I had been told, further, that it was still extant. Fourth, as I tried to form a general picture of sex roles among various East African ethnic groups by reading published accounts and by talking and corresponding with scholars, I became intrigued by the great variation I encountered in assessments of Nandi women's "status." Finally, one East Africanist to whom I wrote for advice about choosing a field site described Nandi District as "one of the most beautiful spots on earth." He was not wrong.

This book, a revision of my doctoral dissertation, is based on fieldwork conducted in Nandi District between April 1976 and December 1977. For eighteen months of this period, my husband and I lived in one community, Kaptel Sublocation of Chemundu Location. I make no attempt to disguise the identity of our major field site, since anyone who wished to learn where we lived could easily do so. I have tried, however, to protect the identities of individuals. In the case studies and quotations in the pages that follow, names and minor details are changed. Our friends and informants will nevertheless recognize themselves in some of the cases related here, and I hope they will feel that I have represented them and their situations fairly and accurately. In several places in the text, I cite the expenses and profits of various economic activities in Kenya shillings. The reader should know that, in 1977, eight Kenya shillings were the equivalent of one American dollar.

Funding for my research was provided by the National Science Foundation and the Woodrow Wilson National Fellowship Foundation Women's Studies Program in 1975–76, and by a National Institute for Mental Health Predoctoral Fellowship from 1976 to 1978. During my stay in Kenya I was a Research Associate of the Institute for Development Studies of the University of Nairobi.

I am indebted to the District Commissioner for Nandi and the government administrative staff for Nandi who facilitated the research. Special thanks for help in starting and continuing the research are due to the following people: Josephine Kamau of the Institute for Development Studies; S. M. Seba of the National Museums of Kenya; Alice Gold, an American historian who began research in Nandi District shortly before we arrived there; Joyce Scott, Michelle and Graham Naude, and other friends at the Kapsabet Bible Institute; Enos Ashimala of the Anglican Church Training Centre; Elijah Terer, then Chief of Sang'alo Location; and Stanley Ng'etich, then Chief of Chemundu Location. The success of the project was due in large part to the work of two first-rate research assistants, Jennifer Jeptoo Kosut (now Maindi) and Peter Kipserem Bungei. Joel Kibiwot Tuwei also served ably, though briefly, as an assistant. Amos Kipchirchir Korir helped me on two continents; he befriended us in Nandi, and later as a student in the United States he clarified various ethnographic points and read and commented on sections of the manuscript.

The people who were most important to this research, and to

whom I must express the deepest gratitude, are the residents of Kaptel Sublocation who generously shared their lives with us. It is impossible to mention them all by name. Paulo Lelei, Subchief for Kaptel at the time of our stay, helped in a great many ways. Kipketer Mosop introduced us to Kaptel, and he and Vincent Karoney convinced us to make it our research site and arranged living quarters for us. William Sang' assisted in the collection of census data in Kaptel. Warmest thanks to Samson and Leah Kerich, their children Willie, Cheruiyot, Sabania, and Chepchumba, and to Grace Chelemek and Kobot Kiberen, who accepted us as members of their family.

I am particularly grateful to my dissertation supervisor, Denise O'Brien, for the extraordinary support she has given me in this project and in all my scholarly work. The other members of my dissertation committee, Peter Rigby, Judith Goode, and Marilyn Silberfein also generously gave me their time, guidance, and valuable insights. Henry Selby, who during his years at Temple was a member of my Ph.D. studies committee, deserves thanks for his help in formulating my original research plans and for methodological advice.

Lorraine Dusak Sexton, Cathy Small, and Diane Freedman also read and commented on drafts of much of the manuscript. Wayne Zachary and Doris Weiland offered advice and help in data analysis. At Stanford University Press I thank Bill Carver and Norris Pope for their interest and the energy they have invested in this project, Shirley Taylor for her editorial work, and Karen Brown Davison for seeing the book through to its completion.

I also thank Altan Tranum, without whose willingness to assume an enormous responsibility I would have felt much less free to go to Kenya for extended research. My mother, Dorothy Smith, has helped me directly and indirectly in so many ways that it is impossible to enumerate them all. The person toward whom I feel the greatest and fondest gratitude is my husband, Leon Oboler. Finally, though they did not assist the project directly, Diana Denise Chelagat and Alexa Helene Jeptum gave me times of happy diversion.

R.S.O.

Contents

Ten pages of photographs follow p. 180

Tables

Women, Power, and Economic Change

The Nandi of Kenya

ONE

Introduction

THE PERIOD of European expansion that began in the sixteenth century, and the accompanying development of European capitalism, literally transformed the world. Confrontations with capitalism and some form of colonialism took place at different times in different places, but by the late twentieth century virtually no society remained unchanged by these historical processes. In East Africa, the critical period was the late nineteenth century, when European powers "scrambled" to gain control of the African continent. Colonial administration was imposed, taxes were levied, wage labor and cash crops were introduced, and cash systems were established. Peoples whose economies had been subsistence-based and relatively isolated became participants in national and world market economies. In the wake of this transformation, social relations of all kinds that had their roots in the process of production were profoundly disturbed. Among these social relations were those between men and women.

In the last decade sociocultural anthropologists have become increasingly interested in understanding the nature of sex and gender roles and how they vary across cultures. One important area of study that has emerged within this broad topic is the impact of colonialism and rapid socioeconomic change. It was once widely assumed, even among anthropologists, that women in traditional societies were typically far more oppressed than women in Western industrialized societies. The corollary assumption was that the imposition of colonial rule brought with it an "enlightened" European attitude toward women, which, reinforced through education, would ultimately lead to women's emancipation or at least to the improvement of their status. There is now a growing body of evidence that colonialism and the penetration of capitalism frequently undermined women's traditional sources of power, wealth, and value, as well as traditional safeguards of women's rights, without substituting any significant advantages (Boserup 1970; Van Allen 1972; Pala 1976; Hafkin & Bay 1976; Guyer 1978; McElroy & Mathiasson 1979; Etienne & Leacock 1980; Sanday 1981).

I present here a case study of the impact of colonialism, capitalism, and a cash economy on sex and gender roles among the Nandi, a semipastoral and patrilineal people of western Kenya. The analysis will focus particularly on the roles of women and men in production, and on women's and men's respective relations to property. Since the sex roles associated with production and property relations are intrinsically connected with sex roles in other areas—in the marriage system, husband-wife relations, kinship, cultural ideals of male and female, ritual relations, participation in community affairs—these areas will also be dealt with where appropriate. Ultimately such an analysis leads to, as it to a large extent grows out of, a desire to know whether the changes that have occurred within Nandi society have been favorable or unfavorable to women. Has women's economic position improved or declined as a result of colonialism and socioeconomic change? Is Nandi society marked by a greater or lesser degree of sexual stratification now than it was in the precolonial period?

Such questions, at some level, involve values. I believe that values inevitably affect analysis and generalization in social science, and that implicit values masquerading as facts interfere with understanding more than do those that are made explicit. Therefore I should like to make clear at the outset my feminist and leftist position.

The account I present has three objectives. The first is to provide an ethnographic description of the Nandi that is current and appropriate for the analysis of gender roles. Most existing Nandi ethnography dates from before 1950, and much of it is written as if it describes a society made up exclusively of males who reproduce themselves by cloning. The second objective is to present a sociohistorical analysis of the impact of colonial policy on the Nandi, and specifically on the roles of women and men. The third objective is to offer a critique of recent sex and gender theory, using Nandi ethnographic material as a starting point. Obviously these objectives are not independent of one another. The development of theories with cross-cultural applicability—whether of the conditions under which male and female roles assume certain patterns, or of the effects of colonialism on traditional societies—depends on the existence of ethnographies with information relevant to the questions that arise from these current theoretical concerns.

Because change is a major focus of this analysis, I deal wherever possible with ethnographic data historically. Information for the period of my fieldwork, however, is obviously much richer than for any other period.

The Research Context

My fieldwork in Nandi District was conducted between April 1976 and December 1977. The bulk of this time, eighteen months, was spent in one community, Kaptel Sublocation, which is in the north-central part of the district and has a population of just over 2,200. A sublocation rather than a smaller area was chosen as the focus of research because it is the fundamental unit within which public, day-to-day interaction takes place, and because it is the smallest formal political unit. Each sublocation has a center, a collection of shops, grain mills, beer clubs, and so on in the midst of an otherwise scattered settlement pattern. Women come here regularly to grind grain and buy household necessities, men come to learn the latest news and engage in discussions with other men, and older people of both sexes come to socialize and drink. Here also are held the meetings called by the chief of the sublocation, which are the main forum of local government, and it is here that elders come together to hear cases in customary law. The sublocation thus presents itself as a natural unit in a way that no smaller unit does. Later research revealed that the sublocation is also overwhelmingly endogamous, whereas no smaller unit is even primarily endogamous.

Kaptel was chosen because the population was homogeneously Nandi, and because it seemed, at least superficially, repre-

sentative of Nandi society as a whole. Later I came to the conclusion that there were certain ways in which it was not quite
typical. Two-thirds of the household heads in this community
profess to be Christians; but whereas the majority of Nandi
Christians are Roman Catholic, most of the Christians in Kaptel
are members of the Africa Inland Church, a fundamentalist body
with ties to American Baptists and Methodists. The average age
of household heads in this community was, I believe, slightly
younger than in most Nandi communities. Of ever-married
male household heads, 16.8 percent were (as of 1976) polygynists. For reasons explained in Chapter 4, I believe the polygyny
rate for Nandi as a whole is about 25 percent. Thus, the rate
in my research community was probably slightly lower than
average. This fact is not apparently explained by religion, as
Christians in my census sample were no more likely than non-
Christians to be monogamous. In terms of most other basic economic and demographic factors, however, I believe that Kaptel
Sublocation is fairly representative.

The Sublocation contains 286 compounds. The average compound has twenty acres of land, a household of eight people,
and nine adult cattle. All households produce maize and milk
for their own subsistence, and most of them also market a portion of these products. The majority of households also grow tea.

I was accompanied in the field by my husband, who was an
active participant in the research. We lived in the compound of a
Nandi family: a husband and wife, their three sons and daughter, the husband's widowed mother, and the husband's sister,
who was permanently separated from her husband. The metaphor through which cultural sense was made of our relationship
with this family was the categorization of my husband as the
younger brother of the male household head. This was merely a
metaphor that worked in certain social situations: we were never
formally adopted into kinship statuses, nor was there ever a per-
fect fit between our behavior and behavior appropriate to kinship roles.

During most of the research period we worked with two field
assistants, one man and one woman. These people were both
Nandi in their early twenties, English-speaking, and the Kenyan
equivalent of high school graduates. Their duties were to assist

in gathering census and numerical data and data on time allocation, to transcribe tape-recorded interviews and recordings of public events, to teach us the Nandi language, and to act as interpreters in interviews until we gained sufficient language skills. Another local man assisted in gathering some of the census data and cross-checking it for accuracy, and other fourth-form graduates filled in for our regular field assistants for brief periods.

We studied Kiswahili, the national language of Kenya, in preparation for fieldwork, and in the beginning used it to converse with most Nandi people. My competence in Nandi gradually became great enough so that I could understand most of what was said to me. I could ask questions on my main research interests, and at the end of the fieldwork could understand overheard conversations. Because the Nandi accent, tonalities, and grammar are difficult for English-speakers to master, I never attained real fluency in speech. My husband's knowledge of Nandi was less than mine, and he conducted fieldwork mainly in Kiswahili.

An early task of the research was a census of the sublocation to collect sociodemographic information. The sublocation chief facilitated the census by making a list of all 286 compounds, by compound head. Surveying all the compounds in the sublocation seemed an impossibly large undertaking, so I selected a 40 percent random sample, or 115 compounds. A local resident assisted in the census, providing introductions and a check on the accuracy of the information, and later he independently surveyed some of the census households. The following data were collected for all the compounds surveyed: a list of all persons living in the compounds; age, age-set, sex, relationship to compound head, educational level, occupation, and religion of each; clan membership of the compound head and spouse or spouses, and their marital histories, including circumstances of the marriage and a description of the bridewealth; a list of all children of the compound head, including sex, age, identity of mother, educational level, religion, date of initiation, date of marriage, name of spouse, clan identity of spouse's father, description of bridewealth, locality of residence, and sex and ages of any children; amount of land held by the household, in the local community and elsewhere; numbers of acres planted in various crops; numbers and types of livestock; whether the household hired a tractor for annual plowing or used resident or nonresident agricultural labor; all economic activities of the compound head and spouses; any community activities of the compound head and spouses, such as serving on sublocation committees; and the length of time the compound head had resided in the local community and, if not a native, the area from which he or she had migrated.

An additional large sociodemographic data set was obtained by asking a group of 50 informants to supply basic information (sex, age, age-set, locality of residence, educational level, religion, occupation, and marriage and reproductive history) for all their own relatives within certain degrees of kinship. This sample of 50 informants was not random, but I believe that it was not systematically biased and that the relatives who were described were representative of the population as a whole.* The advantage of this material is that it provides data with a wide geographical and temporal range (it includes people throughout all of Nandi District and in Nandi settlements outside it, and it includes people long dead).

Data on daily activities were collected by a study of time allocation for all members of eleven compounds. The methodology of this study is discussed in detail in Chapter 6. The compounds were chosen for their proximity to the compound in which we resided and for their representativeness of demographic trends shown up by the census data. The study spanned nine months. Each compound was visited at times selected at random, and the activity of each household member was recorded.

Highly systematic interviews following set questionnaires were conducted on several topics. Eight women and seven men were interviewed on the ideal and actual division of labor by sex. Similar interviews on marital decision making and the re-

---

* A precedent for this approach is found in the ethnographic work of Asmarom Legesse, who interviewed people who frequented a central marketplace about their own personal kin networks. Though this sample was not random and probably overrepresented young males, Legesse writes: "We were hopeful that all other individuals, whatever the probability of their appearing in the marketplace, would have an undistorted chance of appearing in our sample through the reports of the independent males" (Legesse 1973:140).

spective economic rights of spouses were conducted with sixteen men and thirteen women, including nine cases in which both husband and wife were interviewed. Participants in nine of the ten known cases of woman-woman marriage in the research community were interviewed about this institution.

Less systematic, open-ended interviews were conducted with informants too numerous to count on various topics related to sex roles. A great deal of additional information was the result of informal conversation and participant observation. Both my husband and I spent a great deal of time in various Nandi compounds other than the one in which we lived. We tried to participate fully in all aspects of daily life, and attended as many ceremonies and public events as we could.

We tape-recorded almost all legal cases that were heard by the sublocation council of elders during the fieldwork period. These cases were transcribed and translated to English by our field assistants.

The Nandi and Economic Change

The Nandi have been described as traditionally pastoral (Huntingford 1953*a*), though cultivation has always played a major role in their economy (Gold 1977).* Nandi social organization at the end of the nineteenth century (the point at which the Nandi were first described ethnographically as well as the time remembered by my oldest informants as the "traditional" past) was crosscut by a system of seven rotating age-sets for men, localized military units, patrilineal clans (but not corporate patrilineages), and patrilocal extended families. Clans were not localized. The most important unit of interaction was the local community, which was made up of members of many different clans and based on ties of friendship and voluntary association as well as kinship, and characterized by a dense network of affinal relationships. There was a tendency toward political centralization in the person of the chief *Orkoiyot*, a ritual and military leader.

The staple crop of the precolonial period was finger millet, or eleusine. The nineteenth century was marked by increasing pos-

---

*The basic ethnographic information and analytic points sketched here briefly will be developed in detail in later chapters.

session of cattle and increasing emphasis upon them in Nandi culture (Gold 1978).

The imposition of colonial rule in Nandi in 1905 followed a punitive expedition in which large numbers of cattle (some sources say as many as half the total cattle population) were captured. After 1905, the Nandi were confined within a bounded reserve far smaller than their previous territory. The size of Nandi herds was further decreased by a rinderpest epidemic, and land was taken from the reserve for a settlement scheme for soldiers after the First World War.

The early twentieth century saw the introduction of taxation and cash-cropping as a means of getting money to pay taxes. The colonial government made great efforts to convince the Nandi to restrict the numbers of their cattle, devote less land to pasture, and put more land under cultivation. By the 1940's these changes had been largely effected. During the period between the First World War and Independence (1964), great shifts occurred in the Nandi economy, including the introduction of the three mainstays of today's prosperous semicommerical agriculture, maize, dairy farming, and tea. Maize was introduced in the 1920's and by the 1940's had become the staple crop. The dairy industry did not really take off until restrictions on ownership by Africans of European dairy cattle were loosened in the 1950's. The development of African production of tea as a cash crop began in the late 1950's.

One of the most important socioeconomic changes introduced by the colonial administration, one that had far-reaching consequences for social organization and, as I shall argue, for sex and gender roles, was the partitioning and titling of land during the mid-to-late 1950's under the Swynnerton Plan. The introduction of individual land tenure—the holding of land as private property—had an impact that cannot be overestimated on the relations of both men and women to property. An entirely new system of rules for determining rights in and access to land had to be evolved, where previously only the most fluid set of principles had existed. The new system of rules is in the process of being assimilated into Nandi social organization, and will ultimately touch the entire social fabric.

Women, Men, and Property

Nandi women's rights in property are not insignificant. In most of precolonial Nandi, land was not permanently owned. Community members of both sexes had the right to cultivate it. The "house-property complex" (Gluckman 1950) dominated cattle inheritance, as it still does. Divorce in Nandi is almost impossible, but the corollary of this is extremely secure property rights for wives. Each married woman's household has animals that cannot be reallocated to the house of her co-wives, and are inherited by her male heirs. A woman without a son may take a wife in the hope of procuring a male heir (to whom she stands as "father") for her house property (Oboler 1980). Husband and wife jointly control house-property cattle, though the husband's control predominates. Widows keep some of their house-property cattle as personal property after their husbands' deaths. Men, but not married women, can acquire cattle independently (e.g., by raiding or, now, through wage labor), and have total rights to control such cattle. It was always possible, therefore, for men but not women to hold cattle as entirely private property. Traditionally, cattle were thought of in the abstract as belonging to men, and male control of herds was an important Nandi ideological tenet.

The staple crop, the joint product of the labor of husband and wife, is divided between them. The wife's share is used for food. Traditionally, the husband's share was brewed into beer, which was used to discharge social obligations and, when necessary, to recruit communal labor. Today the husband's share is sold, and he controls the income.

Three forms of property are said to belong to women: the vegetable garden, chickens, and milk from the afternoon or evening milking. (Morning milk was in the past consumed by the household's male members; today it is still a male-controlled commodity.) Women are free to dispose of these three items as they wish, though in the precolonial period there were not many options. Normally all three were consumed by the woman's household, though she was free to give away any surplus and could gain prestige in the community through such gifts. Women could also own small stock acquired by trading their agricultural surplus or by performing specialized services such as midwifery and curing. This stock was often converted back into grain in times of shortage (Gold 1978).

The distinction between product and means of production is useful here, since it is apparent that the primary means of production, cattle, was controlled mainly by men. "Controlled" is appropriate rather than "owned," because the not inconsiderable rights of various members of a household in cattle held by that household show that most cattle were never "owned" completely by a single individual. It is thus impossible in the traditional setting to speak of exclusive "ownership" of the means of production by one sex. Men, however, controlled cattle, and some cattle could be held by men individually in a way never possible for married women. Those things said to be rightfully the property of women were never major means of production. They were either clearly products (e.g., milk), or if a means of production (e.g., chickens), their products were insignificant to the economy. Land, of course, was a part of the means of production, but it was not viewed as a form of property. Land in precolonial Nandi was so plentiful that control over it was not a real issue.

Thus it was a principle of traditional Nandi culture that men were the controllers of the primary means of production. This basic principle still has considerable force. In the modern setting, however, great changes have taken place in what constitute means of production. This leads to a great deal of confusion among informants attempting to explicate a coherent theory of men, women, and property ownership. Further, it leads to disparities in the views of men and women about the definition of male and female property, as each sex attempts to maximize or protect its own position by appealing to conflicting traditional norms.

The most significant changes affecting the means of production and therefore the definition of property rights have been full participation in the nation's cash economy and private ownership of land.

Full participation in the cash economy means that insofar as cash can be reinvested, it has become analogous to the means of production. Money can, of course, be converted to either product or means of production. But informants' statements about the rights of husbands and wives in money demonstrate that married women's rights are only in money as product. Wives, for example, should not control money beyond the amounts needed for home consumption, nor should they reinvest profits.

Private ownership of land is the second change that radically altered the nature of the means of production and thereby generated a redefinition of the rules of property ownership. When the land was partitioned, titles were distributed to individual adult males, and it was assumed that land inheritance would follow the same rules as customary law provided for the inheritance of cattle. What this meant for women was the sudden emergence of a situation in which they could, under certain circumstances, be denied access to land. Women perceive, though they only rarely express it in words, that their traditional rights in land have been undermined. They have reacted against this in various ways: with a sudden increase in the incidence of woman-woman marriage; with the currently popular argument that women should have inheritance rights under certain circumstances; and with a clear sense that women have the right and duty to block the sale of land by their husbands.

Thus many of the changes taking place at present in the position of women and men relative to property can be viewed as struggles to redefine in a changing context old norms about various parties' share in the family estate. Different norms can be appealed to by women and men, particularly as wives and husbands but also as mothers and sons, sisters and brothers, and in other roles, as each person strives to improve or protect his or her personal position. On the one hand are the traditional rules allocating certain types of property exclusively to women. On the other hand is the principle that men have the right of primary control over cattle, the most significant form of property and the most visible means of production. Many of the confusions in informants' ideas about men's and women's rights in property, and the competing rights of various family members in the family estate, revolve around competing concepts of what now constitute the means of production. Land, which though always significant as means of production was formerly not even visible as property, is one major focus for this conflict of norms. Money, which can function as product or as means of production, is another. Competition also emerges over whether men should rightfully control property that was traditionally the exclusive province of women but has now emerged as more significant because of its newfound convertibility to cash. Though women in the main accept a patriarchal view of property and marriage rights, they are by no means totally submissive to men's attempts to extend male control over property; instead, they actively evolve strategies to safeguard what are seen as inviolable and traditional women's rights. Nevertheless, I shall argue that the net effect of the many changes in the colonial and postcolonial Nandi economic system has been the erosion of the position of women with regard to property.

Nandi Women and Nandi Men

Though colonialism undermined some very significant rights and sources of power of precolonial Nandi women, I unhesitatingly characterize traditional as well as colonial and present Nandi society and culture as male-dominated. This is very clear in the way the cultural constructs "masculinity" and "femininity" are defined (see Chapter 3).

The relationship between husband and wife is the metaphor for the whole of male-female relations in Nandi. When informants speak about "women" and "men" in the abstract, what they are usually describing is the relationship between wives and husbands. That men are superior to women is a basic Nandi assumption. It is recognized that some women are superior to some men in certain desirable qualities and that women are sometimes owed deference by men because of their position in the kinship or age-set system. These situational peculiarities can be ignored, however, when marriage is the focal institution in which the tenet of male superiority is acted out. Barring a husband's exceptional abrogation of his responsibilities, it is disrespectful for a wife to outdo her husband at anything. Indeed, Nandi wives show great public deference to their husbands. A wife may not argue with or contradict her husband publicly, and she must remain in the background and be inconspicuous when her husband interacts with people other than close kin and neighbors. Except for short visits, wives must ask their husbands' permission to leave their homestead.

Nandi women do not participate in the two political institutions that have their roots in the precolonial period, community meetings and local courts, although they occasionally hold positions in modern political institutions. Ritual experts, except those who direct female initiation, are all men. A traditional institution in which women had the right to punish men under certain circumstances ("the punishment of women") has not been practiced in living memory.

In spite of all this, the tone or "feel" of Nandi gender relations can often seem very egalitarian. When I was deciding on a research site, a social anthropologist who had worked in East Africa suggested Nandi and said he was impressed with the apparently high status of Kalenjin-speaking (Nandi) women and their evident freedom. Indeed, this was my initial impression also. In some of the first social gatherings I observed, women seemed to mingle freely with men and to interact with them in an egalitarian way. Many Nandi women struck me as extremely strong and determined, and surely not easily dominated. Yet it was also immediately apparent that there was another side to this picture. The forceful characters I met were mainly women at least my age, and usually older. Though forceful in private, they still behaved with deference and could fade into the background when men were present. Young wives were shy, and when men were present, could appear positively cowed. The women who seemed to be on more or less equal terms with men were widows or elderly. When I began to interview women about sex and gender roles, I was told over and over that men rule, men own everything, women control nothing of importance, and only men matter. It took some time, and discovery of the proper line of questioning, to get past this ideological veneer. Eventually it dawned on me that at least two things were going on here: first, there was a marked discrepancy between what people said about the relations between men and women and what I observed in practice; and second, a woman's actual freedom of action as well as her access to resources and power varied considerably throughout her life. The same woman could develop from a timid, deferential, perhaps physically abused young wife, eager to do her husband's bidding, into a rich, independent widow, behaving in most matters as the absolute equal of any man.

I shall describe (in Chapters 3–7) the dynamics of Nandi gender relations in a way that makes it possible to understand how different observers have developed contradictory evaluations of Nandi women's status. This account reveals a complex interplay of elements that make statements about the "high apparent status of Nandi-Kalenjin women" or "the patriarchal nature of Nandi society" (Langley 1979:84) equally oversimplifications. I present the various sources of power and autonomy that Nandi women had and have and demonstrate that Nandi society has historically been characterized by a balance of power, albeit unequal, between the sexes.

I argue that forces deriving from colonization and the penetration of capitalism and a cash economy have eroded some of women's sources of power and autonomy. I do not, however, wish to argue that Nandi society is sexually egalitarian, or that capitalism and colonization are the sole sources of contemporary male dominance. I believe that Nandi society is sexually stratified, and in the broad sense of this term has never been otherwise. I understand sexual stratification to mean differential access, based on sex and gender, to rewards, prestige, power, or resources (Schlegel 1977:3). It is quite clear that male is considered the superior status in Nandi, and that where the goals of men and women conflict, particularly when the parties concerned are husband and wife, the male usually dominates. But this does not imply that Nandi women are powerless or that they have no access to rewards, prestige, or resources.

Nandi gender relations, like gender relations in most societies, are complex. Ethnographic description of such a complicated dynamic process is difficult enough; cross-cultural comparison is even more difficult. How is it possible to determine whether Nandi is more or less sexually egalitarian than, for example, the neighboring Maasai or Luo? In Chapter 8 I discuss some of the problems of using our current inadequate conceptual tools such as scales of women's status and male dominance for evaluating the relative positions of women in these three culturally related societies. In considering the Nandi material from a cross-cultural perspective, some of these inadequacies emerge very clearly.

If Sanday's scale of male dominance (Sanday 1981:254–55) is applied to the Nandi case, for example, the modern Nandi fall into the "mythical male dominance" category and the precolonial Nandi must even be labeled "sexually egalitarian" on the basis of the institution of "the punishment of women." I believe that either of these characterizations distorts the data. Though the work of Sanday and other similarly oriented theorists is extremely valuable in pointing out that male dominance is not nearly so ubiquitous as it was once thought to be, simply defining away the ubiquity of male dominance does not, I think, advance the cross-cultural study of sex and gender.

A further limitation in the anthropological study of sex and gender roles is that scholars working in this area have not yet established a common vocabulary. We use such terms as "power," "autonomy," "women's status," "male dominance," "egalitarian," and so on without agreeing on what they mean or, in some cases, even making explicit what we intend them to mean. Rather than relying on these ill-defined terms, I shall use "sexual stratification" as an umbrella term for the whole bundle of concepts used in comparisons of cross-cultural gender roles: power (and autonomy, which though closely connected to power is analytically separable), resources, rewards, and prestige. One of my arguments throughout this work is that Nandi society was and is sexually stratified on at least three dimensions: resources (my primary focus), power, and prestige.

The term "male dominance" is particularly ambiguous in that it has been used to describe situations of differential power as well as of differential prestige (e.g., Rogers 1978). I suggest that we restrict the term "male dominance" to the power dimension, lest in trying to make it mean too much we make it mean too little. Even if we use this term only in the power dimension, how big does the power differential have to be before we have a legitimate case of "male dominance"? It used to be assumed that male dominance was cross-culturally very frequent; now some recent theorists (Rogers 1978; Poewe 1980; Sanday 1981) contend that it is actually rare. What appears to have happened is that the term has been redefined, or at any rate limited in its application to cases—admittedly rare indeed—in which women have almost no power at all. The more usual situation is the one presented here for Nandi, in which very definite male dominance coexists with a degree of power for women—even if the women themselves will not readily acknowledge that this is so.

These points are taken up at some length in Chapter 8, not only in a general way but as part of a discussion of the extent to which the kinds of changes in sex and gender relations that have occurred in Nandi are typical of the impact of colonialism on traditional societies.

The particular forms of present-day Nandi culture and society have resulted from a unique conjunction of historical processes such as colonialism and world capitalism and certain preexisting social, cultural, economic, and ecological conditions. In analyzing what has happened in Nandi society, I wish to give full recognition to its particularity. At the same time, I am aware that Nandi is also an example of a phenomenon that has been noted by many recent scholars in various locations: that certain forces that existed in the colonial situation and for the most part have continued into the postcolonial setting have frequently (though not invariably) acted to undermine and erode women's traditional economic rights and sources of power and influence. One can hope that studies of this altering pattern can be of some influence on national development policy planners, so that development plans can be designed in such a way as to preserve traditional institutions that support women's economic position, or at least to replace old patterns with new ones that offer significant benefits to women.

Nandi Society, Then and Now

THE NANDI are a section of the Kalenjin-speaking peoples of Kenya whom Sutton (1968:80–81; 1970:22) has classified as "Highland Nilotes." Formerly, the Kalenjin peoples, together with the Maasai and Karimojong cluster, were called "Nilo-Hamites" (e.g., Huntingford 1950, 1953a, 1953b), but it is now clear that any similarities between the "Nilo-Hamitic" languages and those of peoples formerly called "Hamitic" (e.g., Galla, Somali, Rendille) are superficial word borrowings that do not reflect a common culture history, though a series of historical contacts between the two groups of peoples has occurred (Sutton 1968:98; Ehret 1968:159).

Sutton, following Greenberg's (1963) classification of African languages, distinguishes three groups of Nilotic peoples. The "River-Lake Nilotes" include the Nuer-Dinka-Shilluk cluster and the Alur, Acholi, Lango, and Luo, among others. The "Plains Nilotes" include the Bari and Karimojong clusters, and the Maasai and related peoples. The "Highland Nilotes" are represented by two branches: the Tatoga or Datog group, which apparently was at one time settled over a wide area in northern Tanzania but is now represented only by the Barabaig and a few other small pockets of Tatoga-speakers; and the Kalenjin (Sutton 1968:81). The Nandi, Kipsigis, Tugen, Keiyo, Terik, and most Ogiek speak languages that are mutually quite intelligible and are distinguished from one another only by intonation and occasional lexical divergences. The other Kalenjin languages—Marakwet, Endo, Sabaot, Pokot, and Sebei—can be understood by Nandi-speakers after prolonged exposure.

The use of the term Kalenjin for peoples speaking these related languages, and the growth of their awareness of themselves as variants of a single cultural and political entity, began during the Second World War. John arap Chemallan, a Nandi who made vernacular radio broadcasts during the war, is credited with coining this term. In his broadcasts he frequently used the terms "Kalenjin" (sing. "I tell you" or "I have told you") and "Kalenjok" (plural), and this usage was picked up by Kalenjin-speakers in the armed forces and multi-ethnic secondary schools to refer to themselves (Kipkorir 1973:72–75). In Kenya, at the time of the 1969 census, Kalenjin collectively numbered 1,194,414, making them Kenya's fifth-largest ethnic group.*

The name Nandi is not of Kalenjin origin. The Nandi originally called themselves, and were called by other Kalenjin, Chemwal (Maasai: Il-Teng'wal). One theory of the origin of the term Nandi is that it comes from the Kiswahili word for cormorant (*mnandi*) and was used by the early Swahili traders to refer to the people who swooped down like cormorants from their heights above the Nandi and Kakamega escarpments to raid those living below. At any rate, "Nandi" has now been completely accepted as the people's name for themselves, and "Chemwal" is no longer in use.

Culture History

The people now called Nandi undoubtedly represent an amalgamation of peoples who found their ways to the present Nandi District in several waves of immigration. Ehret (1971:73) believes that much of south-central and southwestern Kenya was inhabited by Kalenjin-speakers (his South Kalenjin) during the first half of the current millennium. By 1700, these Kalenjin had been displaced by Maasai over most of this area, though pockets probably remained. Nandi traditions refer to the migration from the vicinity of Mount Elgon (located northwest of Nandi District) by a group led by a man called Kakipoch to settle in Aldai, in

*The numbers for the eight subgroups in 1969 were: Kipsigis, 387,762; Nandi, 322,200; Pokot, 158,336; Tugen, 101,356; Elgeyo, 99,555; Marakwet, 71,445; Sabaot, 49,549; and Dorobo, 4,211. Kenya Population Census, 1969, III:71. The current president of Kenya, Daniel arap Moi, belongs to the Tugen subgroup.

the southwest corner of the present Nandi District. Kakipoch's group very likely found the area already inhabited. Although Huntingford (1950: 11) sets the date of Kakipoch's arrival in Aldai at about the beginning of the seventeenth century, Walter (1970) believes it was earlier, and Matson (1972: 5) points out that "Huntingford's date is based on the questionable assumption that the cyclical age-set system, consisting of seven sets spanning 105 years, has remained constant"; Matson also points out that according to the traditions of other ethnic groups, the Nandi and Kipsigis migrated earlier than 1600.* It seems sensible to assume that the Kakipoch migration took place earlier than 1600, though how much earlier is impossible to say.

There is no question about Aldai's being the original area of settlement in Nandi. Presumably the Nandi stayed more or less in that area for a century or more, but in the latter part of the nineteenth century they gradually expanded northward into the area of better pasture lands at the expense of the Uasin Gishu Maasai, who, following their defeat by a coalition of Naivasha and Il-Laikipiak Maasai (Huntingford 1950: 12–13), were vulnerable to the growing strength of the Nandi. The last battle between Nandi and Uasin Gishu took place about 1880 when the latter attempted a large-scale raid and were decisively defeated. Nandi expansion north into the Uasin Gishu plateau was still continuing at the time it was halted by the imposition of British rule.

Ehret (1971: 63) considers both cultivation and stock raising to have been important economic activities of the proto-Kalenjin as early as A.D. 1000, and indeed he regards the South Kalenjin as having had a distinctly pastoral emphasis (1971: 75). He points to the presence of many Bantu loan words for Nandi horticultural terms, and a counterexchange from Kalenjin to Bantu languages, such as some Luhyia dialects, for certain livestock-related terms (Ehret: 1971: 69–71).

---

*Some other Kalenjin have eight age-sets—the same names as the Nandi sets plus another called Korongoro. According to Nandi tradition, the name Korongoro formerly existed for them also but was dropped in the early nineteenth century in favor of Kipkoimet after the Korongoro age-set suffered a disastrous defeat by the Maasai. Is it possible that at this point an entire set was dropped from the system, which previously had eight sets?

The Physical Environment

Nandi District today comprises most of the area that was controlled by Nandi at the end of the nineteenth century. The southwest corner of Nandi District is only 16 kilometers (less than ten miles) northeast of the Kavirondo or Winam Gulf on Victoria Nyanza. Nandi, which occupies the extreme southwest corner of the Uasin Gishu plateau, is an area of 2,789 sq. km. (approximately 1,060 sq. mi.), about 65 km. long by 40 or 50 km. wide on average (Ominde 1975:84; Sanderson 1955). The equator runs through the extreme southern part of the district. On the west and south, the district is bounded by steep escarpments. In the north and east, rolling hills gradually merge into the Uasin Gishu plateau. The area is well drained by several systems of rivers and streams, though there are occasional marshes in flat areas.

In altitude, the area ranges from a low of 1,402 meters (4,600 ft.) in the southwest to 2,316 meters (7,600 ft.) in the east, averaging 1,829 to 1,981 meters (6,000–6,500 ft.). Huntingford (1950:22) reports a typical soil pattern for the district of 26–30 cm. (10–12 in.) of red topsoil with approximately one to three meters of red subsoil.

The rainfall is high and has been constant over the years. At Kapsabet in the north it averaged about 154 cm. (60 in.) annually for three years for which data were available to Huntingford, and at Kaptumo, in the south, it averaged 187 cm. (73 in.; Huntingford 1950:23). Gold (1977:3) reports that "average yearly rainfall in the southwest has been recorded at 85.2 inches [218.5 cm.]." In some parts of the district, two distinct dry seasons occur, the main one from late December through February and another shorter one during part of September and October. Though there may be occasional rains during these periods, usually there are long stretches without rain. The heaviest rains come between April and July. Huntingford in 1950 reported May through August as the wettest months, so a change in pattern appears to have taken place. More important than sheer volume of rainfall, however, is its constancy. It rains in Nandi in almost every month of every year.

Temperatures vary from 25 to 30 degrees C. (high 70's–low

80's F.) on warm, sunny days, to rainy season daytime temperatures of about 15 to 20 degrees C., to frosts at the highest altitudes on the coldest nights. The usual nighttime temperature is around 10–12, sometimes rather less. The combination of soil, temperature, and rainfall makes Nandi District an area of high agricultural potential.

At the time of the 1969 census, the population density of the district was 75 per sq. km. (198 per sq. mi.; Ominde 1975:84). The total population of the district at that time—209,000, mostly Nandi—represented roughly two-thirds of the total number of people of Nandi ethnicity in Kenya (322,200 according to the Kenya Population Census 1969, III:71). Huntingford (1953a:3) gives total Nandi ethnicity figures of 116,681 based on the 1948 census and 50,440 (Huntingford 1950:5) for 1932, based on figures provided to the Kenya Land Commission in 1932. In Nandi District, the increase in population density grew from 128 per sq. mi. in 1948, to 167 in 1962, to 197 in 1969 (Heyer 1974:50–51)—or about one and a half times between 1948 and 1975, mostly from natural population growth although some immigration occurred. This is by no means one of the highest rates of population growth in rural Kenya during this time period, and Nandi population density is still low compared with other high-potential agricultural areas (e.g., figures of over 150/sq. km. in much of Central Province, of 220/sq. km. in Kakamega District, and of 304/sq. km. in Kisii District.) Still, rapid population growth must be seen as one element in recent social change in Nandi. The percentage of the population in Nandi District under the age of 15 is 48.79 percent, which is only slightly below the national average of 51 percent (Ominde 1975:70).

In 1967–68, the cattle population of Nandi was 181,597, including 166,689 native *zebu* cattle and 14,908 "grade" stock, that is, cattle upgraded by breeding with European dairy cattle, primarily Holstein-Friesians (Heyer 1974:37). These figures would make the ratio of cattle to people in 1967–68 approximately 0.9 to one. In 1976–77, in a north Nandi sublocation, I found the ratio of adult cattle to people to be 1.2 to one. Huntingford's figures (1950:5) of a cattle population of 215,441 in Nandi as of 1932 give a cattle/people ratio of 4.3 to one. Various reasons can be offered for the decline in the cattle/people ratio, including the elimination of communal pasture land, the introduction of high-producing dairy cattle, and the emphasis now placed on the production of milk for the market, but the change may not reflect simply a decline from a consistently high precolonial density. Figures cited by Mungeam (1966; quoted by Ellis 1976: 558) suggest a cattle/people ratio of 0.5 to one immediately prior to the 1905 punitive expedition, and it seems probable that the Nandi cattle/people ratio has a long history of significant fluctuation over time.

The Nandi settlement pattern is one of scattered homesteads, with individual families living in compounds on their own farmland. Each sublocation has a business district known as a "center." These areas were set aside by the colonial government after the Second World War as the only locations in which petty businesses could legally operate. In 1976–77, a typical center consisted of a cluster of small shops, restaurants, beer clubs, grain-grinding mills, and perhaps a butcher shop, a tailor shop, a carpenter shop, a bicycle repair shop, and so on. Informal marketing of produce takes place in the center, and also community events such as public meetings and courts, clinics held by traveling nurses at regular intervals, and cattle innoculations. Each local community also has churches, schools, and cattle dips that are not connected with the center.

The Economy

Eleusine, or finger millet (Kiswahili *wimbi*), was long the staple crop of Nandi, as reported by Hobley in 1902 (Huntingford 1950: 57). Other crops with a long history in Nandi include millet or sorghum (Kiswahili *mtama*), beans, tobacco (Gold 1977: 8), pumpkins (Hollis 1909: 18), and several indigenous leafy green vegetables. These crops were often grown in mixed gardens. Eleusine was ground into flour and cooked with water to form a stiff porridge that could be eaten with either milk or boiled vegetables. Sweet potatoes, now a staple in the Nandi diet, are a more recent addition.

Gold believes that sweet potatoes were first cultivated in Nandi during the nineteenth century, after being introduced to the Nandi by the Luo (Gold 1977: 8). The Nandi word for sweet potatoes, *robuonik*, is derived from Luo and Luhyia words. *Bandek*, the Nandi word for maize, is also derived from Luo. Exactly when maize was first cultivated by the Nandi is not certain, but it was probably not earlier than the end of the nineteenth century. In 1909, maize was grown "in small quantities" (Hollis 1909:19). During the 1920's the colonial government began to encourage the Nandi to grow maize as both a food and a cash crop, and maize soon overtook and replaced eleusine as the staple crop. Maize can be ground and eaten as porridge in the same way that eleusine was and with the same accompanying foods, and it gives a much higher yield per acre in most parts of the district (Huntingford 1950:64). Most households today not only grow maize for their own consumption but also produce extra to sell for cash. Vegetables, grown for home consumption and sometimes for sale, include the traditional ones—potatoes and sweet potatoes, beans, pumpkins, and indigenous green vegetables—and also cabbages, onions and tomatoes, which are more recent introductions. Beans are often grown in the same plot with maize; the other vegetables are planted separately. Potatoes and beans (dried and stored) tend to be a main staple of the diet seasonally, potatoes when they are ready for harvest and beans when other foods are scarce.

Tea is the other important cash crop in much of the district (except in the drier areas of the north), and surplus milk is also produced for delivery to the government-operated dairy marketing cooperative. Other cash crops are relatively unimportant, though a few farmers have planted a small number of coffee trees. The growing of fruit trees is limited mostly to the extreme southwestern part of the district, in the lower equatorial zone; sugar cane and bananas grow well there, but the altitude of most of Nandi is too high for any sort of fruit to thrive. Sugar cane is, however, a moderately important crop. According to the 1969–70 Agricultural Census, 77 percent of the land under cultivation in Nandi was in maize, 10 percent in sugar cane (mostly in plantations in the southwest), 4 percent in tea, 4 percent in beans, 3 percent in eleusine and sorghum, and 2 percent in other crops (Heyer 1974:63).

Traditionally, the work of clearing land for its first planting was done by men. After the ground had been cleared, it was broken up using iron hoes and digging sticks. Huntingford (1950:62) says that men traditionally did not do this work, but most of my informants and those of Gold (1977:9) believe that they did.* Planting was done by men, women, and children, weeding mainly by women and children, and harvesting by both sexes (Huntingford 1950:63). My informants say both sexes weeded. Planting was done in March, harvesting in November (Huntingford 1950:64). Huntingford says that the amount of ground typically cultivated by a Nandi nuclear family was three-quarters of an acre (1950:65). The main departure from the traditional process of cultivation is that tilling is now done with a plow pulled by either a tractor or oxen. Plows were in general use by most Nandi families by the 1950's. Exactly when tractors began to become important to Nandi cultivation is not clear, but today a common arrangement is to hire a tractor to break the ground for the first time, and to till the ground the second time using a plow with oxen. In 1977, 62 percent of the households surveyed in the community that was the site of this study were using tractors for at least part of their annual tilling. Plowing is usually done by father and son, brothers, or age-mates, rarely if ever by women. The job of training the oxen to the plow is usually left to the older boys, who look on it as a game. Ground in which maize is to be planted is not finely broken by hand. When ground is broken by hand, both sexes may participate. Today, both sexes also help with the weeding. All the members of the household, as well as any other people who can be attracted through reciprocal work arrangements, help in the planting and harvesting. Maize has to be weeded at least twice during its seven-to-eight-month growing cycle, but at other times people are free to turn their attention to subsidiary crops and cash crops such as tea.

Huntingford (e.g., 1950:39) believes that pastoralism was formerly of overwhelming economic importance among the Nandi. Gold's research (1977, 1978) suggests that it was only during a brief period toward the end of the nineteenth century that cattle even approached the kind of significance ascribed to them by

---

*See also Annual Report, District Commissioner, Nandi, 1940:2: "The Nandi are almost unique in that the menfolk and not the women do the tilling in the fields."

Huntingford, and that Nandi subsistence has always been based primarily upon cultivation. The high point of the cattle/people ratio, 4.3 to one, is in the high range for East African semi-pastoralists; it may be compared, for example, with figures of approximately one to one for the Nuer (Elam 1973: 140), three or four to one for the Jie and Turkana (Gulliver 1955: 38) and two or three to one for the agricultural Pokot (Schneider 1957). Among more purely pastoral peoples the ratio is six–eight to one for the Hima (Elam 1973: 140), between five to one and ten to one for the pastoral Pokot (Schneider 1957: 161), and fourteen to one for the Maasai (Gulliver 1955: 38).

In precolonial Nandi, herding cattle was preferably done by young men of the warrior age-grade, between the ages of circumcision and marriage. The communal pastures were located within a reasonable walk of the homestead—close enough so that the cows could be returned to the homestead at night for milking. The cattle were housed (as they still are) in enclosures separate from but close to the dwelling. Milking was done in both the morning and the evening (Huntingford 1950: 47). Twice a day the cattle were taken to drink at rivers and streams, and about once a month they were taken to one of the ten or so salt licks in the district. Even by 1950, many Nandi were feeding cattle with rock salt in their own compounds (Huntingford 1950: 47). According to Huntingford, adult men were often the herders, or at least the chief herders, who supervised younger men or children doing the actual herding: "Though much of an average day is passed in what the European calls 'idleness,' squatting on a rock gazing at the cattle, or standing on one leg whistling to them, this concentrated apparent doing of nothing is 'work' to a Nandi" (Huntingford 1950: 39).

Today the majority of cattle herding is done by children, though adults of both sexes may do it as well. There are no longer communal pastures. There are still some small grassy public places where children of more than one family sometimes graze their cattle together, and there are public watering places at rivers to which cattle are taken to drink twice a day; but for the most part the cattle of each family graze in a pasture on family land, and in many cases where the piped water system has been extended, they are watered at troughs in their owners' compounds. The drives to the salt licks have disappeared: cattle are given salt in their owners' compounds almost invariably. The only communal aspect of animal husbandry today is a strictly modern addition: twice a week, cattle are taken to communal cattle dips operated by local communities to be immersed in an insecticide solution as protection against East Coast fever. Aside from that, the principle is now that of private ownership. Pasture land is considered private property, and if a farmer wants to graze cattle on land that belongs to someone else, he must buy that right.*

Another feature of Nandi cattle-keeping practices that has declined in the modern setting is what Huntingford (1950:52) calls the "*Kaptich* system" (also known as *kimanagan*). This was a kind of loan or caretaker system in which cattle were loaned out among friends and relatives, so that each owner, while having some cattle with friends or relatives, also was custodian of *their* cattle. Being a custodian gave one the right to use the milk produced by those cattle, but the owner retained the right to reclaim any calves born to his cows while at Kaptich. (The word Kaptich means literally "cattle place," that being the place where the cattle were said to be while they were staying away from the homestead of the family that owned them.) One function of the system was to provide a kind of insurance—against the loss of a whole herd to Maasai raiders or to an epidemic. At the same time, entrusting someone else with one's most cherished possessions served symbolically to dramatize and reenforce ties of friendship. It was common for a man's herd to consist of only a few of his own cattle and mainly of cattle that had been entrusted to him by various friends. The Kaptich system is seldom used nowadays, and it mostly takes place in exceptional circumstances, for practical reasons—when it is inconvenient for the lender to keep the cattle himself, for example, for lack of land, or when a borrower asks a friend to lend him a cow because he himself has no milk-producing cows. The old dangers of loss of cattle to enemy tribes or from epidemics no longer exist; and

*People who own goats, however, have a right to allow them to browse anywhere. According to Huntingford (1950:55), the average Nandi herd included at least ten goats and sheep. The number today is certainly much less. Large herds of goats are rare; most families keep a few at most, and many keep none.

since milk is now produced for cash, milk cows are much more valuable than they used to be and men prefer to manage their own animals. Nevertheless, when cattle lending *does* occur, people refer to the traditional kaptich or kimanagan institution, and stress its friendship-solidifying aspect.

Milk has long been one of the mainstays of the Nandi diet and the major source of protein. It is drunk fresh and also put aside and allowed to sour in charcoal-lined calabashes. The old practice of drinking ox blood has largely died out. Every six weeks or so, according to my informants, oxen were bled by piercing the jugular vein with a blocked arrow. The blood—a good source of protein—was drunk fresh or mixed with sour milk. The reason for the almost total disappearance of this custom may have had something to do with the Christian missions, which of course abhorred it, but the fact that it is no longer current even among people who do not consider themselves Christians suggests an economic reason also. The decrease of herd size that has accompanied the change to individual land tenure means that superfluous cattle are generally not kept, and people cannot afford to risk lowering the productivity of working oxen and milk cows by bleeding them.

Traditionally, cattle were not killed except for ritual purposes. Today, superfluous cattle are sold at regular cattle auctions, whence they go to the canneries of the Kenya Meat Commission or to the local butcheries for sale to the villagers. Nandi is one of the leading beef-exporting areas of modern Kenya (Heyer 1974:40). Most of the meat that people eat comes from the butcher shop, but goats may be slaughtered by the families who own them for special celebrations or to entertain important guests. A common petty business enterprise is to buy a goat or sheep, slaughter it in the Center on the day of a community meeting, and sell the meat at a net profit.

Very few Nandi herds today include bulls, since artificial insemination is readily available and cheap. The government Veterinary Service sends artificial insemination agents (whom Nandi refer to as "*chi ne kirgit*," "the bull man") around the countryside on a regular daily route. The owner of a cow can have it inseminated by any of a number of standard European breeds at a cost of two Kenya shillings (about 25 cents American).

The most common causes of mortality in cattle are pneumonia, East Coast fever (which is erroneously believed to be the same disease as malaria in people), and milk fever (acute calcium deficiency following parturition). Rinderpest, which used to be an important cause of cattle mortality, is now almost completely under control; all cattle are legally required to be vaccinated against it in government-sponsored mass inoculations. Despite dipping to prevent infestation by ticks that carry East Coast fever, some cattle still contract it and it is usually fatal. Various patent medicines for cattle diseases can be bought, and most owners of cattle inject their animals with these medicines themselves.

Certainly, Nandi culture was traditionally marked by values usually associated with the so-called "cattle complex." Wealth was reckoned primarily in terms of cattle, and a man who had no cow at all was looked upon as having very low social status. (Nevertheless, there were periods, according to elderly informants, when to have even one cow was good fortune.) Cattle raiding was an important part of Nandi culture. The number of words for types and markings of cattle found in the Nandi lexicon is impressive, and many personal names are derived from them. In the traditional religious system, cattle, and various things associated with them, were considered sacred. Modern attitudes reflect this belief. No one is even slightly repelled by cow dung; people will casually pick it up with bare hands, and people still wash their hands in a cow's urine if it happens to urinate while being milked. The taboo on eating meat and milk on the same day has disappeared, however: formerly it was believed that to partake of the flesh and milk together was an insult to cattle that would result in a decrease in the production of milk.

Concern with cattle still permeates Nandi life in social matters, nonetheless. Cattle are still essential for bridewealth and homicide payments, and their well-being and relative merits are still major foci of conversation, though criteria for judging their merits have changed.

Most women keep chickens, and eggs and chicken stew are eaten with the staple maize porridge as a dietary change of pace. Chickens and eggs are also sold by women at markets as a source of petty cash. A traditional proscription on the consumption of chickens and eggs by women is no longer in force.

Relations of trade traditionally existed between the Nandi and their neighbors on the south and west, the Luo, Luhyia, and Terik. Certain points along the boundaries were recognized as trading centers, as were certain points within Nandi, though there were not organized weekly markets. Trade that involved foodstuffs was largely in the hands of women. In times of food shortage, women would travel into the territory of neighboring ethnic groups to exchange small stock for surplus grain. In case of a Nandi grain surplus and shortage in other areas, the process worked in reverse. Trade also involved other items such as cattle, pots, calabashes, fish, hides, and tobacco. According to Gold, "the main movement was grain out of Nandi and livestock in " (Gold 1977:17), which stands in opposition to Huntingford's assertion (1950:65) that traditionally Nandi rarely grew enough grain to last a family for a year, much less a surplus. It seems likely that the direction of this trade shifted over time, complementing fluctuations in the people/livestock ratio. In the first half of the nineteenth century, Nandi also traded for metal implements, hoes, axes, and weapons, with the Keiyo, Tugen, and Pokot; Nandi apparently did not work metal themselves at this period (Gold 1977:5). After Maasai blacksmiths came to Nandi in the late nineteenth century, metal working increased there (Gold 1977:5), but today Nandi has few blacksmiths and nearly all tools and metalware are bought in shops.

Clay pots, too, traditionally made by Nandi women craft specialists, have been supplanted, if not totally replaced, by manufactured ware. Aluminum pots and enamelware are common. Though pot making is no longer done by Nandi women, water and beer pots made by Luo and Luhyia potters can be bought by Nandi in local markets. Huntingford (1950:82) says baskets were made by men. Today few baskets are made in Nandi, and the few basketmakers I encountered were women. Men traditionally worked in wood, making such things as three-legged stools and knobbed clubs. Some still make the latter, which they sell for cash. Calabashes for milk storage, with beaded leather tops, are the most important craft item. Most women know how to make them, and make them for their own homes and as gifts, particularly wedding gifts, for other women.

Such items as beds, wooden suitcases for storing clothes, and wooden tables and chairs, bought from professional carpenters, are now common in Nandi households. Richer families sometimes own such things as radios and good-quality kerosene pressure lamps. Western-style clothing is worn by both sexes (though most women seem to have adopted it as recently as the late 1960's), except for the very old, who may still wear traditional garments. Most women wear a "cape" made of a printed cotton rectangular cloth (called *khanga* or *lesu* in Swahili) draped over one shoulder, or wrap such a cloth around their waists while working around their compounds. Many old men (and some women) have replaced their traditional monkey-skin cloaks (later blankets) with European raincoats.

Political Organization

The largest territorial unit in traditional Nandi was the *emet* (pl. *emotinwek*) or "country." At the beginning of the twentieth century, there were six (Huntingford 1953*a*: 7) or seven (Gold 1977: 3) such named divisions. The emet was in no sense a political division: it was simply a geographical division that served to distinguish the various parts of Nandi. The second-largest territorial division in traditional Nandi social organization was the *pororiet* (pl. *pororosiek*), a term that Huntingford (1953*a*: 8) has translated as "regimental area." Originally, the three southernmost countries were divided into a number of separate regimental areas. The men of each regimental area, especially those of the warrior age-grade, formed a fighting unit in the military system. As the Nandi occupied more territory, migration and expansion took place on a regiment-by-regiment basis, so that various regiments came to have sections in several different parts of Nandi. Each localized regiment was divided into a number of local communities, or *korotinwek* (sing. *koret*). The council of elders of the koret was termed the *kokwet* (pl. *kokwotinwek*). (Today the term kokwet is used loosely to mean the territorial division as well as its council.) The size of local communities varied considerably, from twenty to a hundred compounds (Huntingford

1953*a*:6). The regimental area thus probably represented from 2,000 to 5,000 people. The populations of local communities numbered in the hundreds, and the local communities and their councils were the most important units in the daily life of the people—the locus of economic joint efforts, ceremonial cooperation, and settlement of most disputes. The next higher level, the councils of the regimental areas, dealt with affairs concerning all the constituent local communities: warfare, circumcision, and planting, as well as disputes involving members of two different local communities.

Though in theory the ideas of any married man could be aired in the local community council, in fact most men were (and still are) content to let the majority of talking and decision making be done by a few particularly influential and articulate elders. Semiformalized leadership of the local community council belonged to a personage called the *boiyot ab kokwet*, or kokwet elder. This man had to belong to one of the "elder" age-grades, and he attained and held his position on the basis of his personal standing in the community, his force of character, his ability as an orator and knowledge of customary law, his reputation for fairness, and his ability to articulate the consensus of the assembly. Though he was not formally elected, he was accepted and recognized in his position by everyone. A local community also contained at least one man called *boiyot ab tumdo*, ceremonial elder, who was an expert and final authority on ritual matters.

According to Huntingford (1953*a*:34–35), the council of the regimental area was composed of all the kokwet elders from the constituent local communities, the two leaders or "captains" (*kiptaienik*, sing. *kiptaiyat*) of the warrior age-grade, and two *maotik*, representatives of the Orkoiyot, the centralized magico-religious and military leader (see below). Leadership of this council was vested in two elders who came to hold their position in much the same way as did the kokwet elders within the local communities. These elders were called *kiruogik* (sing. *kiruogindet*).

Today, the term *kiruogindet* is used to indicate the government-appointed heads of locations and sublocations, and may be glossed in English as "chief." The current administrative hierar-

chy divides the district into nine locations—location being both
a geographical and a political unit. In the beginning of British
administration, the district was divided into twenty-five locations, roughly corresponding to traditional regimental areas.
Later on, these locations were consolidated in an attempt to do
away with the association between each administrative unit and
a traditional land unit (it was feared that the military associations of the latter might become a source of "unrest"). Under the
present system, the nine locations have been divided into sublocations, varying in number, each under a subchief. The subchiefs
are appointed by the District Commissioner on the recommendation of the location chief, who has himself been appointed by
the Commissioner. Campaigning for both these positions is
done (informally) within the constituencies served by them,
however, and the candidate with the greatest support is virtually assured of appointment.

Within each sublocation are the old kokwotinwek (a term now
used to mean an area rather than a council), though now the
kokwet elder (who these days can sometimes be quite a young
man) is formally appointed. The kokwet elder's main concern is
now the settlement of disputes between people belonging to his
kokwet, because most of the functions that were formerly functions of the kokwet have become functions of the sublocation.
Most community meetings, self-help (Harambee) project committee meetings, local courts at which decisions binding upon
offenders are taken, and so on are held at the level of the sublocation. People today think of the sublocation as an integrated
unit and feel their allegiance is to it. Moreover, it is an overwhelmingly endogamous unit. For these reasons, I consider the
sublocation today to be the most basic "community," and have
taken it as the unit of this study. In the modern context, then, I
use the term "local community" to refer to the sublocation and
"neighborhood" to refer to the kokwet. Sublocations vary in size
of population and number of households. In the sublocation
that was the site of my fieldwork, there were 286 households
(compounds), with a total population of approximately 2,300
people. There are also smaller, named neighborhoods within
the kokwet, but like the largest unit, the emet, these neighbor-

hoods have no distinct boundaries and no distinctive functions as such.

Age-Sets

One of the most important features of traditional (and current) Nandi social organization is a system of seven rotating age-sets (*ibinda*, pl. *ibinwek*) for men. Kipkorir (1973) reports age-sets for women among the Marakwet, and Persistiany (1939) reports that such a system formerly existed among the Kipsigis. Women's age-sets may once have existed in Nandi, but not in the memory of living people, nor does early ethnography report their former existence. Women take their position in the age system from their husbands, being termed "wives of Such-and-such age-set," though one sometimes hears comments such as "She was married by a Nyongi, though she really should have been a wife of Maina."

A man's membership in an age-set is determined by the date of his circumcision; all men who were circumcised within a certain period of time belong to the same age-set. In the traditional age-set system there were at any given time four sets of elders (one of which might not contain any living members), the set of the senior warriors, the set of the initiates, and a potential set of the young boys. Since boys are not circumcised at any fixed age (but usually between twelve and sixteen), at the margins of two age-sets there can be some overlapping of ages. In 1977, men of the Kipkoimet age-set were between the ages of fourteen and thirty; men of the Sawe age-set, twenty-eight to forty-five; men of the Chuma age-set, forty-two to fifty-nine; men of the Maina age-set, mid-to-late fifties to early seventies. The youngest Nyongi men were in their early seventies and the oldest about ninety, and only a handful of men of the Kimnyigei age-set were still alive. The next age-set to be circumcised will be Kaplelach, and a new Kimnyigei age-set will follow them.

The view of the Nandi-Kalenjin age-set system enshrined in East African ethnography and introductory anthropology textbooks, that of Huntingford (1953a:64–68), has been called the "clockwork" approach (Daniels 1982:5). Its underlying assumption is that there has always been a regular periodicity to age-set transitions. Huntingford argues that a new age-set began initiation once every fifteen years, signaled by alternate flowerings of the *setiot* plant, which bloomed every seven or eight years. The time it takes the system to cycle, from the beginning of the initiation of a particular age-set until all its members have died and boys who will bear the name of the same age-set are about to be initiated again, is about 105 years. Daniels, however, convincingly debunks this model and argues that Kalenjin age-sets have always been of variable length. A new cycle of age-set transition and initiation began when "social pressures . . . reached a threshold in a large number of local areas" (Daniels 1982:2). On the basis of the reports of informants and other ethnographers, he views the setiot as marking ill-omened times for initiation.

Huntingford also believes that initiations were conducted for a set period of four years, after which came a long "closed" period that effectively marked off one age-set from the next. Daniels (1982:22) relies on eyewitness accounts to argue that at least since the earliest part of the colonial period, male initiation has occurred more or less annually. Members of an age-set are divided into four subsets (in Nandi these are called Chongin, Kiptaru or Kipalkon, Tetagat, and Kiptoitoi) on the basis of the order of their initiation. Daniels maintains that assignment of members of a marginal initiation subset to an age-set could be an individual decision determined by social factors.

Traditionally, size rather than actual age determined whether a boy was ready for initiation. Only boys considered "big enough" (measured by fitting them with an armlet of standard size) were initiated. Though members of an age-set considered themselves to be essentially equals, and a high value was placed upon sharing and cooperation among all age-mates, those who were circumcised at the same time (a *mat*, or "fire," from the fire they shared as initiates) were considered to have a special relationship within which equality and sharing were absolute.* At some point, the oldest among the initiates began to take on the duties of warriors, while the oldest of the warriors in power married and began to establish themselves as householders. One of the social pressures that contributed most urgently to the occurrence of an age-set transition was the demand of the initi-

---

*Daniels (personal communication) rightly points out the need to portray clearly three levels of age-set solidarity: all members of a set, members of chronological subsets within it, and men who actually underwent initiation together.

ates for their age-set to be recognized as the senior warriors. It is said that the warriors resisted "retirement" and had to be convinced of its advantages.

The transition from one age-set to another was marked by a big ceremony known as *saget ab eito* (slaughter of the ox), which had as its main feature the bloodless sacrifice of a white ox.* At this ceremony, a huge moving-on celebration for all Nandi, the initiates became warriors, warriors became elders, and a new age-set was begun for boys about to be initiated. The saget ab eito probably also served as a public way of assigning men to age-sets so as to enforce age-set exogamy (the rule that forbids a man to marry his age-mate's daughter or a woman to marry her father's age-mate; Daniels 1982:14). A man and his son should not belong to adjacent age-sets: for example, if a man is a Maina, his eldest son should be a Sawe. The eldest and youngest of a set of brothers will in all probability belong to adjacent age-sets.

It is not clear how it was decided to hold a saget ab eito, but presumably the decision involved negotiations among many ceremonial elders. No saget ab eito has been held by the Nandi since about 1892 or 1893, when the Kipkoimet age-set ceded its status to the Kaplelach. The ceremony was due to occur just after Nandi "pacification" by the British, and was forbidden by the new government; it was due to occur again in 1923, but though permission was granted, it was rescinded at the last minute because the colonial government believed the Nandi planned to use the ceremony to stage an uprising. In 1938, permission to hold a ceremony was requested, and denied.

In modern Nandi, though the tradition of the saget ab eito ceremony survives in oral history and in the memory of a few old people, the age-set system functions without the ceremony, and no one seems to feel the need for such a ceremony. The age-set that precedes the one being initiated is still spoken of in English as being "in power." (In 1977, this age-set was Sawe, consisting mainly of men in their thirties.) Circumcision is now not restricted to a specific four-year period but takes place in a local community whenever there are a sufficient number of boys

---

*The best existing description of this ceremony is the one given by Peristiany (1939:32–39) for the Kipsigis. The Kipsigis ceremony was essentially the same as that of the Nandi, though it may have differed in some minor details.

of appropriate age. Though it may not occur yearly in each local community, it most likely occurs somewhere in a group of neighboring communities on a yearly basis. The initiation of an age-set may thus, at present, be spread out over a period of fifteen years. The subset names are still used, but only in a general way, to distinguish those who were circumcised relatively early during this period from those who were circumcised relatively late; there are no clear-cut lines of demarcation between the subsets. On the other hand, the solidarity of age-mates, and particularly those who were circumcised together in the same ceremony, is still an important part of Nandi life; and hierarchy based on age, which includes women as well as men, continues to be a central organizing principle of Nandi culture.

Magical and Political Power

Orkoinatet is a term that denotes a type of supernatural power believed to reside in a category of people known as *orkoiik* (sing. *orkoiyot*). This power includes precognition, clairvoyance, telekinesis, and the ability to control the weather and the health and fertility of animals and people. It is believed to be patrilineally inherited by men only. Orkoinatet is believed by the people to exist in several Nandi clans to a mild degree, and to have always been present. However, it is found to a greater degree, and it became solidified into a sociopolitical institution, in the Talai clan.

In the late nineteenth century, when the Uasin Gishu Maasai had been defeated by the Naivasha and Il-Laikipiak Maasai and were in the process of being displaced from their former homeland by the Nandi, a family of Maasai *laibons* (supernatural practitioners, rainmakers) migrated to Nandi. The role of the *iloibonok* as centralized ritual leaders and military consultants was apparently already established among the Maasai. These Maasai migrants are said to have been assimilated into the Nandi Talai clan.* They were believed to possess particularly strong powers

---

*Later members of the same families migrated from Nandi to Kipsigis and established the same institution there. The assertion that the Nandi orkoiik were originally Maasai may not be literally true. The Maasai apparently have a tradition that their iloibonok came from "outside," in some versions, from Nandi (P. Rigby, personal communication).

of orkoinatet, and gradually they became very influential and rich. By 1890, one Talai lineage had come to stand out as orkoiik, and the Nandi had moved toward a form of centralized political organization under the leadership of a chief orkoiyot. The term orkoiyot thus can be used to denote any man with powers of orkoinatet (and all male members of the Talai lineages descended from the Maasai), but there was also a person known as the Orkoiyot, who was the magico-religious and military leader for all the Nandi people. This position was hereditary, passing from father to son and from elder to younger brother. According to Huntingford: "The chief *orkoiyot* . . . is not an executive authority. He is not the 'chief' of the tribe, he is not a judge, and he is in no way a supreme central authority to whom appeals may be made . . . his real functions are confined to that sort of expertness which is founded on magic and religion" (1953a:45).

The Orkoiyot sanctioned war, circumcision, and planting. It was believed that he performed magic to ensure adequate rain for the crops, and he was thought to have exceptional power to prophesy the success or failure of military expeditions. When a raid was being planned, representatives of the regiment that was planning it approached the Orkoiyot to inquire whether it would succeed, and if he foresaw that it would, to receive his blessing. If the raid was successful, the regiment gave the Orkoiyot tribute in cattle. Since no regiment would be foolhardy enough to embark upon an expedition that did not have the sanction of the Orkoiyot, he functioned as a centralized controller of military affairs. There was no direct line of political authority from the Orkoiyot to the regimental area council, thence to the local community council, but the Orkoiyot had representatives at the meetings of regimental area councils who could report back to him. Very likely the Orkoiyot, simply because of faith in his magical powers, could wield considerable influence to make community affairs go his way if he chose to do so.

It can be assumed that the Orkoiyot was a shrewd military observer and usually backed only fairly sure raids. At any rate, the Talai clan grew very rich on the cattle tributes. Having plenty of cattle to make the bridewealth payments, they took many wives, and they made a practice of "naming" wives—that is, if a man of the Talai clan fancied a girl, he would announce publicly that he intended to marry her. If she married any other man instead, it was believed that this man would be destroyed by orkoinatet. People resented the Talais for this, of course, but little could be done because they were so much in awe of their magical powers. On the other hand, resentments could sometimes boil over. For example, in 1890, the Orkoiyot was stoned to death because a cattle raid he sanctioned was a disaster and a great many Nandi warriors were killed. He cursed the Nandi as he died, and it came to be believed that the British defeat of the Nandi fifteen years later was the result of his curse. In this case, the fact that the Orkoiyot's power had brought this ultimate disaster down upon them strengthened people's opinion of the power of orkoinatet and the inadvisability of crossing the Talai clan.

After the advent of colonial administration, the person of the chief Orkoiyot—Koitalel arap Samoei—became a rallying point for Nandi resistance to British rule. This Orkoiyot was assassinated by a British army officer in 1905 during presumed peace negotiations, and the British then undertook a punitive expedition to "pacify" the Nandi. The Nandi were enclosed within a reserve, and the Talai clan, who were suspected (probably rightly) of having been behind the agitation against British rule, were forcibly moved from wherever in Nandi they had been living and segregated in a separate location, Kapsisiywa.* Non-Talais had to have government permission to enter the location to consult with Talais, and Talais had to have permission to leave it. Nevertheless, they continued to exert influence through relatives and supporters outside their location. At various times during the colonial period the British government deported from Nandi orkoiik whom it viewed as rabble-rousers (Magut 1969: 106–7).

The attitude of the Nandi as a whole to the Talai and the institution of the Orkoiyot has always been somewhat ambivalent. It is certainly true that large numbers of people (whether the majority or not is hard to tell so long after the fact) supported the Talai in their opposition to British rule, and perceived the person of the Orkoiyot as an institution around which opposition

*Kapsisiywa is now a sublocation of Sang'alo Location.

could crystallize. Samoei is today regarded as a great hero of the anticolonial struggle, and public institutions such as schools are named for him. I was once introduced to one of the widows of Barserion arap Manyei, a later Orkoiyot, whose residence in her community was apparently a great source of pride to its members. On the other hand, along with the fear of the Talai for what they could do with their supernatural powers there was also resentment of their arrogance and high-handed use of power, and especially—as mentioned earlier—their behavior in claiming women as wives and having their own way in situations of conflict with other people. Because of their segregation after 1905 or so, the Talais were prevented from experiencing many forces of change to the same extent as other people, and in any event they had a stronger vested interest than others in the maintenance of the traditional system. Talais have a reputation for having maintained more aspects of traditional life than other Nandis. They were late to adopt Christianity, for example, and many of those who have done so became converts to Roman Catholicism, which permits more leeway than the Protestant missions in combining Christian belief with traditional practice.

For all these reasons, the Talai clan still is viewed as quite distinct from other Nandi, and people can be heard to talk about the Talai as opposed to "real" or "true" Nandi. Talai people claim that they are objects of collective discrimination in various forms; Talai young men, in particular, complain that they have difficulty marrying because people deny them their daughters on account of former Talai excesses. Though the missions and colonial administration certainly made efforts to undermine people's belief in the reality of orkoinatet, the vast majority of Nandi, regardless of social status or degree of education or Westernization, believe to some extent that Talai men possess supernatural powers. Many of the educated young Talai men, when asked whether they themselves possess these powers, say that they do not because a high level of Western education is somehow inimical to their expression; but then they say that they know for a fact that orkoinatet is possessed by their fathers and grandfathers. I even heard of a number of recent cases in which it was said that Talai men succeeded in marrying women against their will. The position of chief Orkoiyot, however, has disappeared. Today there is no particular person who is regarded as occupying this status.

Kinship

Nandi descent is patrilineal and residence is patrilocal, though there is not now, nor was there ever, such a thing as a patrilineage with any corporate functions. Patrilineally related people are believed to be more closely related than people who are related through other kinds of links. One calls one's father and his brothers by the same term, and considers one's father's brother's children as effectively equivalent to one's own siblings.* One inherits membership in one's clan (*oret* = road or path) patrilineally. Aside from the clan, the largest patrilineally structured group is a loose conglomeration of households consisting of the families of brothers and patrilineal first cousins, all known collectively by the one name of their common grandfather as Gab-So-and-So (the family of So-and-So). Only occasionally is such a group genealogically extended to a greater degree than through the grandfather. The word that denotes such a group is *gab chi* (a person's house or home), which is probably best translated as "patrilineal extended family." These people, if living contiguously as today they often do, cooperate economically in many ways. Each married couple has its own fields, but cooperative labor among members of a patrilineal extended family is common, as is also mutual aid in the form of both food and money. Cattle may be separately owned but are often herded together.

Aside from clan membership and the presence of small patrilineal extended families, Nandi for the most part reckon kinship cognatically and stress any known kinship links between two individuals as the basis for mutual aid, support, and goodwill. The Nandi word *tiliet* translates as "personal kindred," and *tilianutik* as "kinsmen" or "relatives."

Nandi kinship terminology has relatively few terms, many of which subsume large numbers of kin types. One of its most interesting features is the complexity of the terminology desig-

---

*Children of one's mother's sister, though also called by the term for "sibling," are not regarded in quite the same way.

nating affinal kin types relative to the terminology for consanguineal kin types. In terms of traditional classifications of kinship terminologies, Nandi fits all ten of the criteria stated by Buchler and Selby (1968) for an Iroquois terminology, but it also has features that they cite as diagnostic of Omaha, most notably the terminological merging of members of the mother's brother's lineage. (A list of the most commonly used kin terms and the kin types they denote is given in the Appendix.)

A person expects to be able to call upon anyone for whom he or she uses a kinship term for assistance in times of need or for help in endeavors that require collective labor. Such links are much more likely to be activated, however, if the people involved live in close proximity. Aside from members of one's immediate patrilineal extended family, affines are more likely to cooperate than are consanguines. Since most marriages are locally endogamous, affines tend to live close to one another. The combined principles of age and affinity make brothers-in-law who are age-mates prime candidates for cooperation and mutual aid. Mutual aid ties and friendly solidarity are particularly marked between men related as *lemenyi*, husbands of two sisters. There is a somewhat conscious tendency to convert friendships to ties of affinity where it is convenient to do so. Sisters and close female kin also make conscious attempts to be married into households located close to those into which their sisters have already been married; this enables them subsequently to be in a position for mutual aid and cooperation (e.g., one sister will often help another living in the same neighborhood with domestic chores if the latter is ill or pregnant; or one sister may stay temporarily with another if she quarrels with her husband). This pattern means that men who call each other lemenyi (an extended affinal relationship) also tend to be neighbors, and special relationships of cooperation often develop between them on the basis of the dual criteria of affinity and proximity. People also maintain close ties throughout their lives with their mothers' brothers and their families, even when they live in different communities.

Clans

Membership in a clan is inherited by every Nandi male. After marriage a woman assumes the clan membership of her husband, so that if asked what her clan is she responds with the name of her husband's clan.* The Nandi clan is a corporate unit only in two very restricted senses: in the control of marriage and in the control of homicide. Among the Nandi, unlike some other Kalenjin peoples (e.g., Keiyo), clans are not and were not in the historically recorded past geographically localized. Rather, each clan would have representatives in most if not all Nandi regimental areas and local communities (though there might be a tendency for particular clans to predominate in particular local communities). The exception to this is the Talai clan, which, as explained earlier, is localized around the Kapsisiywa sublocation.

Both Hollis (1909:5) and Huntingford (1953b:25–27) report the same seventeen named clans.† Clans are not segmented into lineages, but each clan has one and sometimes more totemic animals, and the assignment to a particular totem in the case of clans with more than one is patrilineally inherited. There was traditionally a rule against a man's killing his clan animal, but this appears not to have been taken seriously for some time (Huntingford 1950).

The chief function of clans is in the regulation of marriage. For various reasons it is considered good for each Nandi patrilineally extended family to intermarry with as many clans as possible. Marriages can be forbidden between clans if the elders think that one clan has taken wives from the other too frequently in the recent past, or if such marriages have not been successful.

Huntingford (1953b:25) says that clans are exogamous, but that in the case of clans with more than one totem "marriage is

*This tenuousness of a woman's connection with her natal clan is an unusual feature for a patrilineal society. I believe that it is connected with the permanence of the marriage tie and the extremely secure rights a woman acquires in the resources of her husband's kin group by virtue of her marriage. In several ways, a woman's incorporation into the kin group of her husband is unusually well defined in Nandi.

†My own data show some discrepancies with those of Hollis and Huntingford. For example, in recording clan membership in a community census, I found some clan names not recorded by them that informants insisted were neither subgroups of larger clans nor alternate names. Moreover, several informants argued that one name presented by Huntingford and Hollis as a clan name is actually a subgroup of another clan. If groups that were once subclans evolve into clans in their own right, it is possible that such discrepancies reflect a continuing process of change.

allowed between people who have the same clan name but different totems." According to Hollis (1909:6) "there is no objection to [a man's] marrying into his own clan." In 1977, it was widely believed by younger Nandi (and even by some of the older informants) that clan exogamy had at one time been the rule, but that it was no longer adhered to owing to the impact of Christianity. These varying and conflicting interpretations result from the fact that there has never been one simple rule of thumb about which Nandi clans may intermarry. As *boiisiek che bo tumdo* (ritual experts) explained the situation to me, there was never a rule requiring clan or totemic exogamy per se; each clan's ranking elders established the rules that governed the marriage choices of that clan. The details of these rules were probably not completely known to nonmembers (owing to lack of interest rather more than to secrecy), or even to many clan members. Furthermore, marriage proscriptions were constantly subject to change. If several consecutive marriages between two clans were attended by bad luck (early death, infant mortality, barrenness), marriages would be proscribed. At some later time, a match could be permitted to take place and would be watched with care. If no bad luck attended it, marriages between the two clans would again be opened. Marriages between men and women of the same clan were in general discouraged because they did not extend the network of clan alliances, and they were subject to the same proscriptions: if marriages within a clan had not worked, a rule of clan exogamy *for that clan only* would be instituted. Later, if two people of the clan had a strong wish to marry, the arrangement could be tried on an experimental basis. If it "worked," such marriages would again be permitted; but the proscription could be restored at any time. Thus, marriage rules have always been open to change in Nandi, and attempts to classify Nandi clans as either exogamous or nonexogamous can only lead to confusion. The same system of marriage choices exists today, though it is true that strongly Christian families sometimes choose to disregard the current proscriptions.

Clan membership also figured importantly in cases of homicide. If a man killed someone of his own clan, no legal action was taken. If he killed someone belonging to a different clan, he and his relatives were obliged to make compensation to the dead person's family—ten cows for a man and nine for a woman (paid to her husband's family).* If the killer's family was slow in making the payment, the victim's family was considered within their rights in seizing ten cattle of their choice from *any* of the members of the killer's clan.† Snell (1954:64) reports that if a married woman without children was killed, compensation was paid to her father's clan, but that if she had any children it was paid to her husband's clan; also, that if a man should happen to kill his own mother (or any of his father's wives?), compensation was paid to her brother's clan. If this is true, it indicates that women to some degree maintained membership in their natal clans, in spite of informants' denials that this is the case.

Crime and Punishment

Huntingford (1953a) lists as legal offenses the following: persistent disobedience to the kokwet, sacrilege, incest, witchcraft, *chesorbuch* (the birth of a child to an uninitiated girl), homicide, cattle theft, other theft, and assault. Other offenses for which sanctions could (and can) be imposed include: adultery, rape, illicit pregnancy, and vandalism. Persistent disobedience to the decisions of the kokwet council could be punished by expulsion from the community. At the same time, the offender's property would be destroyed by the community's warriors at the order of the elders (Huntingford 1953a:104).

The category of sacrilege as defined by Huntingford (1953a: 105) included mainly acts against the Orkoiyot, such as carrying weapons in his presence or touching his head. The offender was cursed by the Orkoiyot, and no other sanction was needed.

Incest includes sex between people who call each other by relationship terms or who consider themselves *tilianutik*. It also includes sex between a woman and a man of her father's age-set, or between a man and a woman of the same age as his mother.

---

*When I asked who would pay compensation to whom if a woman killed someone, my informants were puzzled, for it seemed that no one had ever heard of such a case; but after discussion it was generally agreed that the woman's husband's family would probably pay. The hypothesis that the victim belonged to the woman's father's clan, however, led to great confusion and the tentative assertion that compensation might not be required.

†Actually, there is lack of agreement about the amounts of compensation to be paid. The amounts I have stated here are those given me by informants.

In the past, incest was punished by women in a procedure known as *njoget ab chebiosok* (punishment of women), discussed in Chapter 3. This sanction also applied to rape resulting in miscarriage (Huntingford 1953a: 106; Snell 1954: 33). Otherwise, a rapist or adulterer might be publicly beaten by his age-mates. Women were beaten by their husbands for adultery (Snell 1954: 31–32).

In cases of suspected witchcraft (e.g., illness or sudden death), the identity of the witch was first divined, after which he or she was expelled from the community. If the witch was believed to have killed someone, he or she could be executed by clubbing (Huntingford 1953a: 107–9). Snell (1954: 86) says that relatives of the witch were required to carry out the execution.

If an uninitiated girl gave birth, the child was killed (though a childless woman on the spot could adopt it), and the girl was thereafter considered unclean, *samis* (Huntingford 1953a: 106–7).

Cases of homicide, as explained above, were handled through the payment of compensation. A habitual offender could also be executed at the orders of the kokwet elders.

Theft of cattle from another Nandi was said to be so repugnant that it hardly ever took place. The offender would be ostracized by the community, and the boiyot ab kokwet would formally and publicly curse him (Huntingford 1953a: 118). Theft of property other than cattle was more likely to occur, though it was, and is, an act looked down upon with great scorn by the community. A thief who was discovered was required to pay compensation greater in value than the item stolen. If the guilt of a thief was disputed, it could be proved or disproved by a curse or an oath.

In cases of assault, there was no penalty if no injury was inflicted. If there was an injury, compensation in the form of meat or a goat to be slaughtered and eaten by the victim was paid. Compensation could (and can) be paid even for minor injury, provided blood had been drawn. Destruction of property was handled through restitution. A man was required to accept responsibility and make restitution for acts of his wife and children (Snell 1954: 59–60).

The Nandi curse (*chubisiet*) can be invoked against either a known or an unknown offender. It is still believed to be effective and is used both as a criminal sanction and in the settling of local disputes. The public announcement that an unknown thief is about to be cursed usually causes the offender to confess and make restitution. A legitimate curse can be uttered by anyone, but in the case of crime it is usually elders who perform one of various sorts of magical actions (e.g., burning something, heating a needle in a fire, snuffing out fire) at the same time saying, "The person who did this thing, may the wind eat him, may smallpox take him, may he be consumed as is this paper, may he suffer stabs of red-hot needles, may he be snuffed out like the fire." It is believed that an innocent person cannot be harmed by this ceremony, and a guilty person cannot fail to be. Chubisiet is not invoked lightly. No one can mount an effective curse against someone for a trivial offense or for an offense that is not universally condemned. A father can curse a child for disobedience, however, and any person, regardless of social status, can curse another if he or she has been truly wronged, and the curse will be effective.

The oath (*mumiat*) is similar to the curse except that it is invoked by the person who has been accused of or is suspected of having committed a crime. The suspect performs certain magical actions and says, "If I am guilty, may [some disaster] befall me." Various forms of oath are described by Snell (1954:81–83).

An important principle in Nandi law and dispute settlement is that cases are supposed to be ultimately resolved in such a way that the offending party makes restitution and is forgiven and reabsorbed into the community. Continuing ill-feeling should be prevented at all costs.

Although the modern system of crime and punishment is a combination of the traditional system and the legal institutions of the national government, the vast majority of cases involving disputes or minor criminal offenses are resolved by means of traditional law within the local community.

The first level of dispute settlement is the kokwet elder who, perhaps together with several respected men of a neighborhood, hears both parties' versions of the dispute and attempts to arbitrate a settlement agreeable to both. The majority of cases (known to the researchers) that were settled by kokwet elders during the period of this research were concerned with accidental property damage (primarily destruction of crops by stray cattle) and domestic quarrels.

The next higher level of settlement (and the level at which most cases are settled) is that of the sublocation. Sublocation court is an informal affair that takes place under a tree in the village center on any afternoon when a large enough number of influential elders is judged by consensus to be assembled. Anyone may attend and listen at these cases, but only prominent elders may speak; other people rarely even attempt to do so. The elders who have reputations for their wisdom and knowledge of customary law will have the most influence. First the elders listen to testimony by people who have knowledge of the case, and then in turns they take the floor to debate its merits. When enough has been said so that it seems there is consensus, a prominent elder will sum up what he takes to be the opinion of the group, including penalties, if any, that should be paid by the parties in the dispute. If no one else stands to air a contrary opinion, a decision has been taken. Cases aired at the sublocation level in the research community in 1977 included property damage cases (not settled to the disputants' satisfaction by kokwet elders), boundary and property disputes, theft, assault, verbal assault, rape, vandalism, adultery, and disputes over inheritance. Internal dispute settlement is considered important to the prestige of the community, and disputants are strongly encouraged to accept it.

If one of the parties in a dispute feels that the decision of the sublocation court has been unfair, he can always resort to the national legal system and file charges with the district police so that the case will be heard in District Court. In the majority of cases, however, the verdict of the elders' court is accepted. Cases of homicide are always police matters. None occurred during the period of the research, but a case of infanticide that occurred was immediately referred to the police and district courts. Several cases of arson, which grew out of skirmishes between Nandi and members of another ethnic group who have settled in Nandi District, occurred during this period in neighboring communities; these cases, too, were referred directly to the police and District Court. Cases involving boundary and inheritance disputes also frequently fail settlement at the sub-location level and are referred to the national legal system. Langley (1979:102) has published accounts of a number of divorce cases heard in the district court at Kapsabet.

Types of behavior regarded by the community as deviant but not criminal (e.g., craziness, homosexuality) are generally viewed with tolerance and/or amusement rather than outrage. Such deviants are not ostracized, but have a place, albeit not a respected one, in the community.

Religion and Cosmology

In Nandi traditional belief, the major controlling force in the universe is *Asis*, a being conceptualized in much the same way as the Judeo-Christian God. *Asista*, the sun, is the metaphorical embodiment of Asis, and should be understood as symbolizing a ubiquitous spiritual being, a view articulated by Nandi informants. Some other names for Asis are *Chepkelyensogol* (nine-legged one) or *Chepkelyenpokol* (hundred-legged one), referring to the sun's rays, and *Cheptalel*, which has been institutionalized as the name for God by the Roman Catholic Mission. Huntingford (1953a:135) offers two possible interpretations of Cheptalel: that "-talel" is the root of *talelyo*, yellow, or that it is a combination of *ta* (meaning "always" or indicating an indefinite future tense) and *lil*, gleam. Swahili speakers often refer to God by using the Swahili term Mungu, and Seventh-Day Adventists and members of the Africa Inland Church use the name Jehovah.*

Prayers to Asis were traditionally said twice a day by both men and women but not by children. The head of a household could pray on behalf of his entire household. Special prayers and offerings to Asis were made at a household shrine (*koros*), made from branches of four ritually important plants, which stood just outside the back door of the house, on the right of the door as one exits. Today it is rare for even a non-Christian house-

---

*I once heard a Nandi Protestant (Seventh-Day Adventist) preacher ridicule the Catholic use of the term *Cheptalel* on the grounds that it means "white girl" (derived from *chepto* = girl and *leel* = white) and therefore characterizes the deity as female.

hold to have a koros, though shrines are sometimes erected for special events such as weddings or initiations.*

Asis was most commonly invoked in individual life-crisis rituals such as initiations, weddings, and funerals, but there were a few communal rituals that involved the whole community, notably the initiation rituals of boys of an appropriate age. The other major community-wide rituals in which Asis was invoked were certain agricultural rituals held by a single regimental area—such as the *Kipsundet* or harvest festival and rituals to bring rain in time of drought—and also rituals at which prayers were offered for the well-being of warriors away on raids.† Except for male initiation, no communal ceremonies of this sort are held today, but it is not entirely clear how long they have been out of use. Huntingford (1950:77) described the Kipsundet festival as "obsolescent" in 1950. It is still common for elderly people to offer daily prayers to Asis, and Asis is still invoked at initiations, weddings, and funerals.

Also important in Nandi traditional belief were the *oiik* (sing. *oiindet*), or spirits of dead ancestors. It was believed that the dead—usually patrilineal but sometimes maternal ancestors—were reincarnated in their descendants. The person himself would have no memory of his former life, but older people who had known the ancestor would be able to see the likeness between the two in appearance, mannerisms, aptitudes, interests, and so on. While souls were waiting to be reincarnated, they

---

*For further discussion of the traditional Nandi shrine and its use in modern ritual, see Langley (1979:26, 128–30). Peristiany (1939:215–16) gives a good description of the analogous Kipsigis *mabwai* and its functions.

†All major sources on the Nandi (Hollis 1909; Huntingford 1950 and 1953; Snell 1954) agree that a communal ceremony known as *Kipsundet* or *Kipsunde Oieng* was held between September and November to celebrate the harvest. Hollis uses the term Kipsunde Oieng (second kipsunde) to denote the communal ceremony, the first kipsunde being the first fruits ceremony celebrated quietly by the women of each household. Snell (1954:4–5) describes an unnamed traditional ceremony that took place during the *Buret* season (July) and was intended as intercession for growing crops. His description of the details of this ceremony is remarkably reminiscent of the descriptions of Kipsundet given by Huntingford and Hollis and also of the postharvest ceremony called *Rootet* described by Peristiany (1939:222) for the Kipsigis. It is not clear whether there were two similar ceremonies and this fact was not discovered by most ethnographers, or whether Snell was misinformed as to the timing and purpose of the ceremony he describes.

lived in the land of the spirits, *koret ab oiik*—the underground land still believed in as a place where life is an exact replica of precolonial Nandi. Traditionally, only old people and children were buried, because they were thought to be already close to the spirit world. People in the prime of life had to be eased into the spirit world, and so their bodies were left to be eaten by hyenas (men lying on their right sides, women on their left). The dead person's spirit would then enter the hyena, and when the hyena burrowed and slept underground, the spirit would leave it and enter the land of the spirits. Spirits could leave the spirit world to visit their living relatives, apparently chiefly because of nostalgia.

"On the whole," Huntingford writes (1953a: 140) "the *oiik* (spirits) are friendly to their people and the Nandi think of them with affection." It was my experience, also, that Nandi view the European fear and horror of ghosts (when they are aware of it or are told of it) as silly and irrational. If you haven't done anything wrong, why should a ghost harm you? It was the traditional belief in Nandi, however, that angry spirits and not Asis were responsible for the majority of disease and disaster (with the exception of crises concerned with the weather and epidemics). When it was ascertained what offense had angered a spirit, a ceremony could be held to placate the spirit, and the descendant's health and prosperity would be restored.

Non-Christian Nandi still believe in spirits and the spirit world. The degree to which Christians nowadays accept this traditional doctrine of the spirits is not clear. Tales abound of people who came near death, accidentally went briefly to the spirit world, and found it exactly as described above. Such tales were related to me even by people who considered themselves Christians. One devoutly Christian informant described his beliefs about Heaven and the spirit world thus: souls of Christian Nandi go directly to Heaven and dwell with God for Eternity; souls of non-Christian Nandi go to the spirit world and continue to be reincarnated in their descendants. I am unable to say how typical or idiosyncratic this view is, but clearly not all Christians dismiss traditional belief as false and illusory. The bodies of both Christians and non-Christians are now buried in family compounds, however, so at least one aspect of the traditional belief has changed.

The traditional Nandi cosmos contained a number of nonempirical beings besides Asis and the spirits. There were *musambwanik*, or evil spirits, invisible beings believed to stay near places frequented by human beings for the express purpose of causing people annoyance and bad luck. People still refer to these evil spirits, but they do not seem to take them very seriously as a cause of misfortune.

Witches, on the other hand, are still believed in by most Nandi—excepting the younger, educated ones—and are credited with causing much evil. Witchcraft or sorcery has several categories. The most common kind of witch is the *bonindet*. This can be a person of either sex but is usually a woman who has no inborn ability but is adept at using magical devices. A *kimetit* is a male member of certain clans who possesses an inborn power that brings misfortune—either at will or inadvertently—upon others. The *sakutindet* is a woman (usually barren) who may cause a newborn child to die if she comes near it, owing to the envy it arouses in her. *Chebusoriot* is a woman who bewitches her husband by putting magical preparations in his food, making him stupid, weak, and easy to bend to her will. In every community certain people, usually old women with few relatives, are thought to be witches and are shunned. Old people lament the fact that it is now illegal to destroy witches.

Thunder, *Ilat*, was another named nonempirical being in the Nandi cosmos. There is also a mythical monster known as *chemosit*, which lived in the forest and was believed to eat people. Some old people swear that once such a creature existed in fact, but it is now mostly spoken of jokingly as a bogeyman to frighten children.

Of the Christian churches, the Africa Inland Church, a fundamentalist denomination, has the longest history in Nandi and is today one of the strongest. The Anglican Church Missionary Society for Africa and the East ran a mission post in southern Nandi District from 1909 to 1912 but found few converts, and in 1914 it sold its station to the Africa Inland Mission. The AIM moved its station to Namgoi (Kapsabet) in central Nandi District in 1924. One of the first projects undertaken by the AIM was the translation of the Bible into Nandi, and Nandi has the distinction of being the first East African vernacular to have a translation of the Bible.

A Roman Catholic mission station was established at Chepterit, also in central Nandi, in 1934, and it has been very successful. According to Langley (1979:8), "in Nandi District today, about 100,000 people call themselves Christians." Of these, most are Roman Catholics, followed by Africa Inland Church adherents, Anglicans, and small numbers of Seventh-Day Adventists and Pentecostals. A tiny minority of people are adherents of the African independent churches, but these have little popularity among the Nandi. There are also (especially in Kaptumo) a small number of Nandi Muslim families; these are mostly descended from early Swahili traders who intermarried with Nandi or from converts of these traders.

Most Nandi, Christians and non-Christians, accept the idea that Asis or Cheptalel and the Christian God are one and the same. Belief in Jesus and ideas about sin and the afterlife distinguish Christians from non-Christians. The Roman Catholic Church allows more latitude than Protestant denominations for the combination of Christian belief with traditional practice (rituals, polygyny, clitoridectomy), and allows dancing and the use of alcohol. The Africa Inland Church and the Seventh-Day Adventists both regard alcohol as sinful, and in areas where the majority of Christians are fundamentalist Protestants this is the biggest source of conflict between Christians and others. All the churches theoretically forbid male members to have more than one wife, but the Catholic Church is said to be more lenient in its view of polygynists. The impact of Christian disapproval of polygyny is, in any case, very limited.

The current pattern of Nandi religion, then, is one in which almost everyone worships a single deity who is regarded by most people as identical to the God of their ancestors. Most people continue to believe in the effectiveness of the spirits of the ancestors to intervene in human affairs. A majority of adults consider themselves Christians, but for a large number of these, belief in the basic tenets of Christianity is combined with continuing observance of traditional ideals of action in opposition to Christian teaching.

Expressive Culture

The rather spare traditional Nandi religious framework has not produced much in the way of mythology. There are few ritual contexts that involve the narration of sacred stories. The bulk of Nandi oral literature consists of folktales told in the evenings by old women for the amusement of children. Circumcised men consider telling folktales beneath their dignity. If they ever do recount such a tale, they make a great point of swearing to its veracity, or they comment on the exceptional character of their actions in narrating events known to be fictional. There is also a standard set of riddles asked mainly of children. Hollis (1909:97–151) has published a large collection of Nandi riddles, proverbs, and folktales.

Music, song, and dance are the most popular form of entertainment and creative activity among adults. People normally dance in sex-segregated groups, and almost always to the accompaniment of song. Drums are used now, though they were traditionally absent; women kept time by slapping their leather skirts. There is room for creativity in composing lyrics for songs sung on special occasions. For example, girls' initiations and weddings are always the occasion for original songs performed by groups of adolescent girls.

Beer drinking is a favorite recreational activity of elderly people, and it is also part of all Nandi traditional celebrations. A common pot of beer is shared by members of a gathering, who sip from it through individual reed straws six or more feet long. Unison and call-and-response singing around the beer pot are common, and people often rise on their knees and perform a kind of dance of the upper torso, swaying in unison in accompaniment to the music. People say that in the past women would never have joined men in beer drinking and singing, but today there is no stigma whatsoever attached to this practice except in the case of very young wives, who are not supposed to drink alcohol at all.

Singing and dancing have been formalized to a great extent

owing to the formation in many villages of men's and women's performing groups, which wear traditional dress and sing and dance at public events such as Harambees (fund-raising meetings for community-sponsored projects) and to entertain visiting dignitaries. During President Kenyatta's administration, performing groups traveled regularly from all over Kenya, including Nandi, to entertain him at his home in Nakuru. Churches and schools also sponsor organized choirs.

The only traditional Nandi musical instruments were three- and six-stringed lyres, illustrated by Hollis (1909:39). Today these instruments are very scarce in Nandi District. A number of Nandi men have learned to play European-style guitars (though women are considered almost incapable of doing so), and these instruments are not uncommon in rural areas. Radios and battery-operated phonographs are common and much-coveted items. There is a Kalenjin-language record industry, but Swahili-language popular music is also very well liked.

Nandi visual art consists mostly of elaborate beadwork, which is used to decorate women's traditional leather skirts and long earrings (both worn on ceremonial occasions), the tops of milk containers, and so on. There is no carving except for useful items such as men's knobbed sticks and walking sticks. In the modern setting, there is growing up all over East Africa, including Nandi, a tradition of wall painting, both interior and exterior, in shops and particularly bars. The themes of these murals are both traditional and modern—battle scenes, the mythical *chemosit*, various wild animals, cars and buses, and well-known public figures.

Ethos

When Nandi informants are asked what character traits are most important in a person, or what traits a man must have to become a community leader, certain ones are inevitably mentioned. A good person can be described as *tala*, polite/gentle/humble. A leader must be *tala ago kiboitio*, polite/gentle/humble and hard working. Another phrase consistently used to describe the ideal character is *chi ne kasyindos ak bik tugul*, a person who gets along well with everyone. A good person must also have respect, *konyit*, which means essentially showing appropriate deference to members of age-sets above one's own in the age hierarchy, and avoiding familiarity with one's seniors and members of certain other categories (e.g., for men, daughters of age-mates). Two essential Nandi terms in evaluating character are *kitalait*, to be polite, and *keng'elel*, to be rude. If people are asked to evaluate someone's motivation in violating a community norm, the response depends on the person's previous reputation. If it is good, an argument will probably be presented that what was done did not really constitute a violation of a norm. If it is bad, the typical response is, "That one is a very rude person."

There is little open conflict in Nandi society. Traditionally, people would be more apt to swallow grievances and move elsewhere than to air them openly. A Nandi finds it difficult to tell another person outright anything critical or unpleasant or to confront another person with a grievance or problem. One of the most valued leadership traits among Nandi is the ability to talk out problems and resolve disputes in ways acceptable to all concerned and restore amity, and people who are always quarrelsome are looked at somewhat askance.

Nandi people are very averse to open displays of any kind of emotion—not only anger, but also joy and grief. They are stoic in the face of pain. Wild shows of emotion do sometimes occur, but onlookers find them embarrassing. Drinking to the point of drunkenness is tolerated good naturedly in old people as a sort of well-earned privilege, but in anyone else drunken behavior, especially if it is aggressive, is embarrassing and strongly censured. The consumption of alcohol and drunkenness among members of younger age-sets and women is constantly discussed as a major social problem.

A good person, man or woman, should be hard working, not only for the family and household but also on behalf of the community. People who participate wholeheartedly in community work projects are looked upon with approval. Accumulating personal wealth is also approved, and the ideal person is one who will increase the material well-being of his or her household through hard work and shrewd planning. It is generally assumed that material wealth will be the reward of hard work, effective planning, and self-control, and therefore wealth in itself is taken as proof of these traits and is an important criterion for assignment of leadership and influence to a man. Wealth is necessary to the highest level of good character.

Other valued traits—for both sexes—include courage, truthfulness (in the sense of not intentionally deceiving someone for a private motive; lying to spare someone's feelings and/or avoid confrontation is more or less expected), and honesty with property (stealing is viewed with contempt). Certain traits are especially favored in men alone, and certain others in women. These will be discussed in Chapter 3.

THREE

General Ethnography of Gender Roles

A NANDI WIFE said to me: "It is true that there is a special love between mothers and daughters. Nevertheless, it is very wrong to wish that your [first] child will be a girl. You must not do that. It is a great insult to your husband."

The young Nandi wife awaiting the birth of her first child wishes for a boy. A family can be complete without daughters, but it can never be complete without sons. Not only are sons necessary to continue the line of patrilineal descent so ideologically important to the Nandi, but also, because of the "house-property complex," only male lineal descendants of a married couple may inherit their property. Failing male lineal heirs, the property must revert to a collateral line, and this is considered a great misfortune. The birth of sons to a woman therefore ensures the proper devolution of her house's property. The importance of the first child's being male is emphasized in other ways, too, such as the higher ritual status accorded to a man whose first-born child is male; only men who meet that qualification are permitted to be sponsors at a male initiation ceremony (Langley 1979: 20).

All children, regardless of sex, are welcomed and loved in Nandi families, however, so if the first child is a girl, disappointment is not great. A girl is an asset to a family because the marriage of daughters creates valued ties of kinship between families and brings to the family bridewealth cattle, which enable a girl's brother to marry. Thus, the ideal Nandi family has children of both sexes, and this is consciously recognized.

Nonetheless, though children of both sexes are equally valued in a family, both sexes are not given the same cultural evaluation: male is very clearly viewed as superior to female. Most Nandi mothers do not acknowledge any great difference between their male and female children in mental or behavioral traits. (This is rather different from the opinions of American mothers in my experience, who tend to view their male children as fussier, more independent, more active, and more aggressive than their female children from birth.) Nandi mothers are on the whole remarkably adamant in their insistence that any behavior differences they observe are not significant.* The profound differences that are held to exist between men and women begin at puberty, particularly for boys, who are thought to be utterly transformed by the rite of male initiation.†

The Cultural Constructs "Male" and "Female"

In Nandi, men are considered superior to women physically, intellectually, and morally. Men pride themselves on feats of endurance, such as being able to travel on foot for very long periods of time without rest or food. They are supposed to be less susceptible than women to cold and able to endure sitting and even sleeping outside in cold and rain without shivering. Shivering is thought to be an unmanly behavior, and it is one of the symptoms of having been affected by feminine-child pollution.

---

*My material on these points is entirely impressionistic. I made no detailed studies of the actual behavior of Nandi children in the field, and I do not know to what extent, if at all, they actually behave differently from American children. American studies of child behavior (e.g., Goldberg & Lewis 1969; Maccoby & Jacklin 1974) indicate that American mothers' evaluations may to a degree reflect actual behavioral sex differences in young children (whether in some sense innate or the product of early socialization is unresolved by these studies). My Nandi observations do not in any way reflect on the question of whether there are sex differences in behavior in young Nandi children, and whether or not these are of a greater or lesser order than those found in American children. My comments refer only to what Nandi mothers think and say about their children's behavior. These data are in the realm of cultural constructs and may have little relationship to behavior amenable to study by observation, but they are relevant to the question of how Nandi culture encodes the nature of sex differences.

†As puberty approaches, boys and girls are said to begin acting more differently from one another than previously in preparation for their adult roles. But they are not dramatically and fully differentiated until the boys have undergone male initiation.

Women are thought to be susceptible to cold, and thus in cold, damp weather to spend their time huddled around the household hearth, which men are not supposed to approach.

The symbolism of the hearth implies more than greater female susceptibility to cold. The cooking hearth of a family dwelling—one for each married woman with children—is the quintessential symbol of womanhood. It symbolizes both the domestic role of the wife and the lines of cleavage as well as the wife's position in the property system. The most basic domestic and property holding unit is that composed of a wife and children. Though a husband may have overarching rights in more than one such unit, he is fully incorporated into none. The dwelling of a family with a cooking hearth in Nandi is called *got*. *Sigiroinet*, another type of dwelling, was traditionally a neighborhood barracks or clubhouse, where warriors and young married men slept and entertained their girl friends. Today, boys and young unmarried men in a family compound occupy a hut called sigiroinet, which is distinguished from the family dwelling by the lack of a cooking hearth, though there may sometimes be a fire for warmth. Traditionally, a married man avoided approaching his wife's hearth and also avoided sleeping in his wife's house if she was nursing a baby.

Got and *sigiroinet* both have subtle implications. Women are associated with the warmth of the hearth, men with the cold and rain; women are associated with house property, men with property not allocated by house; women are associated with the domestic domain, men with the public. Girls may be referred to as *lagok ab got*, children of the house, whereas boys may be referred to as *lagok ab sang'*, children of the outside. The Nandi present a classic case of a symbolic system in which female is represented by "inside" and male by "outside" (Garretson 1972:119), an extension of the identification of women with domestic and men with public concerns assumed by numerous theorists (including Rosaldo 1974:23; and Ortner 1974:77) to be near universal. Whether near universal or not, this dichotomy is not always symbolically elaborated as it is in Nandi. The inside-outside dichotomy, the cooking hearth as a symbol of the wife's domestic concerns and her position in the property system, hence as a general symbol of womanhood, the avoidance of the cooking hearth by the husband (and by adult men in general) and their association with the outside, cold and rain, the assertion that a true man should not shiver, and the idea that men are possessed of greater strength and ability to endure physical hardships than are women are all part of a single system of ideas. A realization of this pattern cleared up my original puzzlement at responses such as "Shivering," or "Sitting near the hearth often," to the question, "What things might a man do that would cause you to doubt that he is truly a man?"

Male is symbolically associated with the right, stronger side; female is associated with the left, weaker side. (In a number of East African societies it is considered to be incorrect to be left-handed; children are strongly trained for right-handedness, and almost all adults are right-handed.) The hearth in a traditional Nandi house is to the left as one enters the front door, and the left or hearth side of the front room is the domain of the women and children. Men entering the front room go to their right, and remain on that side of the room, away from the hearth. The same pattern is carried over to other gatherings of men and women (e.g., ceremonial beer drinking): men sit to the right, women to the left. It is said that in the past it was believed that if a woman passed a man's right side it could be injurious to his physical strength and skill with weapons, and any man had tacit permission to immediately beat a woman who passed him on the wrong side. People still tend to walk toward the right-hand side of a road when passing one another, but women do not seem generally to go out of their way to avoid passing a man's right side. Nor are people any longer very particular about which side of a sitting room they occupy. In any case, in many more modern Nandi houses the hearth is no longer in the sitting room but in a separate kitchen shed.

Men are believed to be more intelligent than women. Women are thought particularly to be incapable of foresight and to lack the ability to make and carry through sensible and realistic plans. For this reason it is generally agreed that husbands should administer the family estate and wives should for the most part concur with their husbands' plans. It is commonly claimed that if a woman tried to manage property, she would very likely make a mess of it.

Along with possessing greater intelligence and the ability to plan and manage, men are assumed to be more decisive and to have greater strength of will. Women are said to be indecisive, contradictory, unable to hold to a course of action. Men are said to be able to think through and carry out a plan of action without being swayed from their course. This is the aspect of manliness that is attacked by women who use witchcraft on their husbands. These beliefs about men's greater capacity for forethought underlie the Nandi tenet that men are the appropriate controllers of property. Beliefs about the nature of male and female thus form the ideological support for the relation of men and women to property.

Men are said to be more likely than women to forgive and forget after they have had a dispute with someone. They are better able to maintain amicable relations in spite of differences. Women are said to be more likely to hold grudges and to let old quarrels interfere with their ability to live harmoniously with people. In other words, the amicability that is such an important value in Nandi culture is attributed to men, and the presumed lack of that quality in women is a mark of their inferiority.

Courage is a quality believed to be of importance to both sexes. Every Nandi should be able to endure hardship or suffering without complaint. For women, this quality is particularly stressed in relation to the ordeal of childbirth. A woman is not expected to be courageous, like a man, in confronting enemies or wild animals. For both sexes, it is disgraceful to cry aloud or openly display fear or pain. Yet uncourageous behavior is a greater disgrace for men than for women. If a woman is not brave during childbirth, for example, her reputation suffers, but not greatly and only temporarily.

There are only a few qualities that are held to be desirable that women are generally said to possess to a greater degree than men. One of these is the capacity for pity and understanding (*rirgei*). Women are also said to have a greater tendency than men to be clean and neat in their personal habits; to be otherwise is a greater disgrace to a woman than to a man. For the most part, however, masculinity is defined as having in full measure those traits most valued in Nandi culture. Femininity is not seen as another completely different set of traits, both positive and negative, but more as the *lack of* the positive traits whose full measure defines real masculinity. There is a Nandi word for masculinity (*murenotet*, literally "manliness") but no corresponding word for femininity.

"Masculine" traits are in fact valued for both sexes in Nandi; it is only that it is assumed that women will usually fail in giving them full expression, owing to their natural inferiority. In this context, it is interesting that the Nandi lexicon contains a term to describe women who display masculine levels of the aforementioned valued traits (and who, it might be added, are also described as more assertive than the average woman, though assertiveness is never listed as an ideal character trait toward which all people should strive). This term is *chemurenyo* or "manly woman," derived from *che* (feminine prefix) and *muren* (man). Informants deny that it is in any sense negative for a woman to be considered a "manly woman" or masculine; it is simply that, women being naturally inferior, there are not many who can be described in this way. When I asked my informants for examples of such women, two women in particular were mentioned. One was the wife of a prominent Christian living in the community. This man was highly respected, though he did not participate to a great extent in community affairs because of his intense involvement in affairs of the Africa Inland Church for the whole of Nandi District. He was one of the earliest Nandi converts to Christianity, who had helped translate the Bible into Nandi, had a degree in theology, and spoke almost flawless English. His wife was one of the most highly educated women of her age group. She was active in organizing women's affairs of both the church and the community and was one of the few women to hold a formal position of influence in the community (a seat on the Board of Governors of the self-help secondary school); and she had managed the family farm single-handedly for two years while her husband was away studying for his theology degree. The other woman commonly described as a "manly woman" was a woman separated from her husband who farmed land that had been pioneered by her mother, then a widow, in the 1920's or 1930's. This woman was not educated or active in community affairs. Her reputation as "manly" was gained from the fact that she successfully managed an estate without the assistance of a man.

If it is desirable for a woman to be "manly," why are there so few such women? The answer lies in the principle that a wife must maintain behavior that shows respect (*konyit*) for her husband. The deference of wife to husband is a central concern of Nandi ideas about respect. It is the metaphor for the whole of male-female relations. Nandi informants realize that not every man is superior to every woman in every way. They know that some women are more intelligent than some men. Elderly women deserve some deference because of their position in the age-set system. But by accepting marriage as the focal institution in which the relationship between the sexes is acted out, the Nandi can ignore exceptions that run counter to stated ideology. Certainly it may be true in individual cases that a man is inferior to or owes deference to individual women; nonetheless, husbands (standing for men in the abstract) should *always* be superior to wives (standing for women in the abstract). This principle must be respected as long as the husband does not abrogate his responsibilities to his family and the management of his estate to such an extent as to be viewed as less than a man in the eyes of the community. Thus, if a man fails utterly in the management of property, because of a drinking problem, for example, it is not considered disrespectful of the wife to assume responsibility. But in the normal marriage, it is disrespectful for a wife to outstrip her husband at anything. Unless the husband is far and away the superior achiever, even to engage in any activity that might bring her prominence or a reputation for manliness is to court community censure for "trying to be bigger than her husband." A woman who openly displays abilities and behavior that might cause her to be classified as a "manly woman" must be either an independent woman or the wife of a very prominent man; otherwise, she runs the risk of being thought lacking in respect.

Women referred to as "manly" are ordinarily in the prime of life. They are rarely widows, even though a widow no longer has to worry about showing appropriate respect for her husband. In the example cited above, it was the separated daughter of the widow who had pioneered land who was described as a "manly woman." Her mother, a very old woman, living in the same household, was not described in this way, though the daughter was only administering what the mother had gained through her independent efforts.

In sum, the Nandi concept of masculinity assumes a high level of hard work, good social relations, physical strength, emotional reserve, stoicism, foresight, and decisiveness—all traits that are generally valued in Nandi culture. "Femininity" is defined not as a thing in itself, but as a lower level of the same generally valued traits—the absence of the full measure of masculinity. But though it is negative for a man to be unmasculine, it is *not* negative for a woman to be unfeminine; there is even a special word, of favorable connotation, for such a woman. This positive evaluation of masculine women exists more in the abstract than in fact, however; in particular cases, the positive "manliness" of a woman is usually weighed against the principles that husbands must be superior to wives and that wives must respect their husbands by not trying to "be bigger than" they.

Men, Women, and the Community

The validity of the distinction between "domestic" and "public" domains is currently being questioned (e.g., Sacks 1976; Etienne & Leacock 1980). I would agree that the fruitfulness of this distinction is by no means universal. Nevertheless, it remains a useful descriptive tool for many societies. For Nandi, I believe it makes sense to consider as a group a number of diverse roles, which all have in common that they are significant for a collection of people that has as its basis physical proximity, and is larger than the minimal compound group that is the basic unit of production and consumption. These are roles that exist in relation to a community.

The community-wide roles that I am concerned with here fall within the following categories: ritual leaders, diviners, practitioners of traditional medicine, judicial leaders, and political leaders.

The *boiyot ab tum*, ceremonial elder or ritual expert, can only be a man. He is responsible for performing and overseeing all details of men's ceremonies and ceremonies that involve both sexes. He does not have authority over women's ceremonies. These are organized and overseen by female ritual experts. There is always at least one such woman in each neighborhood. Traditional weddings must involve both a male and a female ritual expert, though the man is considered to be in charge. The position of female ritual expert is unnamed and is less formal than that of boiyot ab tum; nonetheless, because of their reputations among women, such women can attain significant influence in a local community.

The restriction of female ritual experts to rituals involving women has not always been the case in Nandi society. The post-harvest festival (*kipsunde*), a major ritual that involved an entire regimental area, included a blessing of the harvested crops by both male and female ritual experts. The experts were compensated for this service with grain or small livestock (Gold 1977: 12).

In present-day Nandi, though female experts are in charge of girls' initiation, the lucrative business of designing and renting the costumes worn by the initiates is entirely in the hands of men. These male specialists say, however, that they follow specifications determined by the female ritual experts.

Diviners, who predict the course of future events on the basis of numbers and patterns of stones and other small objects shaken from a calabash, are present in many communities and can be consulted for a fee. They are invariably men. Like the greater powers of *orkoinatet*, the art of divination is believed to run in families and to be inherited by sons from fathers. It cannot be either inherited or learned by a woman.

Traditional curers may be of either sex, but this is an art that seems to be more commonly practiced by women than by men. The traditional Nandi doctor uses both herbs and ritual manipulations. There are a number of male traditional doctors with outstanding reputations in Nandi, and in almost every Nandi community there is at least one female herbalist (*chepkerichot*). The chepkerichot can be consulted for a fee—by persons of either sex—and she dispenses remedies concocted from local plants for complaints such as colds, fever, malaria, diarrhea, nausea, headache, backache, menstrual cramps, and infertility. Occasionally a female herbalist has a male apprentice. One herbalist I knew said that she had taught much of her craft to her son, but he showed no interest in practicing. More and more, however, Western-trained medical practitioners, the majority of them men, are being consulted for illnesses that used to be treated by the herbalists.

Another exclusive province of men is the traditional political mechanism. Women attend community meetings conducted by the chief in the role of observers only, usually sitting in a small cluster in a far corner of the gathering. Women can also observe in local elders' courts. They speak only when they are direct participants in litigation or have been called as witnesses, and even in these cases they are sometimes spoken for by male relatives, since it is assumed that women, especially if young, are shy about speaking in public.

In the precolonial period, there was one institution through which women participated in a community-wide judicial and sanctioning process: the *njoget ab chebiosok* (punishment of women). A man who committed incest, certain other sexual irregularities, rape (especially if it resulted in miscarriage), and other less clearly defined offenses against women (one of which, according to an informant, may have been physical abuse of a woman that resulted in serious injury) was subject to this sanction. This institution was not unlike the Igbo custom of "sitting on a man" described by Van Allen (1972: 170). A similar "council of women" has been reported for the Kalenjin-related Barabaig of northern Tanzania (Klima 1970: 88–94), and for the Kalenjin Tugen (Kettel 1981). In the "punishment of women," naked women, shouting their outrage, surrounded the offender's house, then dragged him out and beat him and set fire to the house, and possibly confiscated some of his livestock. This institution appears to have been lost by the early part of the twentieth century. I found no reference to it in colonial records, and I know of no evidence that the government was responsible for its cessation.

Women do sometimes participate in Western-derived political institutions, particularly as members of governing boards for schools, clinics, cattle dips, the community water supply, and so on. A handful of women in my research community sat on these boards, and I knew of a few women who did so in other communities. The national political party requires that a certain number of seats on local party committees be occupied by women. Women have also served on the district council for Nandi District, and a Nandi woman has been a Member of Parliament.

A local branch of the national women's organization *Maendeleo ya Wanawake* (Progress of Women) was just beginning to be revived as I prepared to leave the field. Maendeleo was active in Nandi during the late 1950's and early 1960's but then fell dormant, apparently—or so I was told—because the local women thought that many of its programs, such as courses in baking and embroidery, did not really do anything to help improve the quality of their lives. Whether or not the attempt to revive the organization has been successful, I do not know. It was my observation, incidentally, that although men are active in providing volunteer labor for community development projects such as building schools, damming rivers, and laying pipe for the community water supply, very few Nandi women participated in community work projects.

Nandi women, though barred from the male-controlled political process, have traditionally occupied some roles in the extra-domestic community that carried with them a certain amount of prestige, influence, and even power. Today, the pattern of women's roles in this wider community is changing. Though women are free to participate in the government at the district and national levels, they have not gained in political participation in the local community, which is the most important political arena, and they have lost the single institution through which they once did have power to affect some area of community life. Further, the public roles of ritual expert and curer, which formerly gave some outstanding women recognition in the community, are on the decline.

Pregnancy and Birth

Motherhood is the most valued role for a Nandi woman. It is also true that a man with no children has little social standing. All women fear the possibility of barrenness, and a woman's first pregnancy is cause for celebration. Hollis (1909:64) describes a formal ceremony that was traditionally held at the time of a young wife's first pregnancy. Today, the celebration is informal and people acknowledge the pregnancy only obliquely, since Nandi believe that it is bad luck to talk openly about hoped-for events or treat them as faits accomplis.

According to Peristiany (1939:89), "It is a great crime for the Kipsigis to frustrate a woman of motherhood." This is also true for Nandi. If a woman's husband is unable to impregnate her, she is considered completely justified in seeking out some other man to do so, and she cannot be treated as an adulteress for doing this. Her husband's inability to sire a child was one of the very few grounds upon which a woman could traditionally ask for a divorce. Every woman has the right to have children, and if a woman is unable to become a mother, she can use other means such as adoption or woman-woman marriage to acquire children for her house.

Sexual intercourse is avoided from the time a woman knows that she is pregnant. It is believed that intercourse during pregnancy can cause miscarriage, or if not miscarriage, that the whiteness of the semen can cause the baby to be born with a skin pigmentation condition characterized by light-colored spots. If a child is born with this condition, it is assumed that the parents violated the rule against intercourse during pregnancy.

If a woman feels ill during her pregnancy and has trouble carrying out her domestic responsibilities, someone—usually an unmarried sister or a teen-age girl from the neighborhood—will come to stay with her and help her. If there is no child in the family old enough to be responsible for helping with the care of another child, a relative or friend will be asked to lend the mother an older child shortly before the birth is anticipated. This child, usually a girl, is called *cheplakwet* (child nurse), from *chep* (feminine prefix) and *lakwet* (child). Older informants say that in the early twentieth century the child nurse was usually a teen-age girl, but today she is usually a girl between the ages of seven and twelve.

The decline in the age of the child nurse is partly a reflection of a marked lowering of the age of marriage and first pregnancy for women. Older informants maintain that in the early part of

TABLE 1
Age at First Marriage for 63 Women Married 1970–1977

Age at marriage	Number of women	Age at marriage	Number of women
14	3	21	2
15	11	22	1
16	9	23	2
17	11	24	1
18	13	25	0
19	5	26	1
20	4		

this century girls in their early twenties were just ready for initiation, and most girls were married between the ages of twenty-three and twenty-five. Langley (1979:86) suggests that the traditional age at marriage for Nandi women may have been as late as twenty-five to thirty, but this seems doubtful. And even though the usual age at marriage was late in the past, there were numerous exceptions. Individual life histories include such events as marriage by abduction at an age judged by the informant to have been the same as that of a child of thirteen. Age at marriage for women has certainly declined; the majority of women now marry before the age of eighteen. For women in my random sample household census (wives, daughters, and daughters-in-law of the household heads) who were married in the period between 1970 and 1977, the average age at marriage was 17.8 years. The distribution of ages at marriage is shown in Table 1.

The decline in age at marriage and first pregnancy is a partial cause of an apparent increase in fertility among Nandi women over time. Matson (1972:13n) estimates that in 1890 the average size of the Nandi family was 2.6 children, as compared with figures of 7.75 for Luhyia (Bantu Kavirondo) and 10.6 for Luo. Langley (1979:86) estimates that in 1973 the average family size was 8–10 children.* Ominde (1975:33) shows a figure of 6.6 for total

---

*Neither Matson nor Langley exactly specifies the source of figures used in making these estimates (Matson refers to "statistics compiled in later years"). Nor is it clear whether estimates of "average family size" are intended to refer to completed fertility only or include women who have not yet completed their fertility as well.

TABLE 2
Average Number of Children per Woman by Age Cohort

Age	Number of women	Average no. of children who survived to adulthood	Average present no. of children
≥70	11	2.9	
60–69	20	3.5	
50–59	21	4.3	
40–49	27	5.5	
30–39	39		5.9
20–29	72		3.1

NOTE: Includes only women married more than one year.

fertility for Nandi District on the basis of 1969 census figures.*
Ominde's figure is more in keeping with my own data. The data
on family size that I collected in the field do not directly demonstrate that Nandi women's fertility has increased (see Table 2).
For women past childbearing age, by ten-year age cohorts, average numbers of children who reached adulthood have steadily
increased, but this could be due to an increasing survival rate for
children rather than to any increase in the number of live births.
(I found it very difficult to obtain accurate information about
children who had died.) Figures for women still of childbearing
age are not comparable to the figures for the older women, because the number of their children who will survive to adulthood is not yet known. My informants certainly believe that
Nandi fertility has increased, and I think it likely that this is true
although I cannot demonstrate it.

The decline in age at marriage and first pregnancy for women
is one factor, certainly, in the increase in Nandi family size. But
one must ask why Nandi family size was so low in the first
place. There is no reason to think that infant mortality in Nandi
was significantly greater than in neighboring societies where
families were typically larger. Two of the reasons that Langley
(1979:86) suggests as accounting for small family size—infan-

*Total fertility is a hypothetical estimate of completed fertility (number of live
births per woman past menopause) that would be the same as completed fertility
if women who have not yet completed fertility continue to reproduce at the rate
for all women during the year in which the calculation is made (Thompson &
Lewis 1965:251).

ticide and female genital mutilation—are, I think, inadequate. It is doubtful that infanticide was practiced frequently enough to be a very significant factor; and if mutilations during clitoridectomy were in the past a significant factor in keeping the birthrate low, they would continue to keep the birthrate down today since the vast majority of Nandi women still undergo clitoridectomy. To explain why Nandi families were small in the past in comparison with neighboring peoples, while today they have increased, we must look for a factor that was significant in the past but has now disappeared or been greatly reduced in importance. Late marriage, and women's role in traveling to seek food during famines—two factors also mentioned by Langley— meet this criterion. I suggest a third, that is, the system of beliefs about the polluting influence of women and young children on men. This could well have been sufficient to ensure that births were widely spaced. Decreased infant mortality owing to the availability of modern medical services helps to explain the increase over time in family size for Nandi, but not the difference between Nandi and neighboring peoples.

Birth control is not much practiced in Nandi. Advice on birth control methods, and devices of various sorts (IUD's, pills, condoms), are available to women and men at a government family planning agency in the district administrative center at very low cost. People will agree with the idea that the growth of population is a problem and that it cannot continue without giving rise to a class of landless people (so far virtually absent in Nandi), but it is a long way from this abstraction to personal practice. Several strong objections to birth control are apparent. There is, first of all, the continuing high value placed on fertility and the notion that no woman should be childless. Women are interested in birth control techniques, and some progressive women are beginning to use such devices as IUD's. A definite stigma is attached to limiting one's fertility artificially, however, so that even progressive women tend to remain quiet about their use of birth control. One of my closest friends in Nandi initially denied to me that she used birth control and only admitted it months later. Artificial methods of birth control, including pills, are viewed with a certain skepticism, particularly for younger girls. Even when people agree that teen-age pregnancies are a social problem, they think that young girls who use devices or pills will have difficulty conceiving a child later on. Also (as in the United States), girls are too embarrassed to go and present themselves at the family planning clinic and in that way admit that they intend to engage in sexual intercourse. Thus, modern means of birth control have so far had a very limited impact on the rapidly expanding Nandi population.

Most births occur at home, with one or two of the local midwives in attendance. The knowledge and experience of the midwives is quite impressive, and they also know when the mother is in such great difficulty that she should be taken to hospital. Midwifery, though a special skill, is not formalized in any way; midwives learn from other midwives and from experience. Today they are usually paid in money, though sometimes with a sheep or a goat.

A woman in labor sits or lies inside her house or outside in her compound—whatever place and position she finds comfortable. During the delivery she squats, supported by the midwives and other women who may be present, and the child is expelled into the waiting hands of a midwife. Men may not be present during a birth—this is considered strictly the business of women. When a woman goes into labor, the husband, if he is at home, immediately leaves the compound (perhaps going first to the home of the midwife to call her) and he does not return until after the birth.

Women know that they are expected to display courage in labor and childbirth. No special techniques are used to reduce pain. The one time I was present at a delivery, the mother, though obviously in pain, did not even moan. One woman who was cowardly during childbirth became the subject of gossip among the women of the neighborhood. It was said that she had cried aloud and refused to open her legs or push to expel the baby when told to do so by the midwife. She apologized later for her cowardice, saying that she did not know what had possessed her to act in such a way. Cowardly behavior does not carry a lasting stigma, however, and the gossip about this woman's behavior as it went around the community for a brief time was one of mild disapproval and ridicule. The incident was soon forgotten.

When the child is born, someone present at the birth goes to inform the father, who is waiting somewhere nearby with a group of male friends. The mother is supposed to be fed a high protein diet for the first few days following birth. Her husband should slaughter an animal to provide her with meat, and sour milk will have been stored for weeks or even months in advance. For the first few days following the birth of a child, a woman is supposed to do nothing but rest and nurse the baby. Traditionally, a man left his wife's house at the time of the birth and was not fully reincorporated into the household until the child was old enough to walk. Today the period of avoidance has been greatly reduced, but there is still the feeling that the husband should avoid the place of birth of his child for a period of days or weeks. Women now may try to arrange things so that their child will be born, for example, in the house of their widowed mother-in-law in the same compound. The woman can then spend the first week or so sleeping in her mother-in-law's house and being looked after by her, while the husband is free to use the house he normally shares with his wife. Traditionally the husband went either to the house of another wife (often cited by informants as one of the major advantages of polygyny) or the *sigiroino*, the communal warriors' dwelling.

On the third or fourth day after birth* the mother and baby would come out of the house for the first time for the naming ceremony, called *king'et Asis* (to awaken God) or *kimong' asis* (to come into the sun), at which the child was given his or her first name, the *kainet ab oiik* or spirit name. Hollis (1909:65–66) implies that this was primarily a woman's feast, but my informants describe relatives of both sexes as being present. The naming ceremony is still held, though it is no longer very formal. Elderly relatives, particularly patrikin, gather round the sleeping baby and go through the list of deceased family members, calling out each name in turn. (A boy can be named for a woman, but a girl can never be named for a man.) When they reach the name of the person after whom the child will be named, the child will sneeze or urinate. The name the child is given may be the name

---

*Hollis (1909:65) says fourth. Some of my informants said fourth, some third, and some third for a girl and fourth for a boy.

of the ancestor, or a name that refers in some way to a characteristic of the ancestor. One of my informants, for example, was nicknamed Kipselem, from *set* (to raid) and *Lemek* (Luo or Luhyia). He had this nickname because the ancestor for whom he was given his ancestral name was killed during a raid in Luo country by being stabbed in the stomach. My informant has a light-colored birthmark on his stomach, and this is taken as proof that he is in a sense the reincarnation of this particular ancestor. A person does not usually use the ancestral name as his personal name, but rather the *kainet am musarek*, or porridge name. Hollis (1909:66) says this is given a few days after the ancestral name, though Huntingford (1953a:144) says it is given at about the age of three months, when the child first eats porridge. At present a child's personal name is given within the first week after birth. This name begins with the prefix *Ki-* or *Kip-* for a boy and *Che-* (*Je-*) or *Chep-* (*Jep-*) for a girl, and has as its root a word that refers to the circumstances of the child's birth— Kiplagat or Chelagat, from *lagat* (evening), for example; or Kiptoo or Jeptoo, from *toot* (guest), or Kip- or Chesang', from *sang'* (outside). Most young people today also take a European name of their own choosing later on, at the time they are baptized, or when they go to secondary school, or just as a personal preference.

Traditionally, the new mother was not allowed to touch any household objects or do any housework prior to the king'et Asis ceremony. After this ceremony, she could touch things with caution, and some informants say that she could begin to cook for herself and her children. Other informants say that she was really not supposed to do any housework at all for at least a month. These pollution taboos no longer exist to any degree, and there seems to be no hard and fast rule about when and to what extent a new mother assumes her normal activities. It is said that it is good for the mother if she waits as long as possible, but it depends mainly on what is convenient for the particular household.

Feminine-Child Pollution

The father's traditional avoidance of his baby and the house where his wife had just given birth had its basis in a set of beliefs

that for want of a better term may be called feminine-child pollution. I use this term because both mother and child were considered polluting to the husband/father, and informants' accounts
are divided on the question of whether the polluting effect of
women was intrinsic or was due merely to their close association
with children.

Beliefs about feminine-child pollution seem to have been very
significant to relations between husbands and wives and between fathers and children. Though the beliefs are no longer observed in their traditional form, traces linger in that new fathers
(even rather acculturated men) avoid close contact with their
children for about a month. They usually say, however, that
they do not really hold with the old beliefs. Most old men hold
these pollution beliefs in very much their traditional form. Many
old women say that there was never any truth in the idea of
feminine-child pollution and treat those beliefs as onerous su-
perstitions that they are glad to be rid of.

Kerek is the Nandi word for a polluting substance believed to
emanate from young children, particularly newborn babies.*
The precise nature of the polluting substance is not entirely
clear. My informants (in roughly equal numbers) thought it was
a substance (of indefinite character) found in babies' mouths, or
the urine and feces of babies, or mothers' milk; some men said
that it had to do with menstrual fluid. The afterbirth was believed to be particularly unclean, and it was buried by the midwife immediately following birth. The new mother was therefore most contaminated just after the birth, and both the baby
and the mother became less unclean as time went on. The popular modern theory is that the primary sources of kerek were the
child's urine and feces, and that women were unclean by association with children because their cowhide garments were in
constant contact with the child's excrement and could not be
thoroughly cleaned. This view is used to rationalize the fact that
kerek is no longer a matter of grave concern: today, women wear

---

*The Nandi word *kerek* is clearly related to the Maasai word *kereek*, though
the concepts are somewhat different. "A woman's skirt is said to be 'dirty'
because it may have been in contact with *kereek*, the lard with which newborn babies are smeared" (Llewelyn-Davies 1978:217). The Kipsigis concept of
feminine-child pollution is very similar to the Nandi concept, though a different
word is used for it, *chepengobit* (Peristiany 1939:76).

cloth dresses that can easily be washed in soap and water. The term kerek is also used for the ritual pollution that characterizes recent initiates during their period of seclusion following initiation. I believe the use of the term in this context emphasizes the "rebirth" symbolism of initiation and is a way of making a symbolic statement about the equivalence of initiates and newborns.

Opinions also vary on the subject of exactly who could be affected by feminine-child pollution. Some informants say that any man could be affected, others say only the child's own father and members of his age-set, and others say only the father himself.* It is also said that the grandfather of the child could be affected by kerek, but that in this case the effect could be nullified if he wore a row of cowrie shells sewed onto his fur cloak.

There is unanimity among informants, however, as to the nature of the effects of feminine-child pollution. It was damaging to a man's *murenotet*, or masculinity. His masculine qualities—courage, strength, foresight, decisiveness, stoicism, and reserve—would be impaired. He would become emotional and "think like a woman," and would lose his skill with weapons and become susceptible to shivering in cold weather.

Traditionally, following the birth of a child, a husband would stay out of his wife's house entirely for a period of from one to several months—informants' statements vary. The end of this first period of prohibition was marked by a ceremony called "washing of hands" (*labetab eunek*), a ritual hand-washing on the part of the new mother and an anointing of the child with congealed milk fat. Following this, the husband would enter his wife's house for the first time after the birth and sit on a bed in the back room of the house (where sheep and goats were kept at night). For several months, he could not enter the main room. After the "washing of hands" ceremony, his wife could cook for him, if she kept herself clean, but the food had to be taken to him in the back room. If beer was prepared in the home, other men could sit in the main room and drink but the husband had

---

*Peristiany (1939:76) implies that, among the Kipsigis, any man who entered a new mother's house could be affected by feminine-child pollution. I was told the same thing by a Kipsigis informant. According to Llewelyn-Davies (1978:217), kereek in Maasai affected equally all members of the warrior age-set but apparently not other men.

to drink his in the back room. After another four months or so, the father was finally permitted to enter the main room, but only through the door connecting it with the back room and not through the front door. At this time he would make it a point to go to the left side of the room (the right-hand side as one enters through the front door), the side that was less polluted because the wife did not frequent it.

The father could not have normal contact with the child or resume normal contact (including sexual intercourse) with the child's mother until the child was weaned and could walk. The father was not supposed even to touch the child until this time. If the child accidentally touched anything normally used by the father, or used in the preparation of his food, it was supposed to be traded to an elderly female neighbor in exchange for a similar item. Many informants describe receiving food from their fathers as toddlers in the following way: the father would place a ball of porridge on the top of his foot, extend his leg, and allow the child to take the ball of food without touching him.

Every day during the period until the child was weaned, the mother had to clean herself in the proper way so that she could prepare her husband's food and handle his possessions. This was a complicated process. She would rise before dawn and go immediately to the nearest stream or river and wash her hands and arms thoroughly with sand and cow dung. Old women told me that they were supposed to continue washing for at least an hour, perhaps two hours, and that if a woman returned from washing too soon, her husband might suspect that she had not done a thorough enough job and beat her and send her back to do it again. They said that husbands sometimes hid in the bushes by the stream so that they could see how thorough the women were in this washing. (Several old men among my informants claimed they had actually done this, and several old women claimed their husbands had done it.) If the husband thought the wife was not washing vigorously, or if she made the mistake of touching her body with her hand in any way, her husband would either leap out of the bushes and beat her on the spot or lie in wait for her on the way home.

On the way home, the woman was supposed to hold a stick across her shoulders to make certain that she could not touch her clothing, which was contaminated from contact with the baby. When she reached home, if the baby was hungry, the child nurse (*cheplakwet*) held it to the mother's breast. If the mother touched the baby, she could not cook for her husband or handle his things until she washed again. Since she was not supposed to touch her own clothing, if she wanted to arrange her clothing or scratch herself, she was supposed to use sticks.

Informants report that for most people at least some of these rules for avoidance of kerek were still in effect as late as the late 1950's and early 1960's. By the mid-1960's they had mainly ceased to be observed. The most popular local theory about why such practices are no longer necessary is that through the use of soap women can now keep themselves and their cloth garments adequately clean without such elaborate measures as in the past. During the late 1950's some husbands began to allow their wives to use soap and water in their own compounds instead of going to the river. Others waited to observe whether these pioneers would suffer any ill effects before going along with the trend. Soap was thought to be a more powerful cleansing agent than cow dung, and therefore one could wash for a shorter time and use less water, so there was no need to make the trek to the river.

The account I have given here is based on what I was told by old people of both sexes. Can such an unwieldy system of prohibitions coupled with such extreme displays of intersexual antagonism have actually been followed? I did not observe it firsthand and am not prepared to present my informants' statements as objective. It seems likely that they are exaggerated—that such a system must have had some built-in flexibility. It is unfortunate that Huntingford, the Nandi scholar who *could* have observed these practices at first hand, had no interest whatsoever in women and sex and gender roles.

Only vestiges of these beliefs and practices still remain. Though most men feel that it is somehow inappropriate for them to have much to do with a newborn baby, within several weeks after a child's birth, most young men are again sleeping in the same house as their wives (though sexual intercourse should not resume for at least three months). By the time a child is about six months old, the father, if a young man, has begun to be very demonstrative and physically affectionate toward it.

Most young men, if asked about feminine-child pollution, respond that there is no such thing. However, several young wives told me that their husbands delayed as long as a month before holding their own children. There are now few absolutely rigid restrictions in the sexual division of labor (a man will do quite a lot of things usually considered "women's work" if there is no woman around to do them), but several of the few that there are have to do with too intimate contact with women and young children. A man would under no circumstances wash the clothes of a woman or a very young baby, nor would he clean up a baby's mess.

Female informants (including very old women) tend to view traditional feminine-child pollution beliefs and the associated elaborate cleansing process as a form of extreme oppression of women, and their abandonment as a major step toward emancipation of women. Most young people of both sexes and many older women believe that feminine-child pollution was not a real phenomenon but rather a silly superstition of the past. Older men, and some younger men, though they will admit that cloth and soap make it possible to control this pollution without elaborate and rigid procedures, have no doubt that it was and is a real phenomenon. People's responses to the question of whether feminine-child pollution actually exists fall into two categories: (1) it doesn't, and the proof is that modern men have close contact with babies and it doesn't do them any harm; (2) it does, and the proof is that modern men are obviously less exemplary of all masculine virtues than were men in the past for the reason that modern men have too close contact with women and babies.

One of the important effects of beliefs in feminine-child pollution and the avoidances resulting from them was the spacing of births and the limitation of family size. This effect is recognized by elderly informants themselves, who say (at least in certain contexts) that this was good because it meant that a child would have its mother's milk for as long as it needed it. On another level, there is a strong cultural value on having as many children as possible, and informants also say they are glad that diminished concern about feminine-child pollution now makes possible larger families than in the past. Thus, ideas about the desirability of spacing children and the desirability of large families are in conflict, and may always have been in conflict, in the Nandi value system.

Other Categories of Pollution

Feminine-child pollution was not the only kind of pollution. Men who had killed someone and mothers of twins were considered to be dangerous persons and were described as being *ng'wan*, literally "sharp," "bitter," or "painful." In most cases, the condition of a man who had killed was temporary; he would go into seclusion for four days, at the end of which a purifying ceremony would be performed. The two exceptions, according to informants, were the man who killed a second time before the purifying ceremony could be performed, and the man who killed a member of his own clan; in both cases, the killer was regarded as unclean for life. The condition of a mother of twins was also permanent, there being no way in which she could be purified. This stigma did not extend to the twins themselves, however.

Ng'wan people were dangerous to cattle. If they drank milk, the cow would sicken and die. They were forbidden to walk among cattle or to cross a cattle enclosure, or to milk. Killers, but not, so far as I could determine, mothers of twins, were also believed to be dangerous to small children. If a man who was thus polluted allowed his shadow to fall across a small child, the child could sicken and die.

Ng'wan people were supposed to wear a particular type of bracelet so that they could be distinguished from ordinary people and not be offered milk to drink. In their own homes, however, there was a way of letting them have milk: a particular cow could be assigned to a ng'wan person, and person and cow together went through a ceremony that involved drinking an herbal medicine from the same trough. This ceremony was believed to nullify the effects of the pollution on the individual cow. Thereafter, the person could drink milk that came from that cow, but no other.

It is difficult to say to what degree these special pollutions still matter in Nandi. Several informants told me that mothers of twins are now viewed as the same as anybody else and that while murderers are not "the same as anybody else" they have no special ritual status. It was impossible to investigate whether people's behavior conforms to this assertion, since I never personally encountered a case of either twin birth or homicide.

I have already mentioned the taboo about a woman's passing too close to a man's right-hand side. This taboo had no special name, but it was carefully observed. A woman passing a man on the road was supposed to walk to his left side; not to do so could rob him of his finest masculine qualities—his skill with weapons, ability to withstand cold and damp, and mental vitality and decisiveness. The effects of error were thus similar to those resulting from contact with feminine-child pollution, except that in the case of passing on the wrong side, impairment of skill with weapons is particularly emphasized—perhaps because that has an obvious connection with the right hand. Men no longer beat women who pass them on the wrong side, but passing on the left is still considered the polite thing to do, particularly if the man is old.

Menstruation seems to have been regarded as only mildly polluting. Some male informants seemed to think that menstruation was one traditional aspect of feminine-child pollution, but others thought it was not really regarded as harmful. Sexual intercourse was avoided during menstruation, and still is, and some men say that in the past a man would avoid touching a woman who was known to be menstruating. Menstrual blood is believed to be dangerous to manly qualities if ingested. One of the ways in which wives are believed to be able to bewitch their husbands and gain control over them is by putting menstrual blood into their food. The activities of menstruating women are not particularly restricted in any way, however, nor were they in the past.

Childhood

It is the common perception among Nandi themselves that one of the most radical changes that distinguishes their traditional way of life from their current one is the easy-going relationship that fathers are now free to enjoy with their young children. On visits to Nandi compounds during moments of leisure today, it is not unusual to see young fathers (especially members of the Kipkoimet age-set, who in 1977 ranged in age from adolescents to men in their late twenties) holding, cuddling, talking to, and playing with their children, particularly infants and toddlers. Nevertheless, the degree to which children have an intimate relationship with their fathers even today should not be overstated. In fact, small children are with their fathers only rarely, because men spend most of their time away from their compounds, either at work in their fields or visiting with their age-mates in other compounds or at the sublocation center. Children rarely accompany their fathers on such excursions. During five months of a study of time allocation conducted as part of this research, of a total of 345 random observations of adult married men, in only one case was a man observed in direct interaction with a small child (Oboler 1977a: 11).

As the child grows older, though he or she may spend more time in the father's company, perhaps helping in work, the distance and reserve in the relationship increase. Nandi mothers say that by the age of five a child should have been trained to show respect for the father by not playing roughly or making noise in his presence, by refraining from physical contact, and by paying attention when spoken to. So far as I could tell from observations, the child's sex does not determine the degree of contact between father and child during early childhood. Later on, fathers begin to spend more time with their sons (but also occasionally daughters), cooperating in such chores as taking care of the cattle, plowing, and fencing, and teaching them to do types of work associated with men.

Mothers, too, spend less time in direct interaction with infants and toddlers than a Euro-American observer might expect. In my study of time allocation, I found that adult women spent only 6 percent of their time, and married women only 6.5 percent of their time, in activities defined as "child care." * Even the mothers who spent the *most* time in such activities (those without helpers) spent no more than 10 percent of their time in this way. It must be remembered that *all* Nandi mothers (as well as mothers in most other African societies) are working mothers, with heavy work loads aside from the care of children. The vast

---

*This category includes direct interaction in all care-giving activities (e.g., feeding, bathing) as well as holding, talking to, and playing with infants and toddlers.

majority of interaction that any young child has with other people is with older children, and it is therefore children who are responsible for the bulk of the socialization of other children.

The person most likely to have primary responsibility for the care and socialization of an infant or toddler is the *cheplakwet* or child nurse, a girl (usually) between the ages of seven and twelve, sometimes an older sibling, often a relative. A boy may occasionally be given the care of a younger child if no girl of the appropriate age is available but this does not seem to be as common in Nandi as in some other Kenyan societies (Ember 1973; Weisner & Gallimore 1977; L. Binagi: personal communication). If a family does not have children old enough to take care of little ones, they borrow a child from relatives for a period of some years—usually someone on the mother's side (a younger sister, or the child of a brother or of a sister). The child nurse is clothed and fed by the baby's parents, and if she goes to school her school fees, uniform, and so forth are paid by them. Sometimes the youngest girls in a family may escape the responsibility of being a child nurse, but most girls have one taste at some point during their childhood.

The corresponding role for boys is that of *mestowot*, or herd boy. Traditionally, the care of adult cattle was the work of young men of the warrior age-grade, between the ages of circumcision and marriage. It could be a hazardous business, since defense of the herds from enemies and/or beasts of prey was sometimes required. Younger teen-age boys and girls frequently accompanied the young warriors to pastures away from the homesteads, and cattle herding was a time of sociability and courtship as well as work. Today, the majority of the work of herding is done by boys between the ages of seven and fifteen. As in the case of child care, families that do not have children available for this task may borrow a child from another family—sometimes the husband's or the wife's younger sibling or a sibling's child.

Because of this pattern of child labor—the economic near-necessity that every household include children of a certain age, and the fact that not every married couple has its own children of this age category—the practice of fostering is very common. Though I do not have statistical data on this point, it is probable that the majority of adult life-histories reveal a period during

TABLE 3
Activities of 22 Nandi Girls, Aged 7–18

Activity	Age 7–9 (N=10)		Age 10–12 (N=4)		Age 13–15 (N=4)[a]		Age 16–18 (N=4)	
	No. of observations	Pct. of all observations	No. of observations	Pct. of all observations	No. of observations	Pct. of all observations	No. of observations	Pct. of all observations
Housework	14	5.5%	21	21%	16	21.9%	25	24.8%
Farm production	58	22.9[b]	14	14	11	15.1	10	9.9
Other work	6	2.4	3	3	5	6.8	—	—
Wage labor	—	—	—	—	—	—	5	4.9[c]
School	15	5.9	9	9	12	16.4	12	11.9
Child care	43	17.0	17	17	7	9.6	10	9.9
Leisure	104	41.1	35	35	19	26.0	29	28.7
Other	13	5.2	1	1	3	4.2	10	9.9
TOTAL	253	100.0%	100	100.0%	73	100.0%	101	100.0%

SOURCE: R. S. Oboler, "Work and Leisure in Modern Nandi: Preliminary Results of a Study of Time Allocation," Working Paper no. 324 (Nairobi: Institute for Development Studies, 1977).
[a] One of the four was away staying in another household during part of the study period.
[b] Mostly herding animals (19.3%).
[c] One individual.

TABLE 4

Activities of 19 Nandi Boys, Aged 7–18

Activity	Age 7–9 (N=4)		Age 10–12 (N=3)		Age 13–15 (N=7)		Age 16–18 (N=5)	
	No. of observations	Pct. of all observations	No. of observations	Pct. of all observations	No. of observations	Pct. of all observations	No. of observations	Pct. of all observations
Housework	2	2.5%	4	5.6%	4	2.4%	2	2.1%
Farm production	36	45.0[a]	20	28.2[a]	70	42.7[a]	13	13.4
Other work	—	—	4	5.6	12	7.3	9	9.3
Wage labor	1	1.3[b]	—	—	—	—	3	3.1
School	9	11.2	6	8.5	21	12.8[c]	7	7.2[c]
Child care	3	3.7	—	—	—	—	—	—
Leisure	24	30.0	28	39.5	47	28.7	36	37.1
Whereabouts unknown	1	1.3	2	2.8	3	1.8	20	20.6
Other	4	5.0	7	9.8	7	4.3	7	7.2
TOTAL	80	100.0%	71	100.0%	164	100.0%	97	100.0%

SOURCE: R. S. Oboler, "Work and Leisure in Modern Nandi: Preliminary Results of a Study of Time Allocation," Working Paper no. 324 (Nairobi: Institute for Development Studies, 1977).

[a] Mostly herding—37.5%, 19.4%, and 32.3%, respectively.

[b] Assisting an older person.

[c] Excluding boarding students (one in each age group). 10.4% of the total observations of the 13–15 group and 17.1% of the 16–18 group were "away at boarding school." This table analyzes only the time spent in Kaptel. "Away" observations are not counted as school because there is no way of knowing that school activities are actually being performed at a given time. The school category is actually underrepresented in these data because the two boarding students are not ever counted as at school.

childhood when the person lived in a household other than that of his or her own parents. Children are strongly socialized to be friendly and outgoing, willing to leave their parents or caretakers and accompany relative strangers. People greeting young children frequently say teasingly, "Let's go stay at my home." A child who readily agrees receives strong approval, though there is no disapproval if a child refuses. Almost every newly married couple who set up a residence independent of the husband's parents (as is becoming increasingly common) foster a child of each sex who fill the roles of child nurse and herd boy. The contribution of these children to the growth and prosperity of the new household (in terms of both production and reproduction) is symbolized by the participation in the traditional marriage ceremony of a child of each sex referred to in the context of the ceremony as *cheplakwet* and *mestowot*. Thus from an early age the sexes are differentiated in terms of the types of labor deemed most appropriate for each. Nevertheless, these distinctions are not absolute, and it is common to find girls herding animals or (somewhat less common) boys caring for babies. Boys and girls are equally likely to become foster children.

Up to the age of seven, there are no significant differences in the activities of boys and girls (Oboler 1977a: 16–17). Tables 3 and 4 show the activities of boys and girls aged seven to eighteen. At about the age of seven, both sexes begin to learn and assume work that will be appropriate to their adult roles, but even so, through the early teens, the lives of girls and boys do not differ markedly. Both sexes have roughly equal amounts of play and leisure time, and play groups are normally made up of children of both sexes. Girls seem just as likely to range widely and to engage in rough-and-tumble play as boys. By the age of ten, a boy, but not a girl, spends nights with other boys away from adult supervision in his own small hut within the compound of his parents or the parents of one of the group. This pattern is a preparation for later courtship behavior; after his initiation, a boy is free to bring an uninitiated girl to spend the night in his hut. It is only after the age of sixteen (the usual age at which boys are initiated) that great differences can be observed in the activities of boys and girls. Up to late adolescence, boys and girls do approximately equal amounts of work. In fact, boys in early adolescence are reputed by informants to work especially hard (voluntarily) because they are trying to show that they are adult and responsible and therefore ready for initiation. This behavior on the part of boys changes drastically at circumcision. There is no longer anything for the adolescent male to prove: he is a man, and everyone knows it. At this time, the work activity of young men shows a dramatic decline. Parents can be heard to complain of the laziness of later adolescent sons. Boys of this age also have a marked tendency to disappear without informing anyone (see the "Whereabouts unknown" category in Table 4). A great number of these unaccounted-for absences are undoubtedly courtship activity. Girls in late adolescence spend much more time working than do boys (though there is still a decline from the younger age-groups). A girl is supposed to demonstrate that she is hard working, for this is one of the most desirable traits in a bride.

School experience is one area in which boys' and girls' life patterns have differed until recently. Up until about 1972, males were still significantly more likely to attend school than were females, though the gap between male and female school attendance has narrowed over time. The educational achievement of adults aged nineteen and above is shown in Tables 5 and 6.*

Today, though there are still differences between boys and girls in educational attainment, they are not nearly so great as before. The vast majority (89.3 percent) of unmarried children of both sexes below the age of eighteen are in school. But an educational bias in favor of boys exists. Almost all the boys in the household census had started school by the age of twelve, whereas 25 percent of girls (including married women) between the ages of thirteen and eighteen had never been to school and probably will never go. Far more girls than boys (15 vs. 2) left school between standards 3 and 7, most of them to be married. Most girls are married by the age of eighteen—and in my census, only three girls were currently continuing school past the age of eighteen whereas there were five times as many boys (9.5 percent of male students) still in school past the age of eighteen.

---

*My census data refer only to households in Kaptel. I assume that these generalizations hold in broad terms for other Nandi communities, but this may not necessarily be the case.

TABLE 5
Educational Attainment of 183 Adult Nandi Males

Number in age group	Level achieved							
	None		Std. 1–4		Std. 5–8		More	
	No.	Pct.	No.	Pct.	No.	Pct.	No.	Pct.
19–24 (40)	4	10.0%	5	12.5%	15	37.5%	16	40.0%
25–29 (36)	3	8.3	5	13.9	21	58.3	7	19.5
30–34 (21)	2	9.5	1	4.8	15	71.4	3	14.3
35–39 (15)	1	6.7	10	66.6	3	20.0	1	6.7
40–44 (14)	2	14.3	5	35.7	7	50.0	—	—
45–49 (16)	8	50.0	8	50.0	—	—	—	—
≥50 (41)	31	75.6	5	12.2	5	12.2	—	—

TABLE 6
Educational Attainment of 215 Adult Nandi Females

Number in age group	Level achieved							
	None		Std. 1–4		Std. 5–8		More	
	No.	Pct.	No.	Pct.	No.	Pct.	No.	Pct.
19–24 (55)	14	25.5%	15	27.2%	14	25.5%	12	21.8%
25–29 (31)	3	9.6	14	45.2	14	45.2	—	—
30–34 (25)	9	36.0	8	32.0	6	24.0	2	8.0
35–39 (18)	10	55.5	8	44.5	—	—	—	—
40–44 (17)	14	82.4	3	17.6	—	—	—	—
45–49 (24)	23	95.8	1	4.2	—	—	—	—
≥50 (45)	45	100.0	—	—	—	—	—	—

In the period of my study, among children younger than twelve, there were no differences in school enrollment between boys and girls. The vast majority of children of both sexes started school between the ages of seven and nine. (Before 1974–75, however, most children seemed to have started school somewhat later.) A recent government policy whereby no school fees are charged for Standards 1–4 probably accounts for the fact that today almost all children of both sexes at least begin school.

Initiation

In the preceding sections of this chapter it has been shown that Nandi ideology holds that women and men, but not female and male infants, are fundamentally different from one another.

Further, male and female adult roles are highly distinguished and are set apart from one another by complexes of symbols (right side, weapons, physical prowess, ability to endure cold, outside; left side, the hearth, nurturance, susceptibility to cold, inside). The roles, activities, and life experiences of preadolescent girls and boys, however, show only minor differences according to sex. Thus, before puberty sex roles are not strongly distinguished, but after puberty they are. This change in role expectations is marked for both sexes by dramatic rites of initiation that signal assumption of the status man or woman.

Initiation is considered the most significant event in the preadult life of the individual. Parts of both male and female initiation ceremonies are public, but important parts, specifically instruction in appropriate sex-role behavior and the genital operations that are the focal point of the ceremonies, are secret and (with a few exceptions) can be witnessed only by members of the same sex who have themselves undergone the ritual.* Infertile people, people who are unable to produce male offspring, or people who have lost by death a large number of close relatives in quick succession are sometimes admitted to the secret portions of the opposite sex's initiation ceremonies in the hope that their condition will thereby be rectified. The focal point of initiation is the operation of circumcision for boys and clitoridectomy for girls. During the operations, initiates must mask fear and pain and display courage and fortitude, or suffer a loss of face in the community. In both cases, the initiation ordeal is considered a test of the initiate's fitness for aspects of the adult role: boys must display the courage befitting the role of warrior, and girls must show that they will be able to withstand with stoicism and dignity the pain of childbearing.

Initiation, particularly male initiation, is an important mark not only of adult status but also of ethnic status. The operation of circumcision as traditionally practiced by the Nandi is a two-stage procedure that is somewhat different from the simple circumcision as practiced in Euro-American and many other soci-

---

*Because only men can attend the whole male initiation and only women who have undergone clitoridectomy can attend the whole female initiation, I was unable to witness all of either ritual. I attended the public portions of five female and two male initiation ceremonies.

eties (see Hollis 1909:55 for a description of the second stage of the operation). A man who has not been circumcised in this way is ridiculed and not considered fully a Nandi. For this reason, attempts by missions to promote infant circumcision and/or circumcision in hospitals have been rejected. It is today as important as it always has been for a Nandi man to be circumcised at adolescence, Nandi-style, by a traditionally trained Nandi circumciser,* though doctors are sometimes present to treat circumcision wounds and administer antibiotics. Christian families sometimes choose a modified traditional ceremony in which certain symbolic elements defined as "pagan" have been dropped, and in predominantly Catholic areas a priest may take part in the ceremony and substitute portions of the Catholic liturgy for such "pagan" elements.

Missionary efforts to eliminate clitoridectomy for girls have been rather more successful.† Today, about 20 percent of women who are the appropriate age to be wives of the Sawe age-set (early twenties to late thirties) or younger have not been initiated.‡ Though there is a correlation between religion and educational achievement (more girls from Protestant than from Catholic or traditional families attend secondary school), educational achievement alone is a better predictor than religious affiliation alone of whether a girl will undergo clitoridectomy. Two-thirds of women (wives of Sawe or younger) who were not initiated

*Kipsigis circumcision is essentially the same as Nandi, and no stigma is placed on a Nandi man who may have been circumcised in Kipsigis.

†The usual European argument against clitoridectomy is that it is a barbaric mutilation designed to keep wives under control by reducing their pleasure in, and therefore desire for, sex. When I pursued this issue, Nandi women refused to confirm this point of view. They viewed this interpretation mostly with puzzlement, sometimes with amusement. Women who had had sexual intercourse both before and after initiation denied that their sex drive was reduced; and surely if the function of clitoridectomy is to reduce the incidence of adultery, it is a dismal failure. Goldschmidt's conclusions about Sebei clitoridectomy are similar: "Europeans often try to explain clitoridectomy as an effort to reduce the level of sexual desire of women, but the Sebei offer no such explanations, and the behavior of women, and what Sebei men expect of their women, renders such an explanation implausible" (Goldschmidt 1976:299).

‡These data are taken from questionnaires answered by a sample of 50 individuals, not chosen randomly but believed not to be systematically biased, in which the informant answered questions about all his or her relatives within certain degrees.

TABLE 7
Education and Initiation for 156 Nandi Women

Level of education	Number of women	
	Initiated	Not initiated
≤Std. 4	73	2
Primary >Std. 4	46	11
Secondary	1	23
TOTAL	120	36

NOTE: These data are for wives of Sawe age-set or younger women for whom information is available on both level of education and status relative to initiation.

had attended secondary school, and almost all noninitiated women had gone to school beyond Standard 4. The vast majority of women with below Standard 4 education (97 percent) were traditionally initiated. Most girls from Christian families (84 percent of Catholics and 65 percent of Protestants) are still traditionally initiated, unless they attend secondary school. There is a tendency for men of high educational achievement to seek wives whose relative achievement is also high, and people tend to believe that only these men, who have absorbed a lot of modern ideas, will marry a woman who has not been traditionally initiated. Except among the educated elite, initiation for a woman is considered a prerequisite for marriage. Table 7 shows the close correlation between educational attainment and female initiation.

Traditionally, male initiation was coordinated throughout Nandi during whatever period was regarded as "open," and occurred yearly during this period. The initiations were usually large, community-wide ceremonies, with many boys being initiated simultaneously. Girls were traditionally initiated in small groups whenever they were judged ready for initiation and marriage, and this is still the custom. Since the Second World War, the formal structure for timing male initiation has broken down. At present, some boys are initiated every year in probably several Nandi communities, though not necessarily every year in every community, nor are the ceremonies always large or community-wide. Sometimes a male initiation ceremony may be privately sponsored by a few families. At a community-wide initiation that took place in Kaptel in 1976, twelve boys participated. Female initiations are sponsored privately by one or a few families and involve usually two or three, rarely more than four or five, initiates. Many girls are now initiated hurriedly when they are already in the early stages of pregnancy in hopes that suitors will come with offers of marriage in the weeks following the initiation.

Both boys and girls are normally initiated between the ages of twelve and eighteen. Fifteen or sixteen is the most common age for boys. For girls, the most common age is slightly younger, about fourteen or fifteen. Informants unanimously insist that traditionally the average age of initiates was a good deal older than at present, commonly over twenty. Whether this testimony represents selective memory and glorification of the past (since the older age is considered closer to the cultural ideal), or whether there has actually been a sharp lowering in age at initiation is difficult to judge. Hollis, writing in 1909, stated that the commonest age at initiation for boys was between fifteen and nineteen (Hollis 1909:52).* One can say the same for today: in other words, though there has been some decline in age at initiation, it is probably not so great as informants claim. The decline in average age at marriage for women probably has a parallel in decline in age at initiation.

The initiation ceremony for boys is completely controlled by men of the community. Elders have important roles in the actual ceremony, but the main planning and the instruction of initiates are in the hands of young men of the age-set next senior to the one that is being initiated. Old women of the neighborhood who have a reputation for their ritual knowledge take charge of the initiation of girls, except that, as mentioned earlier, costuming the female initiates is the province of male specialists.

The costume worn by girls during initiation incorporates items of dress (e.g., colobus monkey skin, thigh bells) traditionally associated with warriors, as well as more modern items of dress associated with men and particularly with the military (dress shirt and tie, crossed bandoliers, knee socks). Hollis (1909:58) makes it clear that traditionally girls being initiated wore men's

---

*Hollis gives no exact age for girls—only "marriageable age" (Hollis 1909:57).

garments, specifically warriors' dress borrowed from their boy friends. I have emphasized that prior to initiation, male and female roles are not strongly distinguished. Initiation is the threshold beyond which the role of the opposite sex is utterly repudiated, and I believe that wearing clothes associated with the opposite sex during initiation is a final dramatization of the role that is about to be repudiated. Nandi informants themselves do not disagree with such an interpretation for the initiation dress of girls. There are elements of ritual transvestism in male initiation dress, also. Male initiates wear cloaks of goat skins that are much like the cloaks worn by women as part of their traditional costume. In the ceremony held at Kaptel in 1976, several of the cloaks worn by the boys were actually borrowed from women. During the public portions of the ceremony, female relatives and friends give the boys headscarves and beads to wear as tokens of their support. Hollis (1909: 53) also speaks of male initiates attiring themselves in female clothes. In spite of all this, Nandi informants deny any elements of ritual transvestism in the male initiation ceremony. I was told that the cloaks the boys wear are traditional boys' cloaks and not the same as those traditionally worn by women, and that the headscarves and beads are merely given as tokens so that the boys will know that their owners are thinking of them throughout the secret ritual and operation.

I shall not include here a detailed description of initiation rites or analyze the symbols that are important in them. A full treatment of this subject would be impossible without the revelation of details that are strongly held to be secret knowledge. Such of these secrets as I know about were told to me in strict confidence, and I have promised not to reveal them in print. Langley (1979), however, has recently devoted an entire volume to Nandi life-crisis rituals, including initiation ceremonies. There are few major discrepancies between her description of the details of these rituals and my information on this subject.

Following the actual operation, initiates begin a period of strict seclusion from members of the opposite sex. For boys, this period lasts until the circumcision wounds heal. For girls, the period is now usually six weeks to a few months. Traditionally, a girl's seclusion was supposed to last until her marriage, and informants claim that it was frequently a year or even longer. Following the period of seclusion, initiates reemerge in their adult gender roles following a ceremony that incorporates symbolism associated with birth. The initiates therefore may be said to be reborn as adult men and women.

After initiation, a girl should ideally be married as soon as possible. Only uninitiated girls are free to engage in sex play with young unmarried men. Cases in which girls emerge from seclusion without any marriage having been arranged for them are, however, becoming increasingly common. Initiation for boys marks the beginning of a period during which they were traditionally warriors and were not permitted to marry (at least for the early part of their warriorhood). They were, however, expected to engage in regular sex play (everything short of full penetration) with uninitiated teen-age girls. During this period they would guard the cattle and raid neighboring tribes but were otherwise exempt from adult responsibilities. Today the military function of the "warrior" age-grade has been eliminated, but newly initiated males still enter a period of relative sexual and social license, with pursuit of formal education seen as one desirable course of action. Such young men normally will not marry for several years.

Courtship

Young men begin a period of intense courtship and sexual activity following their initiation. In the past, the warriors of a neighborhood would spend nights together near the cattle in the communal dwelling, the *sigiroino*, and would bring their girl friends to spend the night with them there. Courting couples were expected to satisfy one another sexually without actually engaging in penetration and full sexual intercourse.* Ideally, a girl was supposed to be still technically a virgin at the time of her initiation. A girl's virginity was ascertained by the old women as a part of the initiation process. Girls who were virgins were allowed to sit during the operation of clitoridectomy on a stool normally reserved for male elders. This was a special mark of honor. They also participated in a ceremony in which they

---

*See Peristiany (1939:51–52) for a description of Kipsigis sex in courtship, which so far as I can tell is also accurate for Nandi.

danced with their fathers, while the fathers' age-mates sang songs of praise for the honor they had done their fathers and the respect they had shown them by maintaining their virginity. Moreover, the girls who were virgins would be given cows of their own by their fathers, and sometimes livestock by other relatives. Whether or not most girls were actually virgins upon initiation is impossible to know. Today, girls who are virgins at initiation may still sit on a stool and be given livestock, though the celebration by the fathers' age-mates seems to have been dropped. Though I have no statistical data on this point, informants claim (probably exaggeratedly) that today the initiation of a virgin is a rare occurrence.

In the past, premarital pregnancy, and particularly the birth of a child out of wedlock, was very much frowned upon. Nandi informants recognize that premarital pregnancy has always occurred, but they insist that in traditional society it was rare. A child born to an unmarried girl was supposed to be killed immediately by the midwife by stuffing dung into its mouth and nose. A child's first cries were believed to signal the entry into its body of an ancestral spirit; if it could be suffocated before it made any cries, it was held never to have really lived. The exception to infanticide of illegitimate children was that if a barren woman was present at the birth, she could claim the child as her own and adopt it. It is said that a warrior who impregnated a girl was severely beaten by his age-mates, though there is disagreement about whether he was required to pay a fine or indemnity.

Today there is no longer a communal warriors' dormitory for a neighborhood, but every young man (or perhaps a group of brothers near the same age) has his own hut inside the compound of his parents. It is still the case that well brought up girls—even daughters of Christian families—will spend nights with young men in their huts without any social stigma. Girls are still supposed to be virgins at initiation and/or marriage, but informants claim, and the incidence of premarital pregnancy makes it seem likely, that full intercourse now takes place with greater frequency than formerly.*

* This point is echoed by Langley (1979:46): "Due to a decline in the use of the warriors' communal hut, today it is more than likely that a young couple will meet in the boy's private living quarters and engage in full intercourse."

A young man who impregnates a girl does not usually feel a great responsibility to marry her, nor does he usually come under community pressure to do so, especially if he is still in school, landless, jobless, or otherwise not well set in life. In one case I was close to, a young man impregnated the daughter of a prominent community member and refused to marry her. He received only minor disapproval, and this was mainly focused on the fact that he was not a native of the community but was only working there: "Why should strangers come to seduce our girls?" However, disapproval became much more intense and he was warned by community elders when he appeared to have impregnated a second girl. In another case, when a girl was impregnated by a young man from another community, the elders of the young man's home community brought pressure on him to marry the girl, since he was of the age to marry and already had land and a good job. The marriage ultimately took place.

In most cases, a girl who becomes pregnant cannot expect her child's father to marry her, nor is she usually considered a good marriage choice by other young men. Most girls believe that men are absolutely not to be trusted in sexual relationships: they take perverse pleasure in "ruining" girls, and promise to marry them with no intention of following through. When a girl becomes pregnant and it is clear that her lover will not marry her, the usual course is for her to be initiated as quickly as possible in the hope that someone will come while she is in seclusion to ask for her in marriage. Anyone is free to come and negotiate to marry a girl who has recently been initiated, but informants say that a girl who is already pregnant is more likely to be married by an old man, a widower, or a woman (all viewed as less desirable candidates than young men) than by a young man.

Some pregnant girls, particularly those with a relatively high education, refuse to be traditionally initiated or married. A girl in this situation has the right to remain on the land of her father or brother, as does also a woman who is separated from her husband. The children, however, have no right to inherit that property, and for that reason these independent women try to raise money through their own economic pursuits and use it to buy land and provide an inheritance for their children. Theoretically, then, it is possible for women of this sort to achieve a very high level of personal autonomy, but most do not. The fate of the growing number of illegitimate children whose mothers fail to make adequate provision for their inheritance is a social problem widely discussed in modern Nandi.

Most Nandi women spend the greater part of their lives as wives. Nandi informants conflate the cultural constructs "man" and "woman" with "husband" and "wife." When asked about the roles of women and men in the abstract, their immediate response is in terms of spouses. The next chapter will deal with the institution that is of primary importance in Nandi ideas about the nature of the relationship between the sexes: marriage.

FOUR

Marriage

THERE IS NO DOUBT that Nandi marriage is essentially inegalitarian. Wives owe husbands a great show of public deference. A wife must have her husband's permission to go very far from home or for very long. A wife should never contradict or disagree with her husband if other people are present. Yet relations between husbands and wives are normally harmonious. I was told repeatedly that good husbands share the making of important decisions with their wives. In many cases the wife's public "respect" for her husband is a façade that masks a true relationship that is, if not egalitarian, at least much less one sided than it looks to an outside observer. If conflict arises in a marriage, however, a wife is at a distinct disadvantage. A wife's opinions and feelings *can* be disregarded by her husband if he so chooses; and unless he blatantly and persistently violates her rights, no outside agent will intervene. If a wife fails in any wifely duty, or in respect, her husband is not only permitted but expected to subject her to physical punishment. A wife's ultimate strategy is to leave her husband's compound; for a reconciliation to be effected, grievances on both sides will be aired before disinterested arbiters. In seeking solutions to or escape from marital difficulties, women turn to other women for help. Nandi women are active in arranging marriages, in reconciling estranged couples, and in defending the rights of wives when their husbands act in clear violation of social norms. Though wives are at a disadvantage they are by no means powerless. Marriage in Nandi (as in other societies) is an active give and take between husband and wife. In this account I wish to delineate some of the features that give this interplay in Nandi its peculiarly Nandi flavor.

Arranging a Marriage

Much anthropological theorizing about the arrangement of marriages in lineage-based agnatic societies portrays it as a process in which groups of men, with little involvement of women, negotiate to give and receive rights in marriageable girls as if the latter were objects. This characterization has been criticized by Van Baal (1971) and Singer (1973). Such an approach may or may not be a fair representation of events in some societies; but it does not fit the Nandi case. Many marriages are made by mutual choice. Even when a groom and bride do not know each other and the marriage is decided for them, their roles can be viewed as equally passive. Certainly, the culture's formal ideology holds that the people who have the most power over the process are the fathers of the bride and groom, with advice and assistance from their close agnatic kinsmen. However, women from both sides are members of the groups between which marriage negotiations take place, and this is not a recent innovation. A girl must see her suitor and consent to the marriage. It is the duty of her kinswomen to ascertain that she is a willing partner (which does not, of course, imply that girls are never pressured into consenting to marriages for which they lack enthusiasm). Informants say, too, that even traditionally it was the mothers of the bride and groom who usually took the first informal steps that ultimately led to marriage negotiations. During informal day-to-day meetings, they would discuss the fact that the daughter of one was nearly ready for initiation and the fact that the son of the other was ready to marry, and they would ascertain that the families were mutually receptive to the potential match and not related in any way that would preclude the marriage.*

At the present time, the bride and groom also have a fair amount to say about the choice of their future spouses. Though parents have the final say and apparently have always exercised it when their child's personal preference is considered unsuitable, an attempt is usually made to take the personal preference of the principals into account. This is apparently not traditional. Elderly informants claim that in the precolonial era, the family

*Peristiany (1939:57) describes the process similarly for Kipsigis.

rarely permitted marriage between two young people who were lovers. This is a recurrent theme in the narratives of old people: in the old days, parents bestowed their children in marriage with no consideration for their feelings, and, someone will say, "even though I was in love with someone, I was forced to marry someone else; young people today are lucky because they get to marry the person of their own choosing." One old man described the arrangement of his marriage to his devoted wife of many, many years as follows:

I came home one day and found my wife already in the house. I was surprised when I was told to stay outside for a while in the evening, and after a while I was told to come in through the rear door. So I knew there was going to be a ceremony. There was a girl waiting for me inside. So the wedding ceremony was performed and she became my wife. I did not know what was being done to me. After we had been brought together as husband and wife I started asking them what they had done to me and they told me that I had married. So they had given me this drumheaded [stupid] wife of mine. I was not satisfied about the whole thing, but what could I do?

Whether or not such marriages were common in the precolonial period, they have been rare at least since the 1930's. In 45 percent of marriages on which I have data, dating back to the 1930's, the informant claimed that he/she and his/her spouse were lovers before marriage. As part of the household census, I collected from household heads or their spouses accounts of the circumstances surrounding their own marriages. The vast majority of these cases fell into one of three broad categories: (1) the bride and groom were not lovers before marriage, nor was either instrumental in the choice of partner—their parents arranged the marriage; (2) the bride and groom were not lovers before marriage, but it was the groom himself who initiated negotiations for the bride, either on his own account if a mature man with his own cattle, or by expressing to his parents a desire to marry a particular girl who had recently been initiated; (3) the bride and groom were lovers before marriage who expressed to their parents their mutual desire that the particular marriage be arranged. Table 8 shows the division among the three categories of the random sample of marriages on which I have data.

Though the numbers involved in Table 8 are in some cases too

TABLE 8

Initiative in Arranging 120 Nandi Marriages, 1920's–1970's

Decade of marriage	Type of marriage			Mutual choice as pct. of total
	Arranged by parents	Husband's choice	Mutual choice	
1920's	1	2	0	0%
1930's	0	3	3	50
1940's	0	4	6	60
1950's	1	17	14	44
1960's	0	23	13	36
1970's	1	14	18	55
TOTAL	3	63	54	45%

small for statistical analysis to be of great significance, a few points are clear. One is that at least since the 1930's, totally arranged marriages have been very rare. Mutual-choice marriages and marriages in which at least the husband has a voice in initiating the process are about equally common. Another important point is that from the 1930's to the present there has been very little, if any, change in the distribution of cases between these two categories.

The formal process of engagement (*koito*) usually takes place while a girl is in seclusion following initiation. If the girl has not been initiated, her suitor's family lets her family know that they plan to come and negotiate the marriage on a particular day. If the girl is in seclusion, a party may come with or without advance notice to the compound where she is staying. The suitor's party consists of his parents, probably some of their close relatives (for example, the suitor's father's father, father's brother, and mother's brother and their wives; some parties I know of included sister's husbands and sister's sons), some of the suitor's family's neighbors, and friends or relatives from the girl's family's neighborhood—usually six to eight persons altogether, often ten or more. It is considered desirable, too, that the party include an elder highly respected in the community and connected in some way to both families. Members of the party show their purpose by carrying leaves from two sacred plants—*nokirwet* for men and *senetwet* for women.* Only the suitor himself does not carry

*Hollis (1909:60) identifies nokirwet as *grewia sp.* and senetwet as *cassia didymobotrya*.

these, and by this he can be easily identified. A smaller number of people representing the bride's side are usually present, but at least her parents, her father's brother, and her mother's brother should be included.

If a girl has been initiated and there is no advance arrangement between two families, several suitors' parties may come to negotiate. In this case, each is interviewed in turn. I was told that unsuccessful parties are told to go home, taking their plants, and wait for further word from the girl's family, though subsequently they will not be contacted. The successful party departs without its sacred plants. Marriage negotiations may be concluded in one visit, or may require more than one. The actual negotiations (which may be delayed to a future date) open with the question, "Who are you?" The suitor's spokesman replies with the suitor's clan identity. This leads to a discussion of the history of marriages between the two clans and families. At any given time there are proscriptions on intermarriage between certain clans (see Chapter 2). Further, it is considered important to gain as many affines as possible, so that conscious value is placed on a family's intermarrying with the maximum number of different clans. Ideally, five sisters should marry into five different clans, and it is forbidden for sets of siblings to marry one another.* Thus another factor mitigating against a particular engagement is if it is felt that too many members of the family of either potential spouse have recently married into the other's clan.

The parents of the potential spouses do not negotiate directly, but a man of each party is its spokesman (some informants said that the spokesman on the girl's side should be her father's brother). Discussion proceeds to the reputation of the groom's family, his own character, their financial resources, and finally bridewealth. I was told that it is preferred that bridewealth not be discussed on the first visit, but in cases known to me this rule was not followed. The bride's spokesman opens the discussion by asking the groom's party to "open their quiver." The groom's

---

*Both the marriage of a brother and sister to a brother and sister, and that of two sisters to two brothers are considered improper (sororal polygyny being viewed as an instance of the latter). The former type of marriage is rather less scandalous than the latter, however, and a few cases have been known to occur. The main reason given by informants for this difference in evaluation is that in the latter case all the cattle are given by one family to the other, not spread about as they ideally should be.

spokesman then reveals how much money the family is prepared to give as part of the bridewealth. If the amount is acceptable, they are requested to "open the other quiver." This starts
the discussion of cattle. The groom's spokesman must describe
each animal to be given in detail, saying, for example, "It is a
heifer, black with a white spot on one leg, part Friesian, its name
is . . ." If he pauses and the bride's family doesn't think that the
animals already described are enough, they will urge him to
continue. It is very unusual for more than six animals to be requested. When all the cattle have been enumerated, the bride's
father's brother says, "Now open the quiver of the *njor* [*njor* being
the back room of a traditional Nandi house, in which sheep and
goats spent the night]." This is the signal for the groom's party
to state how many sheep and/or goats they are prepared to give
as part of the bridewealth. The groom's party is required to
make a second payment of money, ostensibly to pay the bride's
family for the oil with which the two parties anoint each other
to seal the engagement. The amount given is between 25 and 50
Kenya shillings (about $3–$6), and must be given by the mother
of the prospective groom. At this point, the bride, for the first
time, enters the room in which the negotiations are being held.
She brings with her the oil for the anointing, and also at this
point is formally asked if she consents to the marriage. Presumably she will answer yes to this question, since her consent has
been ascertained informally beforehand, but I heard of one case
in which the bride backed out at the last minute. All the members of both parties then put oil on their hands and anoint the
heads of the engaged couple. The members of the bride's family
also anoint the groom's relatives and the two families address
each other as *bamwai*, the kin term by which they will subsequently call each other (derived from *mwaita*=oil). This act seals
the engagement.

The following account of an actual marriage negotiation gives
a picture of how this normative procedure is played out in real-
life situations:

The engagement party arrived in the early morning at the compound of
the girl's father's brother, where she was spending her period of seclusion. They had sent word the previous day that they would be coming.
They were seated in the compound while other members of the girl's
family were summoned. The party included the suitor, his mother, and

his father's brother (his own father is deceased), his sister and her husband, two other elderly patrilineal kinsmen who live in the girl's family's community and are well known there, and an unrelated mother and son who know the suitor's family well and are neighbors of the girl's family. The girl's party, when finally assembled, included her parents, two father's brothers and the wife and daughter of one, two mother's brothers and their wives, two brothers and a sister, and several neighbors, both men and women. The two parties sat facing each other. The girl's father's brother did most of the talking for her side. The suitor's sister's husband did most of the talking for his side. The prospective bride remained inside the house, where she could not be seen but could hear most of the conversation.

The prospective groom's family live in a government settlement scheme in Kitale, an area about forty miles [64.5 km.] distant.

The discussion was opened by the girl's father's brother. The suitor's clan identity was not asked, possibly because it was assumed that everyone already knew it. The first question was: "Has anyone from your family ever married ours?" A (by suitor's sister's husband): "Yes." Q: "How long ago?" A: "During the time of Maina." (Probably during the 1940's.) Q: "Was there any problem?" A: "No." Q: "Who is coming for engagement?" A: "He is" (indicating the suitor). Q: "Has he ever been married before?" A: "Yes, once before." Q: "How many acres does he have?" A: "Twelve." The questioning was now taken up by the girl's father: "Why did the first wife leave?" A: "She ran away to another man after only a month of marriage. The bridewealth had not yet been delivered. He (the husband) followed her to Nandi Hills, but she refused to return." Someone on the girl's side who knew the suitor pointed out that the woman who went to Nandi Hills was his second wife; the first wife also left after a very short time. Q: "Was the second woman really his wife, or had she been married before?" A: "We don't know if she had been married before. All this happened two years ago." The prospective bride's mother's brother now asked: "Did you come here from Kitale just for a visit, or did you plan to come for engagement?" The suitor's mother responded: "We came for engagement." The girl's mother: "Why haven't you brought any of your neighbors, since one usually takes neighbors along when one goes for engagement?" A: "None of our neighbors [on the settlement scheme] are Nandi, so we brought only our relatives." The girl's mother's brother turned to her father's brother and commented: "The relatives live near here; we know them. The family is all right. What we need to know about is the man's character/behavior [*atebet*]." Q: "Do you own your own cattle, or are they rented from the settlement scheme?" A (mother): "They are ours." The next question is addressed to the man's sister's husband: "What concerns us is that this man has been left by two wives. We wonder if this shows that his character is bad." A: "No, it was the girls who were not good. They came from the town and were used to wandering around." The suitor's mother now addressed one of the men in the girl's party: "Do you remember that we met in the past? You rested from a journey at our place and I gave you food. I fed you then because some- how I knew that we would someday be relatives."

After this, the suitor's party moved slightly apart so that the party of the prospective bride could have privacy to talk over the proposal. The men asked the women to give their opinion. Two of them responded that they would agree with whatever the men decided. The sister of the girl said: "Why did he deny that he was married twice? Some people say the wives left because he smokes *bhang* [marijuana], but we really don't have any evidence of that." A female neighbor: "The other wives were married in town. He will respect this one more." Another woman: "We should urge him to remember that she is very young and he should treat her well. Actually, it is the responsibility of the mother-in- law to see to that. She is the one we should urge." The girl's father's brother summed up the discussion: "If we have accepted, then the nor- mal bridewealth is four cattle." The girl's father: "We don't really know he has that many cattle. Let's ask for four, but the number must be at least three." Everyone agreed. The spokesman turned to the girl's brother: "What about money? Should we say 600 shillings?" Everyone nodded in agreement. The brother: "Why not 500?" The girl's other brother and her mother's brother proposed 450 shillings. The mother's other brother said: "The money will probably be spent immediately anyway no matter how much it is. Why not ask for 300 shillings? Chil- dren these days are very unreliable. It will be years before we can be sure she is really married." Girl's father: "Let's ask for 600 shillings, be- cause we are not sure we'll get four cattle." Mother's brother: "Could we really repay 600 shillings, in case she runs away?" Father: "We hope she will stay. Don't worry about her leaving. My sons must also go for engagement." There was some quibbling about the amount. The father was willing to accept 450 shillings, others felt 300 shillings would be enough. The girl's brother asked the group of women for their opinion. The girl's father's brother's daughter said: "Why not start by asking for 500 shillings and be willing to accept 300?" The men accepted this proposal.

The two parties again took up their positions. The girl's father's brother: "We have nothing more to say. Open your quiver." The suitor's sister's husband: "There is a black pregnant cow and it has a calf." Nod- ded acknowledgment. "Another is being milked. It is a Friesian. . . . There is a heifer, black with red spots [*mukye*]. . . . There is a black ox, fit for plowing." Q (addressed to suitor): "Were any of these from your sister's bridewealth?" A: "No. I bought them." Q: "What about sheep/goats? If there are no sheep/goats then we need a young ox." The sister's husband offered a pregnant European sheep, but this was vetoed by the mother and others in the group. They settled on offering a black ox. The girl's father's brother's daughter remarked that they really should give a sheep, which is traditionally given to the woman who fed the girl during her seclusion (who happens to be her mother). Five hundred cowrie shells were offered and accepted. The suitor, his sister, sister's husband, and father's brother's son moved apart to discuss the money. They returned and the sister's husband handed money wrapped in paper to the girl's spokesman, who counted out 300 shillings. Suitor's sister's husband: "There is no more." Women on the girl's side began to chide him jokingly: "You must give more." "Why did you come for engagement with so little money?" etc. He got up and went aside to check in his pocket, and returned with 50 more shillings. The women continued to chide him: "You can promise more and give it later," etc., but when they got no further response, they stopped. The girl's father's brother then said: "We are giving you our daughter. Since Kitale is far, we must know how you will care for her. Tomorrow one of her brothers will come to see the animals (and the home)." The amount of money to be given for oil was discussed (with all the women taking an active part), and 320 shillings was agreed upon. Then all the people in both parties who were actually related to the bride and groom entered the house. The girl brought the oil. All her relatives, in order of seniority, rubbed their hands with oil and anointed the man's relatives, in order of seniority, also spitting into their palms and rubbing them on the others' cheeks. The women also anointed the feet of the women in the other party. Then the leaves were collected and put in the eaves of the house.

After the suitor's relatives had gone outside, the girl's relatives remained behind to discuss the division of the money. Her father got 100 shillings, each father's brother got 50, and each mother's brother got 10. Everyone else got 2.5 shillings each. One hundred shillings was theoretically due to the girl herself to buy new clothes, but the men were talking about dividing it among themselves. The girl's father's brother's wife demanded that the girl get her share, and the men capitulated. There was technically another step in the procedure (tying grass on the couple's wrists) to be performed, but all the men began to wander off toward the Center—presumably planning to do it later (or not at all?). The women protested, but to no avail.*

*This account is taken from the field notes of my husband, Leon Oboler.

One of the most interesting aspects of this account is its illustration of women's role in the negotiations. Though the formal spokespersons are men, women also question and respond. Women are asked for their opinions, and the women are the ones who raise points relevant to the girl's welfare. When the men in the girl's party reach an impasse on the question of how much money to ask for, it is a woman who proposes an acceptable compromise. In so far as there is bargaining, it is done by the women while the men maintain their dignity. Finally, it is a woman who stands up to the men to make certain that they do not cheat the bride of her rightful share of the marriage payment.

I was present in another case when a suitor's family made their formal first visit to the home of his prospective bride. Since both families in this case were strongly Christian much of the ritual was dispensed with, but there was still a great deal of formality and speech making. The mothers of both bride and groom were conspicuous in taking the most prominent roles, while the fathers remained in the background.

In no sense is the group that is concerned on either side in the arrangement of a marriage a lineage group. It is a loose collection of people including the parents of bride or groom, father's brothers (but not necessarily any other agnates), mother's brothers, and various other relatives, friends, and neighbors.

The above case study also illustrates the easy-going and flexible character of bridewealth negotiations. The numbers of cattle exchanged are not a matter for strident haggling. Both sides know in advance more or less accurately the number of cattle that will be decided upon. Though there was some disagreement between the two sides about the inclusion of a sheep and the amount of money, neither of these points was a subject for prolonged argument. It is characteristic of the Nandi ethos that a negotiation is managed without overt confrontation.

Bridewealth

At marriage a woman receives house-property cattle from her husband's family. (The actual categories of cattle involved and the structure of rights in them are discussed in more detail in Chapter 7.) The endowment of a woman with such an estate may be viewed as a sort of marriage settlement. Among the northern

Kalenjin (e.g., the Tugen—Kettel 1980:85–86) it was the *only* form of property transfer used to secure a marriage. Among the Nandi, the institution of house property coexists with the form of property transfer at marriage more common in African patrilineal societies, bridewealth.

In Nandi, marriage involves the transfer of bridewealth in cattle, small livestock, cowrie shells, and cash. The institution of bridewealth in Nandi is in some ways peculiar for East Africa. Schneider (1979:82) notes a general correlation for East Africa between a high (or low) ratio of cattle to people and high (or low) numbers of cattle transferred in bridewealth payments. The Nandi appear to be an exception to this generalization. The current Nandi cattle/people ratio (in Kaptel) is 1.2 to one, a ratio not unusual for cultivating pastoralists. It has been as much as 4.3 to one, however, and this ratio is in the high range for cultivating pastoralists (Schneider 1979:87). Traditional Nandi bridewealth, on the other hand, was low. Hollis (1909:61) reported it at one bull, one cow, and ten goats (though he also notes that "formerly the price was higher"—how much higher is unclear). Today, typical Nandi bridewealth is higher than this (four to six cattle, one sheep, and 300–600 shillings), but it is still lower than bridewealth for other East African pastoralists and semipastoralists where I am aware of typical amounts involved. Further, the Nandi data run counter to the hypothesis of a direct correlation between cattle/people ratio and amount of bridewealth because during the period in which the proportion of cattle relative to people has declined, the numbers of cattle involved in typical bridewealth payments have increased.*

An analysis of bridewealth for 49 cases of marriages that occurred between 1925 and 1976 shows that there has been a gradual, steady increase in the numbers of cattle, and value of other items, given as bridewealth. There is no point at which bridewealth amounts show a sudden upward leap. The highest amount in this sample (see Table 9), given during the 1950's, is seven adult cattle, three sheep, and 600 shillings.† The second highest,

---

*Admittedly, there are reasons for this that are related to the commoditization of cattle and other resources, so that even if such a phenomenon is widespread it does not necessarily invalidate a correlation between cattle/people ratio and bridewealth for non-cash economies.

†Cowrie shells are included in bridewealth, but amounts are considered insignificant.

TABLE 9
Bridewealth Cattle, 1920's–1970's

Decade	No. of marriages	Average no. of cattle
1920's	2	2.5
1930's	8	3.5
1940's	7	3.7
1950's	13	4.7
1960's	10	5.3
1970's	9	5.4

seven adult cattle, one sheep, and 450 shillings, occurred in 1976. The first of these two was a case of woman-woman marriage, and the second a case in which the couple eloped and had the marriage ceremony performed secretly. These were special cases in which higher than average bridewealth may have been given to compensate for the fact that the circumstances were less than ideal. In all other cases, six adult cattle and 600 shillings were the maximum amounts recorded. The lowest bridewealth in the sample was two adult cattle and two goats, in the case of a marriage that took place in the early 1930's.

The first appearance of cash as part of a bridewealth (for this data set) occurred in 1950, but it was not common for cash to be part of bridewealth during the 1950's: in 11 marriages that took place between 1950 and 1957, cash figured in bridewealth only twice. In 1958 money became a standard part of bridewealth, and only three of 21 bridewealth amounts recorded after 1958 failed to include money. At that same time, there was a marked decline in the numbers of small livestock included in bridewealth. During the 1930's and 1940's, three to five sheep or goats were commonly a part of bridewealth, but only two of 21 cases from 1958 on included more than one sheep or goat. The partitioning of land in the mid-1950's helped to open cash-cropping opportunities that had previously been unavailable (as will be seen in Chapter 5) and thus helped to create a more plentiful supply of cash. At the same time, the restriction of grazing through land partitioning caused most households to sharply reduce the numbers of small stock they kept. The important socioeconomic shift brought about by the partitioning of land is reflected in typical bridewealth patterns as in other areas of social organization.

Bridewealth cattle are more highly valued if they symbolize certain kinds of social relationships. I was told that ideally at least one animal included in the bridewealth given by a man should be one that was given as bridewealth for his father's sister (or its descendant), and another ideally should be one that was given as bridewealth for his own full sister. I was also told that a bride's family would be willing to accept a smaller number of animals if the animals they were given included sisters' and/or father's sisters' bridewealth cattle. However, because of the commoditization and frequent buying and selling of cattle, these criteria are now less likely to be met than they were in the past.

During periods in the past when cattle/people ratios were low, it was not always possible for men to accumulate sufficient numbers of bridewealth cattle. Informants say that in such a case a girl's family might allow a man to marry her without bridewealth, if he left a bow and arrows with them as a symbol of his intent to acquire cattle through raiding and pay the bridewealth at a later date. Even today, part of a bridewealth payment is still sometimes deferred, but it is preferable that it all be paid within a few weeks of the wedding ceremony, and informants say that this is what usually happens. A marriage is not usually considered irrevocable until bridewealth has been paid, and marriages broken in the first few weeks do not count as divorces. Once bridewealth has been paid, a woman's children are considered to belong to the man who paid it regardless of the circumstances of their birth. If a woman dies childless, bridewealth received at her marriage should be returned. In a case that occurred in Kaptel in 1977, a large wedding feast was held, but within three days the bride had returned home. Her husband's family tried to persuade her to go back to him, but she refused. The husband was much older than the bride, and the reason she gave for her refusal to go back was that she couldn't bear being married to such an old man. No one who discussed the case with me questioned her right to break the marriage if she wished, but she was criticized for the way in which she did it: she could see how old the man was when he came for engagement and she should have refused then, people said, and thus spared his family the expense of the large wedding feast. Within a month, it seemed as though the marriage had never taken place. The bride continued living at her parents' home. The groom's family, outwardly unperturbed, said that they would get another woman.

The group concerned in bridewealth transactions is not a lineage or large-scale kin group, but primarily members of a single extended-family or compound. Only rarely is bridewealth collected from or distributed to a wider group. The father's brothers, and less frequently the mother's brothers, may contribute to a man's bridewealth, but such a contribution is at their own discretion. In the case described in full on pages 103–6, all the cattle were kept by the parents and brothers of the bride. Only the money was divided among members of the party present at the negotiation, and the father's brothers were the only people outside the immediate family to receive significant amounts, though the mother's brothers received more than other members of the party. In precolonial times, goats included in the bridewealth would have been divided according to similar principles, but the transfer of cattle, which constitute the bulk of the bridewealth by value, is a matter between families.

The Wedding

Between engagement and marriage, a period of weeks or months or even longer may elapse, depending on circumstances. The groom's family may need time to collect enough money to finance the wedding feast. It is here that the cooperation of a kin group larger than the immediate family comes into play. The groom, bride, or both may be still in school, in which case the actual wedding will take place after they finish. Traditionally, a girl would remain in seclusion until after the wedding ceremony. Today this is not necessarily the case, since engagement may not follow initiation closely and a significant number of girls are not initiated.

I did not witness a traditional Nandi wedding ceremony, though I attended the festivities following the ceremony on four occasions. The ceremony takes place at night, and the celebration goes on all the next day. Like other Nandi ceremonies, the traditional wedding ceremony is secret and closed to people who have not themselves been principals in it.* This means that unmarried persons and people married in Christian or civil

---

*An exception is made in the case of the two children who enact prescribed roles during part of the ceremony. They are considered too young to understand what is going on.

rather than traditional ceremonies are barred from attending. As in the case of initiation, some of the details of ritual acts and symbolism associated with them were confided to me with the stipulation that I should not divulge them, since they are considered ritual secrets. Some of the features of the ritual (though not advice and admonitions given to the bride and groom) have been published by Langley (1979:76–81).* The day following the ceremony is devoted to beer drinking, singing, and celebration in the compound where the wedding ceremony has been performed (usually that of the bridegroom's father). The groom may join the celebration, but in the wedding celebrations I have witnessed, the bride was in all cases very inconspicuous. I was told that she assumes her household duties immediately and with great diligence to prove that she will be a good wife. One highlight of the public events of the day following the wedding is the formal pointing out of the bridewealth cattle. As the father of the groom indicates to the father and brothers of the bride the cattle that were promised during the marriage negotiations, the groom touches each animal in turn with a leaf-tipped branch. The formal acceptance and transfer of the animal are indicated by the bride's touching it with a similar branch.[†]

Hollis (1909:62) gives an account of the ritual procession in which a bride was escorted from her own parents' compound to that of her husband, where the wedding ceremony was performed. I never saw such a formal procession escorting a bride. Traditional weddings now usually involve partners whose families live in close proximity, and it seems that the secrecy that now surrounds traditional rituals has caused this public aspect of the wedding ceremony to be played down.

In modern Nandi Christian weddings the ceremony in the church has replaced the traditional ceremony in the compound of the groom's father. The timing of the ceremony has also changed—it usually takes place in the early afternoon instead of after sundown. In the case of a modern wedding, it is imperative that the groom hire vehicles to transport the bride and her

---

*Langley's account is apparently based on interviews with Christian converts who no longer consider it desirable to safeguard the secrecy of traditional rituals.

†Langley (1979:80) says that it is the male relatives of the bride who indicate acceptance by touching the cattle, but in the case I witnessed, the bride herself performed this role though her brothers were present, and this was said by informants to be normal procedure.

family, neighbors, and other important members of her party from their compound or home community to the church (located in the groom's home community), from there to the groom's parents' compound where the wedding feast is held, and back home. This is true even if the bride and groom are from the same community; the vehicles are essential no matter how short are the distances involved. Informants consistently mentioned this responsibility, adequate performance of which is regarded as indicative of the groom's future respect for his wife and in-laws. At one wedding that I attended, the late arrival of the vehicles was very badly received and threatened to disrupt the entire event.

A modern bride wears a long white dress and veil. The service in church is very similar to an American wedding, except that the comments of the minister or priest on the duties of husband and wife relate to Nandi expectations. When the wedding party arrives at the groom's father's compound after the service, unmarried girls from the area surround the car in which the bride is riding, beat on the roof, and shout pleas to her to come out. The girls from the bride's home area meanwhile leave their vehicles and stand on the other side of the car, urging the bride not to leave them. The bride refuses to leave the car until her mother-in-law comes to escort her personally. Girls from the groom's area sing lyrics they have composed for the occasion, like this one sung (in English) at a wedding feast in Kaptel in 1977 (the names are pseudonyms):

> We are warning Jepkemei:
> You are now Mrs. Tarus.
> You must never meander
> Like a meandering river.

Speeches are made by important actors on both sides. Themes that are stressed are illustrated by the following excerpt from my field notes:

Every speaker commented on the fact that the families come from far apart. The groom's relatives urged the bride's to consider that they are gaining a son-in-law, not losing a daughter. Also frequently reiterated was that they realize they are fortunate to be getting such a fine girl, and they will take good care of her and/or see to it that her new husband does so. The groom's mother said that she didn't know why her son had succeeded in attracting this girl—certainly it wasn't because he was much more handsome than all the young men of her home area—but these things just happen. The bride's mother replied in her speech that the groom's family was really lucky to be getting "this girl of mine" and they should be thankful and show her family a lot of respect. Several men from the groom's side commented in their speeches that if the young men from the girl's community were annoyed that a girl was being taken from them, they should "come and take one from us."

After the speeches, recorded music is played and all the visitors are given a big meal. The bride and groom sit at a table apart from the festivities, where they receive a constant stream of visitors who give them cash gifts and words of advice. In at least one Christian wedding I know of, the groom's age-mates and their wives and girl friends were entertained with dancing and European bottled beer in the evening when everyone else had left.

One detail of the traditional wedding ceremony is noteworthy from the point of view of my major concern, the property relations of husband and wife. The ceremony is marked by the bride's refusal to proceed at certain points unless promised the gift of an animal. Further, in one of the last steps in the ritual, the groom refuses to eat food prepared by the bride (and by implication subsequently to consummate the marriage) unless she cedes control of at least one such animal to him (Hollis 1909:63). This feature is common to wedding ceremonies in a number of East African societies, and in Nandi it is one of the few features of the traditional wedding ceremony that I have seen carried over into the modern Christian ceremony (though it is not always or even usually a feature of Christian ceremonies). The fact that it has been maintained demonstrates, I think, its real symbolic importance. As I shall show in detail in Chapter 7, the fact that property is held by a woman, but she cedes control of it to her husband, represents the dual principles of the Nandi system of marriage and property relations: female house property and male control.

Relations between Husbands and Wives

We once went to visit an elderly, very traditional Nandi couple. Because they were the parents of a special friend, we took each of them a gift. They reciprocated this gesture by slaughtering a goat (one of a large herd) and roasting meat in our honor. Later in the day, I discussed marriage with the old lady, who made the following comment: "A good marriage is one in which the wife makes a suggestion, the husband sees that it is good, and they do it together; the husband makes a suggestion, the wife sees that it is good, and they do it together. Like today—I said to my husband: 'These guests have brought us gifts and we can't give them a meal with only vegetables—let's kill a goat.' And he said: 'You are right; we will do it.'"

This same woman's husband behaves toward her in a very domineering way, and speaks about her disparagingly. One would never guess from his statements and behavior alone that their relationship is anything but entirely male-dominated. By the time I left the field, I had the feeling that this relative egalitarianism and climate of free discussion and participation in joint decision making in private, masked by a public façade of extreme dominance/deference, is the typical pattern of interaction in Nandi marriages.

In a normally harmonious marriage, husband and wife are partners in the enterprise of building an estate for their children. As long as they both put this goal ahead of their personal interests, there is rarely cause for conflict between them. Of course, the husband's will is supposed to be dominant. The wife expects this—it is also her ideal—and she is not likely to be assertive over trivialities. At the same time, the husband is supposed to take his wife's opinions into consideration, and not to be too domineering or autocratic. Relations between husband and wife are regulated by community censure through gossip, and people's concern about maintaining good reputations. I can attest to the fact that relations between husbands and wives are the subject of a great deal of gossip. I was constantly hearing about offenses that certain men had committed against their wives (and, more rarely, wives against husbands). Some men were criticized for drinking too much, for working too little, for not providing their wives with money to buy household items or clothing for the children. Others were criticized for being overly restrictive of their wives' activities—as one man who, I heard from several sources, doesn't allow his wife freedom to travel and visit friends and doesn't let her have a discretionary budget even though she works for wages. This man was rich, but for various reasons—including his treatment of his wife—he had little prestige in the community. When one man slaughtered an animal his wife had acquired through her own initiative, the community scandal that resulted was enough to cause him public embarrassment. Finally, I heard several men criticized repeatedly for beating their wives too much. Women were also censured through gossip: for being lazy, for drinking, for behaving disrespectfully (i.e. being publicly defiant or contemptuous of their husbands), for carrying on blatant sexual affairs with other men (women whose behavior was otherwise good were rarely commented upon disapprovingly for discreet adultery).

The themes that recur in censure through gossip highlight the normal expectations of marriage: both parties should be sober and hard working; the wife owes her husband respect and deference and certain wifely duties such as cooking for him, washing his clothes, keeping the house clean, caring for the children well; as long as she performs her duties adequately and is respectful, the husband should not restrict her autonomy, though he theoretically has the right to do so; if a wife fails in her duties or in respect the husband not only may, but should, punish her by beating, but if he beats her frequently for minor offenses, he is considered harsh.

In general, Nandi husbands and wives spend much less time in each other's company than each spends with a same-sex peer group. Both spouses act and make decisions autonomously in day-to-day life. Wives are steadfastly loyal and supportive of their husbands' actions and decisions in interactions with people who are not of the family, and otherwise largely do as they please. It is considered beneath a man's dignity to be concerned about or to interfere in the minutiae of his wife's affairs. When an important joint decision must be taken in a harmonious marriage, husband and wife do confer, but a wife whose husband takes a strong position on an issue doesn't usually disagree with him unless she also feels exceptionally committed to an opposing position. In such cases arguments occur—wives do not invariably defer to their husbands in private discussions. If the husband is intransigent, however, it is the wife who (except in extreme cases) backs off and allows his will to prevail. It is not uncommon, though, for a wife to persuade her husband to her point of view (as will be seen in a case cited below).

One cannot easily illustrate the dynamics of successful marriages with concrete examples. When things go right there is little, on the surface, to be observed, and less that arouses comment from other members of the community. A few excerpts from my field notes illustrate observations of the functioning of "good" marriages.

In one compound I know that the wife is responsible for distributing small pieces of land to other compound residents or neighbors on loan; also, she clearly has control over giving away whatever part of the produce she wishes. When she wanted to go on a trip to Nairobi, she said that all she had to do was tell her husband she wanted to go and it was all right. She got a teen-age girl from a neighboring household to take care of her children and cook for the husband. She considers that she has freedom of movement as long as her specific duties are taken care of. (This was during the less busy agricultural season, though; on another occasion, during the weeding season, I noted that this woman's husband refused her permission to travel.)

A couple with whom we are friendly have figured out that they can make more money by not planting maize after this year and buying cattle instead—turning all the current maize fields to pasture. When we visited them, they were explaining the figures to us—multiplying and adding to prove their point. What was interesting in this conversation was that the wife was just as familiar with all the information as the husband, and just as forward in putting the case. They have obviously discussed it at length.

An informant described the relationship between his parents as one of free give-and-take. The father worked away from home for many years and returned on weekends only. Informant says his mother was really the one responsible for developing their farm when he was young. When his father came home, the whole family would have planning sessions about the farm. Even the children got to have a voice. If they were instructed to do something they thought wasn't such a good idea, they could say why they thought so and have their reasons considered. The father didn't give harsh commands to his wife, and was accepting when she became angry and argued with him in private.

In all these cases it is noteworthy that wives have far more autonomy and input in family decision making (especially in matters of farm management) than one would expect from informants' idealized abstractions about the rights and powers of husbands vs. those of wives and observation of public wife-to-husband deference. The first case also illustrates that this situation has limits: even in the best marriages, the wife's autonomy is not complete and her husband can deny her permission to do something she wants to do. However, the husband is not overstepping himself; harmony is maintained because the wife agrees that his position is reasonable.

At first I made notes of examples of such harmonious and relatively egalitarian interactions, but these notes became less frequent as I realized how normal this state of affairs was. On the other hand, my field notes are virtually full of cases of marital discord. Though not the norm, such cases may be even more valuable than cases of harmonious interaction for understanding the nature of the husband-wife relationship. The expectations of the parties to a marriage are demonstrated very clearly by the complaints that ensue when appropriate behavior has broken down. Therefore I shall present and discuss four cases of marital discord.

Case #1. Jerono left her husband Kibet because he beat her frequently and with insufficient cause and went to stay with her sister Jepkoech, the wife of Arap Birirei, who lived in the same neighborhood. She took her children with her. She had been there between one and two weeks when the following incident occurred: Kibet passed the compound on his way home from drinking at the Center. Seeing nobody around, he entered to look for Jerono. He found her bathing behind the granary and began to beat her. She ran to the house of the sister of Arap Birirei, who lived in the same compound. This woman stood in the doorway with a piece of firewood and defied Kibet to try to enter. He went away. After about half an hour he returned, again found Jerono alone, and began to beat her. At this point Jepkoech returned and began a verbal argument with Kibet. Meanwhile, she sent one of her children to fetch her brother (and Jerono's), Kibor, who also lived nearby. When Kibor arrived, Kibet and Jepkoech were still arguing. Kibet was demanding that Jerono return the children, and was trying to push past Jepkoech to reach Jerono. Kibor threw himself on Kibet and the two men fought. Kibor grabbed a clay bellows and began to beat Kibet about the head with it. Jepkoech and her sister-in-law physically restrained him, and Kibet went his way. Shortly after this, Arap Birirei arrived. Normally an extremely "polite" and self-controlled man, he was livid at the lack of respect Kibet had shown him (made worse by the fact that they are related as *lemenyi*, husbands of sisters, and should have a close, harmonious relationship) by beating Jerono in his compound. He almost immediately rushed off for the District Center to file charges against Kibet. Jerono was saying she wanted a permanent separation and would not go back to live with Kibet (who had a general reputation as a bad actor) under any circumstances. Later, she retreated from this position, saying it would be very difficult for her to separate from him permanently and keep the children. Arap Birirei returned and said he had been told that he could only file trespass charges, that Jerono herself would have to appear to file assault charges. Arap Birirei insisted that he wanted Kibet jailed and that Jerono must go with him next day to file charges. Jepkoech talked with him and convinced him that it was not a good idea to file charges because if Jerono caused Kibet to be jailed she could never hope to live with him peacefully. Arap Birirei was mollified and agreed not to prosecute Kibet. Jerono suggested she send the children back to Kibet's compound next day to appease him, but Arap Birirei, with the support of Jepkoech, absolutely refused to let her do this. Next day, tempers began to cool down. Kibet did not pass near Arap Birirei's compound again for weeks. Eventually Kibet's mother came and convinced Jepkoech that if Jerono returned she would see to it that Kibet let her alone. At Jepkoech's urging, Jerono eventually did return. She and Kibet continued living in the same compound, not on good terms but without open hostility.

Case #2. Chesang' left her husband Kipketer, who lives in the same sublocation, and went home to her parents. Her complaints were that her husband made her work too hard and beat her. However, public opinion was almost entirely on his side. People said he didn't ask her to work especially hard, she was lazy, and he had good reasons for beating her. Some women did say, though, that he had a reputation for giving her (and his previous wife) particularly brutal beatings. Arap Sisei, a neighbor of Chesang's parents, talked her into returning to her husband and trying to make a go of it. He asked us to transport her and her belongings in our car. Arap Sisei's wife, Rael, was also a member of the party. When we arrived, Kipketer invited us inside for tea, but Chesang' remained in the car. One of the children was sent for Kipketer's brother, who arrived in a few minutes. Chesang' came in a few minutes later. She and Kipketer sat with their backs toward one another. At one point, all the men went outside. When they returned, discussion began. Kipketer's grievances were as follows: Chesang' is lazy—she refuses to do such jobs as taking milk to the road (to be picked up by a truck from the marketing cooperative) and giving water to the calves; she works harder at her parents' home than at his; she always goes to visit her parents when it is time to weed the maize; he has sold cattle to hire workers to help her, but she does no better; she mistreats the workers, and has tried to get them to collaborate in selling maize on the side and keeping the money; she can't get along with his mother and one of the older children, and treats them very badly; she cooks special meals for herself, and gives him and the children ordinary meals; she doesn't hold milk aside for him, so that when he wants to drink milk at home he finds that it has already been drunk; she has a boy friend, and when this man comes and plays his radio loudly on the road near their compound, she goes out to talk to him; she gossips about his (Kipketer's) private affairs with outsiders; if he sleeps late, she doesn't come to wake him or find out if he is sick, but sends the children; she doesn't teach the children manners and doesn't require them to work hard; she doesn't treat him with respect. Chesang' sat staring daggers at Kipketer throughout this recital. Kipketer had one very specific grievance. When Chesang' went to the hospital to give birth to her last child, he gave her 80 shillings, which she squandered. When she left the hospital she asked people for money, claiming that Kipketer had not given her any. At this, Chesang' started to say something in her own defense. Kipketer's brother told her to be quiet. Sisei and Rael both began pleading eloquently with Kipketer to give Chesang' another chance. Sisei did most of the persuasive talking, but Rael also spoke forcefully at times. Finally, Kipketer agreed, as he said, only because of respect for them. We all left, and Chesang' remained. I asked Rael if Chesang' shouldn't have been allowed to present her side of the story. She said normally yes, but in this case the woman's behavior is *very* bad and everyone knows it. Also, Rael was shocked at the disrespectful way Chesang' had looked at her husband. She said that a wife should always behave respectfully, and that this behavior had completely alienated her from Chesang's cause. If Chesang' couldn't live with Kipketer this time, she (Rael) would do nothing to help her in the future.

Case #3. Mary left her husband, Anderea, and went to stay with her sister Dorcas, who lived in a neighboring community. After a few weeks, Dorcas and her husband Joshua decided to take Mary back to her husband and reconcile the two. The father of Mary and Dorcas also accompanied them. They sent word ahead that they were coming, and were met at the compound by Anderea, his mother, some of his age-mates, his mother's co-wife, and several respected elders of the neighborhood and other neighbors. Joshua explained why they had come, and Mary was asked why she left. Her complaints against Anderea were that he beats her frequently without good cause, that he doesn't provide enough money to feed and clothe the children even though he does contract labor for cash, that the house is in disrepair and he won't provide money to fix it, and that he has sold several cows against her wishes. Her mother-in-law supported her story, and stressed that she believes her son is the guilty party. Obviously anxious to maintain the relationship, she kept exaggeratedly addressing Mary's father as *bamwai* (the kinship term used between the parents of a married couple). Anderea complained that Mary is disobedient to him, and that she drinks and brews liquor, and is so busy brewing that she neglects her duties at home. Mary said that it is true that she brews, but she has to because Anderea gives her no money. She is angry because he wants to sell another cow. He says it is to get money for plowing, but she thinks he will squander the money on his own amusement. She said they once had twelve cows, but he has sold five. There is a long history of conflict in the nine years of the marriage. Both parties have left home for extended periods. Anderea has also quarreled violently with his mother and once set fire to her granary. Mary and Anderea were asked to go some distance away while the elders discussed the matter. When they returned, both of them were warned to change their ways. However, the elders also said that they felt the biggest fault was with Anderea and he should be the one to do the most changing. If possible, he should find some way to get the money for plowing other than selling a cow. Joshua, however, spoke sternly to Mary, and told her to give up brewing and drinking entirely. (He is a dedicated fundamentalist Christian.) He said that her conduct must be above reproach so they can argue more vigorously in her favor if there are any more problems.

Case #4. Emily and her husband Kiplimo seemed to have a very harmonious relationship, so I was surprised to learn that she had gone to stay with her sister Susanna, who lived in the same neighborhood. She took her seven-month-old baby daughter with her. Emily's version of the problem was this: Nandi practice prescribes a three-month minimum (preferably longer) wait after the birth of a child before sexual intercourse is resumed, and also that sexual intercourse be discontinued after the first three months of pregnancy. Kiplimo began demanding that she have sex with him after only a month. Now she is four months pregnant again and he still wants her to have sex. Finally they quarreled bitterly over what she considered his excessive desire for sex, and the quarrel ended with Kiplimo beating her. So she left. Susanna's husband, Kiplimo's *lemenyi* and friend, took it upon himself to patch things up between them. He also urged Kiplimo not to get Emily pregnant so often because too-frequent pregnancy is bad for a woman's health. He told him the close space between these two children would look bad in the eyes of the community and he should wait longer next time. Kiplimo agreed, and Emily returned home.

In all these cases, marital grievances were aired and some resolution of them attempted because the women concerned left their husbands. In three of the cases, they took refuge with a sister, a common pattern and one reason given by sisters for trying to marry into the same neighborhood. The wife's immediate complaint in all cases had to do with the husband beating her: too frequently, too brutally, or for no good reason. Wives' complaints have to do with physical abuse, excessiveness in husbands' demands for services supposedly due husbands by wives, husbands' failure to provide the material support that is the due of wives and children, and in one case the husband's unilateral alienation of joint property (which may be viewed as an aspect of failure to provide support). Husbands' complaints center around wives' failure to perform wifely duties and lack of respect for the husband and/or his relatives. In one case, the wife's drinking and decision to brew beer is a factor, as is her alleged adultery in another.

In two of these cases, the woman's sister's husband was instrumental in helping to effect a reconciliation. This is also a common pattern. Two men who have married sisters are related to each other as *lemenyi*, a relationship that implies solidarity, comradeship, and mutual respect. In Case #1, resolution was complicated because Kibet's behavior in attacking Jerono in Arap Birirei's compound nullified the premises of this relationship. Ultimately, an informal resolution was arranged between Kibet's mother and Jerono's sister. In the two cases that were resolved with the greatest formality, it is noteworthy that a married couple acted together as go-betweens. Note, too, that Arap Birirei's wife convinced him to follow the course of action she and Jerono favored, though he initially favored a different one. Note, further, that, although ordinarily a woman's mere presence in her sister's compound affords her sufficient protection from her husband, in the one case where this norm was breached Arap Birirei's sister was willing to confront Kibet physically in order to protect Jerono (though instances of Nandi women fighting men physically are extremely rare).

The case of Mary and Anderea is interesting because it is the only instance I encountered of a wife's actually succeeding in blocking her husband's intent to sell livestock through recourse to a public forum. (Other instances may have occurred during my field stay without coming to my attention.) In this case, Mary was in an extremely strong position. The cow Anderea proposed to sell would be the sixth he had sold—the family herd was rapidly dwindling to nothing because of his poor management—and even his mother sided with Mary against him. I believe that a wife can succeed in getting the community to intervene in her husband's herd management only in such extreme circumstances.

Since wife beating and male physical aggression toward women have entered the theoretical literature as possible indices of male dominance (e.g., Sanday 1981:164), a brief account of this subject is appropriate. Wife beating is common in Nandi, approved, and expected under certain circumstances. This attitude is held by members of both sexes. I heard of innumerable instances of wife beating in private, and witnessed several cases in which husbands beat wives publicly. There are marriages in which the wife has never, to my knowledge, been beaten by her husband—beating is not universal Nandi male behavior. But if a wife behaves badly toward her husband in the view of the community, he is obliged to beat her or lose face. A highly acculturated Nandi graduate of an American university told me that he was personally attracted to the kind of relationship between husbands and wives he had seen among educated couples in the United States. The thought of wife beating now repelled him: he viewed it as an unfair use of force, since husbands are usually stronger than wives. I asked him if he would in the future beat his wife. He answered, "You see, that depends on what *she* does. If she does certain things, I will *have* to beat her or people will lose respect for me." I asked a number of women why they did not fight back when their husbands beat them unjustly. The reply was always that fighting back might so enrage one's husband that he would inflict really serious injury. "You only fight back if you are eager to die." In other societies, similar considerations do not always prevent women from fighting back. But the Nandi ideology upholds passive behavior as appropriate for a wife when her husband beats her. For certain offenses (e.g., passing a man on the wrong side) I was told it was formerly appropriate for any man to beat any woman, but during my fieldwork I only heard of cases of husbands beating wives, not of men beating women to whom they were not married. I also heard of a number of instances of rape, which, though hardly approved, was not considered a terribly serious offense, particularly if the woman who was raped was unmarried (and unless the woman involved was pregnant and the rape resulted in miscarriage).

Relations between husbands and wives in marriage can be summed up as usually harmonious, normally allowing for a great deal of autonomy and input in decision making on the part of the wife, and even where not harmonious, marked by a lively give-and-take in which the wife is far from powerless. In cases of disagreement in a marriage, though, the husband clearly has the edge. He can make decisions unilaterally that affect the entire household; he does not *have* to permit his wife input. Only if things become extremely bad as a result of his mismanagement of family affairs, or if he blatantly violates his wife's rights, does she have any recourse. Normally, however, her autonomy is protected by her husband's concern about his reputation. Excessive concern about a wife's comings and goings is considered beneath a man's dignity, and a husband who displays such concern is subject to ridicule. In the cases cited above, women are shown as important actors in arranging and maintaining marriages and protecting the rights of other women as wives.

Polygyny

Prior to the conversion of large numbers of people to Christianity, most Nandi men aspired to have more than one wife. This was, as in most African societies, a mark of wealth and status, showing that a man had attained success in life. A great many of the richest and most important men still do marry more than one wife, in spite of belonging to Christian denominations. Men of more moderate means, if they are Christians, contend that they have no desire to become polygynists, because plural marriage is contrary to their religion. The actual impact of Christianity on the incidence of polygyny is slight. Among the ever-married male household heads in my census, for members of the three eldest age-sets,* 31.8 percent of non-Christians were polygynists, but so were 25.9 percent of the Christians, including a number of the most active church members. Whether Christianity (or some other factor) will keep younger men from taking second wives remains to be seen.

In my census, 16.8 percent of ever-married male household heads were polygynists. I consider this figure to be somewhat low when compared with figures for Nandi District as a whole, probably because there are more household heads of the two youngest circumcised age-sets in Kaptel than in most Nandi communities. In the three oldest age-sets, 28.6 percent of household heads were polygynists. In a survey of 454 men of the Nyongi, Maina, Chuma, Sawe, and Kipkoimet age-sets, spread throughout Nandi District, I found 30.6 percent to have had more than one wife (see Table 10). I think that in some cases in this data set, the phrasing of the question was not clear to informants, who may have reported consecutive rather than simultaneous marriages. Further, not all these men are still living. Langley (1979:84) found a 31 percent incidence of polygyny among families with children at primary school. It is possible that because of the method of examining only families with children at school, certain categories of men least likely to be polygynists (the youngest and poorest married men) were undercounted. For these reasons, I view 30 percent of married men as the probable maximum incidence of polygynists for Nandi as a whole, the actual incidence probably being closer to 25 percent.

Table 10 reveals a lower incidence of polygyny for men of the two youngest age-sets than for older men. This does not necessarily mean that the polygyny rate is declining; it may mean only that these men have not yet reached the age at which they are likely to marry a second wife.

A wife does not have a right to object to her husband's desire to take a second wife, as long as it does not involve using cattle that have been clearly assigned to her house. A number of se-

*I excluded members of the Sawe and Kipkoimet age-sets because most of them have not yet reached the age at which a man is most likely to take a second wife.

TABLE 10
Polygynists as Percentage of Ever-Married Men,
by Age-Set

Age-set	Number of polygynists	Percent of married men
Nyongi	29	39.2%
Maina	56	40.5
Chuma	42	36.2
Sawe	11	11.2
Kipkoimet	1	3.5

nior wives in polygynous marriages told me that they urged their husbands to take second wives, helped to find appropriate candidates, and were members of the marriage negotiation parties. Still, the common assumption is that it is difficult for co-wives to get along well together. People of all age and sex categories constantly reiterated this theme: "A husband has always got to love one wife more than the other—he cannot love them both equally." The preference expressed by most people is that the husband should maintain two entirely separate farms, in separate communities if possible. A number of polygynists I knew had wives in more than one community, and they seemed to spend the majority of their time with one, traveling to visit the compound(s) of the other(s) on a regular basis. Greater proximity between co-wives is more usual, however. Of sixteen pairs of co-wives in the census, twelve lived in the same compound or on the same farm, one pair lived in the same community but on separate farms, and three lived in different communities. During my stay in Nandi, I witnessed very few instances of overt hostility and aggression between co-wives, particularly in view of the fact that the culturally endorsed expectation is that such women will not be friends. Nandi norms of "politeness" and avoidance of open conflict prevent continuous bickering between co-wives, even those who don't like each other. If co-wives don't get along easily, they choose widely separated house-sites on their husband's plot and for the most part conduct their affairs independently of one another. Among the four sets of co-wives I knew best, three pairs were friends and one pair was not. The unfriendly pair lived far enough apart so that it was not immediately obvious that they shared a farm, and interacted as little as possible. Informants denied that there is a significant amount of co-wife solidarity that involves taking a joint stand against the husband, but I did record one such instance. This incident took place at the feast after a traditional wedding.

The second youngest wife of the groom's father (the third of four) was sitting inside drinking beer with everybody else, and Arap Maiyo came and told her that she should be out cooking food for the guests as were the other wives. She objected that she had worked all day the previous day when the others were drinking and now it was her turn to rest. Maiyo was threatening to beat her when Kobot Kiplimo (the groom's mother) entered the room. She accused him of always picking on the third wife, and challenged him to beat her (Kobot Kiplimo) instead if he wanted to beat someone. Maiyo said (in effect) that he just might do that. One word led to another, and Maiyo shoved Kobot Kiplimo and knocked her to the floor. Men took him aside and calmed him down, telling him to think of how bad such a scene was when guests were present. Women gathered around Kobot Kiplimo and told her the same thing. The younger wife stayed where she was and didn't do anything. Arap Maiyo left the house, and Kobot Kiplimo sat down and began drinking with the guests. Eventually Arap Maiyo came back and took a place among the men, calm again and apparently unconcerned that his wives had succeeded in thwarting his will. Kiplimo (the groom) was extremely embarrassed and sat outside sulking. Later when we were leaving, he apologized to us for the behavior of his parents.

All wives in a polygynous marriage cook for the husband at every meal and set his portion aside—the husband, without prearrangement, may decide to eat at the house of any of his wives. If the wives are on good terms they may, with the husband's agreement, make an arrangement whereby one cooks for the entire compound on a given day if the other is busy with some other work. A husband may decide to spend the night in the house of any wife. There is no strict rotational schedule, but it is considered wrong for a husband to neglect a wife entirely, particularly sexually. It is a woman's intrinsic right to be impregnated and bear children. If her husband doesn't impregnate her, she is justified in seeking this service elsewhere.

It is often said by young Nandi informants that polygyny is on the decline—that in the age-set of young men that is currently being initiated, few men will be polygynists. They attribute this change to Christianity and to high levels of education and the spread of a "modern" attitude toward marriage. It is said both that modern, educated young men prefer monogamy, and that education for women will have a negative impact on polygyny because girls who have attended secondary school do not like the idea of becoming second wives. It is true that I knew of only one case in which an educated woman became a second wife, but there are going to be plenty of less educated girls in Nandi for the forseeable future. I am not prepared to make a prediction about the future of polygyny. Certainly for the three elder age-sets, though Christianity may have had some effect on reducing the rate of polygyny, it has been slight.

In my opinion, any decline in polygyny will be due at least as much to economic factors as to either Christianity or education, though it may be rationalized by reference to religion. Land partitioning and inheritance mean that people are beginning to take cognizance of land as a finite resource. If a family landholding is small, it may be impossible to divide it among a large number of sons. Under such circumstances, women may become resistant to the idea of their husbands taking second wives, if they realize that this will probably mean that their sons will inherit smaller portions. Further, a corollary of land partitioning has been the replacement of large numbers of low-milk-producing cattle with small numbers of high-milk-producing cattle. Even though the total amount of the product may have remained the same—or even increased—there has been a major shift in the size of the herd it is possible to accommodate on one family's holding, and holdings are still decreasing in size. The house-property system means that the family herd is continuously subdivided. It is easy to divide many animals into several parts, but not so easy to divide a few. Therefore the difficulty of dividing the modern estate—both land and cattle—into parts will be one of the things that works against polygyny in the modern setting. On the other hand, individual wealth differences are increasing and, as the result of the commoditization of resources, solidifying across generations into incipient relations of social class. For the rich, who have plenty of resources, polygyny is still an attractive possibility, and I should expect to see the richest Nandi men, regardless of their level of education or religious affiliation, continue to marry more than one wife.

The Levirate and Woman-Woman Marriage

A Nandi woman, ideally, is married only once. Divorce with remarriage is rare, though if a woman leaves her husband before children are born, and the bridewealth is returned, the marriage is effectively annulled. In this case, the woman is free to marry again. A widow may not remarry; she continues to live on her dead husband's land, and if still of childbearing age, to bear his children.

A woman's house property should be inherited only by her own son or sons. It should never revert to a collateral line. The levirate is one method of ensuring that a widow bears a son to inherit her house property. Informants report that according to Nandi customary law a widow should be taken over (the verb used is *kindi*, which means "to inherit" in a more general sense) by a brother (or classificatory brother = FBS) of her deceased husband. The widow and levir do not live together. He comes to her house as a visitor only. His role is to father children if her family is not considered complete and (normatively) to help manage property held in trust for the widow's minor sons and provide her with the types of material support that a husband provides. Children born of a levirate relationship count as children of the deceased husband and inherit his property, as do children a wife bears after her husband's death whether or not they are fathered by a levir.

A widow is not required to accept a levirate arrangement, and in fact such arrangements are rare. Of my close associates who were widows (at least fifteen women), I know definitely that all but one were *not* involved in levirate relationships. Older widows, whose families are complete, hardly ever practice the levirate; they depend on their grown sons to provide cash assistance and perform the male role in the sexual division of labor— or hire men with their own money. If such a widow takes a lover, this is a man of her own choosing and, because the community is not agnatically structured, not likely to be an agnate of her husband. Younger widows are expected to go on bearing children, and I was frequently told that they *should* practice the levirate. However, of three widows under age forty in the research community whom I knew personally, only one had a levirate husband. In all cases of levirate marriage of which I heard any details (a total of about five), the widow involved was under the age of thirty-five.

Thus the levirate is rare and, when practiced, is practiced by young widows only. A young widow, especially one without a son, is under considerable pressure to have more children as quickly as possible. An older widow is not likely to engage in the levirate for three reasons. First, through her first marriage she has secure property rights (examined at length in Chapter 7), which she does not need a levirate marriage to secure further. Second, a woman's house property is inherited by her sons regardless of the identity of their genitor, who need not be a brother of their pater. Third, because of general affluence, a typical Nandi widow's house property is enough to support her and her children without a levir's help. A widow does not *need* a levirate husband and becomes more free than a widow in a less affluent society to form a liaison with a man (or not to) based on personal preference alone.

There is a marked discrepancy between reports of male and female informants as to what usually happens in cases where a young widow is left with minor children. Male informants tend to report that the dead man's brother takes the widow in levirate marriage, manages the house property, and provides for the children materially (e.g., clothes, school fees). Female informants tend to report that widows manage their property and provide for their children themselves. This discrepancy may arise at least partly from the fact that a brother of the dead husband may be declared by his family to be the widow's levir, though he never performs any aspect of the levir role. Nonintimates, however, may assume that he is doing so. If he is not fulfilling formal role expectations, he is much less likely to reveal this fact to his male associates than the widow is to reveal it to her female associates. Thus the fact that levirs do not always act as levirs would become more widely known among women than among men. In general, my observations and discussions with informants lead me to believe that a brother's role in property management is slight unless he is also an active levir.

Langley (1979:73) says that "the levirate is looked upon with distaste and is resorted to only in secret." It is true that the levirate is not frequently practiced. It is also true that, although there is no particular secrecy surrounding it, the levirate may not be immediately obvious to the outside observer, because it is treated very casually and because widows and levirs do not co-reside. Still, it is viewed by most informants as the respectable and socially correct thing for a widow and her husband's brother to do, and in the one case of the levirate I was close to, the relationship was treated as a source of pride by all members of the family and almost bragged about. The woman's behavior was considered exemplary: she was considered a "good woman" because she stayed with her husband's brother instead of "going outside" to find a man. I believe that the infrequency of the levirate is an example of widows using their autonomous position to do as they please *in contravention* of social norms. It seems likely that before ready access to cash and the commoditization of resources, including male labor, gave widows the kind of autonomy they now enjoy, the levirate was more common. The penetration of Christianity—which disapproves of levirate marriage—may also have had an impact on its occurrence among Christians.

If a woman finishes her childbearing years without a living son, she may decide upon a woman-woman marriage to secure an heir for her house property. I have dealt with woman-woman marriage at length elsewhere (Oboler 1980) and shall discuss it only briefly here.

A postmenopausal, sonless woman uses some of her house property to pay bridewealth for, and thus marry, a younger woman. The two women are considered husband and wife, and the older woman becomes the social and legal father of any children her wife may bear. The female husband is said to have been "promoted" to male status (*kagotogosta komostab murenik*, literally "she has gone up to the side of the men"). She discontinues sexual intercourse with men, and though there is no evidence that her relationship with her wife is in any way sexual, she nonetheless has all the nonsexual prerogatives of a male husband with regard to her wife. The wife is free to engage in sexual liaisons with men of her own choosing, and any children she may have as a result belong to her and her female husband. Formerly, it is said, it was the right of the female husband to arrange a regular consort for her wife—normally an agnate of the female husband's male husband of the wife's generation, usually the son of her co-wife or of her husband's brother. Today, sexual freedom is cited as one of the advantages of marriage to a female husband.

The children borne by the wife of a female husband belong to the clan of the latter woman's male husband and inherit property that originally was his. The arrangement in no way involves the natal clan or family of the female husband herself. My informants agree unanimously about this, although Langley (1979:73) writes that the female husband "raised children either to her own or her husband's clan," and that the genitor was approved by the female husband's own family.*

Woman-woman marriage is not uncommon, though far from all women who are eligible to become female husbands actually do so. Among wives of the two oldest age-sets—the only women who are certain to have completed their fertility—39 percent ($N = 7$) and 27 percent ($N = 6$), respectively, of women with no male heir married wives (that is 6.8 percent and 6 percent, respectively, of ever-married women ultimately become female husbands). In my research community, 3.5 percent of households (10 of 286) were headed by female husbands. A sonless woman must have enough house property, after bridewealth, to warrant an heir before she will consider this option. Further, since most girls consider marriage by a man preferable to marriage by a woman, it is not always easy to find a desirable girl who is willing to agree to such a marriage. Despite disapproval of Christians, however, woman-woman marriage does not seem

---

*Langley (personal communication) says that her information on these points does not conflict with mine. However, I want to record the discrepancy between what she has written, implying either that an option exists or that informants are uncertain on these points, and my many informants' absolute and unanimous certainty that the female husband's natal clan and family have nothing whatsoever to do with the arrangement in which she takes a wife. This relationship is rooted in *property*, and it is the source of this property that is crucial.

to be losing popularity. It is more likely that its incidence is increasing. I discuss reasons for this at greater length in Chapter 7.

An alternative to woman-woman marriage is the institution known as "marrying the house" or "marrying the center post" (*tunisiet ab got, kitunis toloita*). In this form of marriage, the sonless woman's youngest daughter is retained at home, and her "husband" is said to be the house or its center post. This daughter will have children by self-selected sexual partners and her sons will inherit the house's property. The custom is said to be a recent innovation, but it has not gained much popularity relative to woman-woman marriage.

Separation and Divorce

Divorce is so rare that people commonly regard it as impossible. There was, however, a traditional divorce procedure known as *kebet lol* or *betet ab lalet* ("tearing a bag" or "the tearing of a bag"), which is described in detail by Langley (1979:96–98). She says that this procedure was only possible in the case of childless marriages. Hollis (1909:69), too, says that "a woman who has a child cannot be divorced." Today, certainly, there are cases on record of divorces taking place even after the birth of a child, but they are still very uncommon. In nearly all such cases, various parties have claims on a woman, and/or competing traditional, Christian, and civil marriage and divorce norms are involved. This is exemplified in the following case.

A secondary school girl was impregnated by one of her classmates. After they finished school, they were married traditionally, she had the baby (a daughter), he went to work, and she went on to Teacher Training College. While there, she met and fell in love with another man and decided that she wanted to leave her first husband and marry him. They went to the D.C.'s office and were married in a civil ceremony. The second husband paid bridewealth to the girl's family, and they returned the bridewealth they got from the first husband. The first husband was mad with rage and wanted to kill the second husband. The woman swore that even if the second marriage didn't stand, she would never live with the first husband again. When he realized she was serious, he gave up and allowed her to be divorced. Because the child was a girl the first husband didn't even try to keep her, though informants said he would have insisted on keeping a son. What caused a great deal of attention to be attracted to the case was that the second husband's father committed suicide out of shame that his son had stolen another man's wife.

Langley (1979: 100–108) provides a good account of several recent divorce cases on the basis of court records.

Though true divorce is close to impossible, separation occurs. Separation is not usually viewed as a prelude to breaking a marriage, and temporary separation is not infrequent. A separated woman and children born to her do not lose house-property rights. A woman who is incompatible with her husband may leave him for years, and return and take up her status as his wife and her rights in her house property. What this means is that even if a separation is long-standing, it may be regarded as temporary, especially if the woman leaves children behind in her husband's compound. I recorded numerous cases in which elderly women, long since separated from their husbands, returned to take up property rights at their husband's homes. This could occur either while the husband was still living or after his death, and in a significant number of cases the woman was sought out and persuaded by an adult son whom she had left behind with his father. Permanent separation is rare, though not so rare as divorce. Of 123 marriages of male household heads for which I have complete data, six ended in permanent separation. Of the 168 adult women living in 115 compounds in the census, eight were separated from their husbands on a long-term basis, and living permanently with other relatives. This latter figure probably underrepresents the extent of separation, since women who separate from their husbands also frequently migrate to large towns. In any case, these figures show that permanent separation, though it occurs, is not very common.

Conclusion

Nandi marriage is extremely stable. This is bound up with the fact that marriage confers upon a woman inalienable rights in an estate. However, I am not prepared to conclude that one of these facts is "caused by" the other.

A Nandi wife owes her husband public deference, but this

often masks a less public situation in which, though wife-to-husband deference is not entirely absent, it is much less marked, and wives have input in important household decisions and effective autonomy in daily activities.

Though such a pattern of marital interaction is not totally one-sided, it makes no sense to say that Nandi marriage is egalitarian or that the Nandi husband's dominance over his wife is merely "mythical" (a term used by Rogers 1978 and Sanday 1981). Especially in situations of disagreement, a Nandi husband has a very real advantage over his wife. He controls family property in the last analysis, and to a large extent he can even control his wife's person. She has no reciprocal control that she can wield effectively. It is possible for a husband to choose to ignore his wife's rights, and except in extreme cases, she has no recourse. A woman can get marital grievances heard by outside arbiters by leaving her husband temporarily. Usually she looks for refuge and help in reconciliation either to her parents or to a sister and her husband, who stands to her own husband in an important relationship, *lemenyi*.

Women are important public actors in relation to marriage, an institution that is viewed as essentially about the transaction between male and female. Women participate in marriage negotiations, in protecting wives' rights in cases of marital discord, and in arranging reconciliations of separated spouses. Chiñas (1973) has introduced the concept of "nonformalized roles" into the theoretical literature on sex and gender roles. These are patterned behavior-sets that are not "clearly perceived or rigidly defined by members of the society . . . even persons filling such nonformalized roles may perceive their own behavior as individual action without structure or pattern in the larger system." The observer becomes aware of such roles "by observing repeated instances of similar behavior by many different individuals in many different contexts" (Chiñas 1973:94). Chiñas further points out that in societies where women lack formal extradomestic roles, their importance may nevertheless not be confined to the domestic sphere. They may be active in nonformalized extradomestic roles. Nandi women's active participation in the arrangement and maintenance of marriages, both within and outside their immediate kin network, is an example of this type of situation.

Marriage serves as the idiom in which the relation between male and female is expressed in Nandi, and though the theme of male dominance is played out in Nandi marriage, it is by no means absolute.

Colonialism, Neocolonialism, and Economic Change

THERE ARE two primary points about the history of Kenya that are critical to all other events, economic and noneconomic, in its history. The first, it has in common with all colonies: it was intended to pay for its own conquest and administration by a product expropriated from it and exported. In Kenya's case, since there are no mineral resources to speak of, this meant agricultural produce. From this follows automatically the development of profitable cash crops as a major plank in the colonial government's economic program. The economic history of Kenya therefore is to a very large extent the history of agricultural change. The second essential point, though not unique to Kenya, is shared by only a handful of other colonies: Kenya was a settler colony. A large body of opinion among both the British public and the colonial administration held that Kenya's destiny was to become a "White Man's Country" in which the major part of productive privately held land would be in the hands of a permanent European citizenry superimposed upon a black labor force. This meant that the development of a cash crop economy took a markedly different course in Kenya from that of nonsettler colonies like Uganda, where independent African peasants were the major cash crop producers. In Kenya, the idea was to protect European farmers from competition with independent African producers, and simultaneously to force Africans into the labor market by cutting them off from other potential sources of income. The Africans were thus effectively restricted from participating in the independent production of many cash crops during most of the colonial period. In other words, there was an almost consciously articulated policy of underdevelopment for the African sector of the economy. (This argument is perhaps best developed by C. Leys 1974.) At the same time a second body of opinion among the public and colonial officials held that African countries should remain African. Colonization should be restricted to the economic arena and not be physical expropriation of the country for white occupation; ideally, development should further the interests of the African population. Kenya's economic history, particularly the history of agriculture, reflects the tension between the two views on policy for the colonies. Africans were sometimes permitted access to some cash crops, sometimes denied it, sometimes forced into labor for Europeans, sometimes encouraged to become peasants as circumstances and the strength of these competing ideologies shifted. Throughout, the European settler lobby was effective in assuring that the basic primacy of the interests of the settlers was never seriously challenged. African interests could be given consideration only when they did not pose any real threat to the interests of the European farm sector.

The economic history of Nandi or any other particular area of the country during the colonial era cannot be understood outside the context of such shifts in colonial policy. Further, these shifts are tied to events in the larger world economic and political scene such as depressions and wars. At the most general level, then, a discussion of the development of Nandi men's and women's economic position vis-à-vis one another during the colonial era must acknowledge the impact of the world economy on the Nandi.

Kenya's Agricultural Economy in the Colonial Era

The Uganda Railway, linking the Kingdom of Buganda with the East African Coast, was begun from Mombasa in 1896 and reached Kisumu on Lake Victoria five years later, in 1901. Agricultural development of the region between these points—at least in part with the intent of repaying loans taken to build the railroad—soon became a governmental priority. Two logical possibilities presented themselves: (*a*) the development of African peasant agriculture, and (*b*) the development of European-owned commercial farming.

Early explorers in Kenya and what was at that time Eastern Uganda (from 1902 part of the British East Africa Protectorate) had long commented on the suitability of this region for European settlement.* From 1897 Europeans could acquire twenty-one-year renewable land leases in Crown Lands (all land not actively used by Africans at this time); by 1915 the length of such leases was 999 years. Beginning in the first decade of the century, tribal reserves were demarcated, and by 1926 all African rights in land were restricted by law to such reserves (Van Zwannenberg 1975:34). Thus, agricultural development of "unused" lands early became an exclusively European prerogative. By 1902, there were already enough Europeans in Kenya that they organized to promote further European settlement (Bennett 1965:266). By 1920, there were 1,183 European landholders in Kenya, and ten years later the number was something over 2,000 (Brett 1973:175).† The type of farming to which most of the early settlers aspired was relatively small-scale mixed cultivation of the sort they were familiar with in England—primarily wheat, with some sheep and cattle, for wool, meat, and dairy products. This type of farming could be carried out in Kenya, but hardly at a level of productivity that was competitive with other parts of the world. In the first decade of the twentieth century, it became clear that this type of agriculture was not going to succeed economically in Kenya.

Labor was the great need of European farmers in trying to

---

*There was discussion of importing Indian peasants to Kenya, but the idea was abandoned. Though Indians came to form a substantial community in Kenya, they were not primarily involved in agriculture. Some came originally as indentured laborers on the railway, and many were merchants. There was also early discussion of ceding land in Kenya to the Zionist Congress for Jewish settlement, but the Zionists rejected this idea (Bennett 1965:266–67).

†Van Zwannenberg has argued cogently that settlers early on the spot lobbied successfully for land concessions on terms that made it possible for them to accumulate large amounts of land and engage in land speculation. By 1915, 20 percent of all land alienated for European settlement was held by five individuals or companies. These same interests, now even more powerful, subsequently lobbied for further development of European settlement to provide customers for their highly profitable land transactions (Van Zwannenberg 1975: 37–38).

make their land productive, since acreages were huge by the standards of a peasant economy. One major aim of taxation of Africans (first enacted as a hut tax in British-controlled areas in 1901) was to force them into wage labor. However, the result of taxation and the introduction of consumer goods was also the commoditization of certain African products. Up until the First World War, Kenyan export production was African-dominated, though most of the revenue it generated supported the expansion of settlement (Brett 1973:176).

In 1905 the Colonial Office took over administration of the Protectorate. The European settler lobby, through positions in the Colony's political machinery, sought rather single-mindedly to see that laws and the diversion of resources would be limited to its interests. On the other hand, there was opinion within the Colonial Office that supported attempts to foster (or at least appear to foster) African interests. At this point, some resources were directed to efforts to further extend African agriculture. In 1907, one exceptional instance was governmental support of peasant cultivation of cotton in Nyanza Province. The failure of this experiment has been attributed to efforts to force Africans into the labor market as workers on European farms (Wrigley 1965:223). The pro-European lobby at this time saw it as evidence that Africans were not competent to succeed as independent producers in a cash-crop economy. This episode dampened enthusiasm for the development of African peasant cultivation and furthered the idea that future economic prosperity would depend on European settler production (Van Zwannenberg 1975:39).

Beginning in 1910, there was an upswing in the world prices of two crops that Kenya could produce at a competitive advantage, coffee and sisal. European landowners put large tracts of land under these crops, which at times required heavy labor inputs. The role of small-scale planter, dependent on African labor, rather than independent farmer, thus emerged for many Europeans in Kenya.

Formal conscription of labor had been ended by the 1908 election of a Liberal government in Britain (though less formal methods of persuasion were still in use). Taxation was being used to bring Africans into the labor market. A poll tax of three rupees on adult males had been introduced, and the hut tax raised to that amount. The settlers demanded that more reserves be created and that the size of existing reserves be reduced, not because they needed land but because they hoped to force still more Africans into the labor market (Wrigley 1965:230). Overcrowding was already a problem in African reserves, and thus the Africans' need for land and the European settlers' need for labor coincided. The result was the Resident Labour or 'Squatter' System. Under this system, a European landholder would allow African families to reside and cultivate plots and graze animals on his land in return for a certain amount of part-time labor each year. The subsequent role of this system in the colonial agricultural economy was extremely important.

The First World War intervened at this point. A large proportion of able-bodied men, both European and African, became involved in the war effort and governmental resources were also diverted to it. Many Africans were employed as porters, and some even as soldiers in the campaign in Tanganyika. The economic problems created by the war were exacerbated by a rinderpest epidemic beginning in 1916 and a severe drought in 1918. These events had a more significant effect on African producers than on Europeans, whose position was aided by a postwar boom in the world commodity market. Under Sir Edward Northey, who became governor of the Protectorate in 1919, colonization began to increase as a result of the Soldier Settlement Scheme, which set aside several large parcels of land to be subdivided into small (200-acre) farms for British war veterans.* The year 1920 saw a great political victory for European settler interests when the settlers got formal representation on the colony's Legislative Council and the British East Africa Protectorate formally became Kenya Colony.

Labor continued to be an issue during this period. The Native Registration Ordinance that was enacted in 1915, which required all adult African males to register with the government and carry a card, known in Kiswahili as *kipande*,† had made labor re-

---

*Most of this land, 337 sq. km., or 130 sq. mi. (Van Zwannenberg 1973:94), was taken from the Nandi Reserve. This point will be developed at greater length in the following section.

†This system is still in effect, and in 1979 was extended to include adult women. It is an irony that an African government recognizes women's rights by

cruitment much easier and more effective. At the same time, the squatter system had developed in such a way that some land-holders were allowing Africans to live on their land not as la-borers but with payment of "rent" in the form of produce as the condition. Squatting under relatively easy terms provided a safety valve for land pressure in the reserves and mitigated the impact of rigid reserve boundaries as a device to force Africans to become laborers. As a result of lobbying on the part of Euro-pean farmers, the Resident Labourers' Ordinance was enacted in 1918. This ordinance provided that labor—at least 180 days per year—at a fixed rate of payment should be the only legal ex-change for the right of an African to squat on European-held land. The African resident laborer thus became, in the words of Colin Leys, "a kind of serf" (Leys 1974:34). The European de-mand for labor came to a head in the furor over the Northey Circulars of 1919, which were intended to make clear the condi-tions under which African entry into the labor force should be promoted:

The instructions of the labor circular were that it was the "wish" of the government that "tribesmen" should "come out into the labor field," and administrative officers were to encourage them to do so. Chiefs and elders should assist "as part of their duty," and lists were to be prepared of those who were "helpful" or "not helpful"; employers and recruiters "will be invited and encouraged to enter freely any native reserve" to recruit; and in areas near the farms women and children should also be recruited. By implication the encouragement of African farming within the reserves was not part of government policy. [Middleton 1965:355–56.]

Further, the poll tax was raised the following year (1920) from 12 to 16 shillings (Middleton 1965:356), and administrative officers were encouraged to make sure any "idle" young man had paid his tax. The policy outlined in the Northey Circulars was not far short of forced conscription of labor (especially in view of settler lobbying at around the same time to have African wage rates re-duced by one-third). This situation was dramatized by the anti-colonial lobby in Britain.

_____

including them in a system that is a legacy of a colonial policy long regarded by the Africans themselves as repressive.

Despite all their obvious advantages, the European settlers were having a bad time. In 1920 the bottom fell out of the world commodity boom, and the general slump in world prices of their major crops greatly hurt the prosperity of the settlers. The East African currency crisis of the same year, following which rupees were revalued as shillings on terms that increased the settlers' real debt, was a further blow. A new administration led by Winston Churchill as Colonial Secretary assumed the Colonial Office in 1921. One of its first acts was to revoke the Northey Circulars. This government was much less tolerant of the position of the settlers and inclined in favor of the development of indigenous peasantries in colonial countries. In 1922, Northey was replaced as governor by Sir Robert Coryndon. Under pressure from the Colonial Office, the new governor, for a brief time, encouraged the development of African agriculture, primarily in terms of investing resources in extension services and promoting maize as a cash crop that could be sold mainly as food for plantation workers rather than exported (Brett 1973: 178–79).

The change in policy at the Colonial Office and the constitutional controversy over Indian rights in Kenya led to the so-called Paramountcy Declaration of 1923, contained in a document entitled *Indians in Kenya*. This document stated that "the interests of the African native must be paramount and that if, and when, those interests and the interests of the immigrant races should conflict, the former should prevail" (quoted by Brett 1973: 180). The document went on to state, however, that no policies detrimental to the interests of current European settlers would be undertaken.

By the time of the Paramountcy Declaration the European farmers were already on their way to economic recovery as a result of a general upturn in world prices. The growing of maize for export was encouraged, accompanied by reduced rail rates for European producers of maize to make its export profitable (Wrigley 1965: 235). The economic position of the Europeans was further bolstered by the 1923 Tariff Amendment Ordinance, which placed heavy duties on imported wheat, wheat flour, butter and cheese, bacon and ham, sugar, tea, ghee, and beer (Wrigley 1965: 236). This ordinance is important, too, because of its later indirect impact on the development of African agriculture. Once a protected internal consumer economy was created, it had to be supported. Leys (1974: 39) sees an attempt to stimulate this internal economy by increasing African purchasing power at a time when Europeans were in financial difficulty as one reason that the Colony's government put some resources into developing African agriculture during the 1930's.

The report of the East Africa Commission (Ormsby-Gore Commission), dispatched from London in 1924, reflected the conviction that the protection of settler interests was essential to Kenya Colony's well-being. In practice, the result was the continuation of policies favoring settler production at the expense of African peasant production; attempts to foster the development of African agriculture were thus toned down during the remainder of the 1920's (Brett 1973:181–83).

Throughout the colonial period, Africans were systematically denied access to the most lucrative agricultural activities. The Coffee Plantations Registration Ordinance (1918) required every coffee planter to buy a license, costing 30 shillings. During the 1920's, by government policy, Africans were not eligible for licenses. From 1925 on, Africans lobbied for the right to grow coffee, but European settlers were successful in blocking the lobby on the grounds that badly tended African coffee would only encourage pests and diseases that could spread to European coffee. Dairy production was also restricted to the settlers. After experiments by Delamere with crossbreeding African and European cattle to get disease-resistant but high-producing dairy stock began to pay off in the 1920's (Marsh & Kingsnorth 1972: 147), large-scale European landholders saw the opportunity to put their unused tracts of land into production as pasture. Africans were prevented from owning high-producing dairy cattle on the grounds that they could not care for them properly and that cattle theft would increase if there was no visible distinction between European and African cattle. The struggle of Kenyan Africans for the right to own dairy cattle became a major theme of later colonial history. In the 1920's, however, African interest in acquiring dairy herds was not yet significant. The issue on which African and European interests came into opposition was the conflicting needs for pasturage of African squatters and the new European dairy farmers. For many Africans, the primary purpose of entering into a resident labor contract was the right to pasture land for animals (some of which might well be held in trust for relatives living in a reserve) that were necessary to their subsistence. Squatting served as a safety valve for population pressures of animals as well as people within the reserves. This safety valve was now eliminated as European dairy farming took over land formerly used by African herds. In 1925 a new Resident Labourers' Ordinance set a limit to the number of animals a resident laborer could graze on his employer's land (Middleton 1965:346).

The 1920's also saw the beginnings of large-scale, plantation production of tea; by 1938 tea was second in value to coffee as an export crop (Wrigley 1965:250). As with coffee and dairy stock, access to tea was denied to individual African producers on the grounds of predicted inability to attain sufficiently high production standards. But the growth of tea did have a positive effect on the economic situation of African producers in that it gave them a market for maize, which would be needed by the many African wage laborers employed on the tea plantations.

Aside from the developing market for maize, the thrust of the economic events of the 1920's was toward the expansion of European agricultural production and the consolidation of the position of the settlers at the expense of their African competitors. Wrigley (1965:243) says: "In 1912–13, at a conservative estimate, 70 percent by value of the agricultural exports had been 'native produce.' In 1928 the proportion was less than 20 percent."

The final delineation of Reserve boundaries for all the peoples of Kenya in 1926, which limited African rights in land to the Reserves (Van Zwannenberg 1973:34), resulted in a marked intensification of population pressure upon scarce land for Africans. African resentment began to build, and there were petitions demanding the reinstatement of land that had been alienated. This agitation, and the growing population pressure, culminated in the Kenya Land Commission (Carter Commission). Between 1932 and 1934 when it published its report, the commission undertook a thorough investigation of the territorial claims and customary systems of land tenure of all Kenya's ethnic groups. (Its evidence, taken from a great many sources, produced a report on the Kenya land situation that filled five volumes.) In spite of all this, the recommendations that stemmed from the work of the Carter Commission were very limited. In a few cases, it was decided that land occupied by a particular ethnic group had indeed been unjustly alienated for European settlement, and additional lands were added to the group's Reserve as restitution. In other cases of extreme overcrowding of Reserves, extension of Reserve boundaries was recommended. But these changes were insignificant when set against the Commission's implicit acceptance of the basic policy assumptions that had created the land crisis in the first place. In spite of growing population, Reserves were to remain. In most cases their boundaries were unchanged, and even where extensions were recommended they were miniscule in relation to land needs. Further, boundaries were fixed for areas in which only Europeans would be legally able to hold land (the "White Highlands"). In other words, the impact of the Carter Commission was not in any sense a solution of the land problem but rather a formalization of the existing land situation.

Bad times for both European and African producers in Kenya began in 1928. In 1928 and 1929, the crops were attacked by locusts, and between 1931 and 1934, there was a major drought. At the same time, world commodity market values plunged. The value of coffee was reduced by half, that of maize and sisal by two-thirds (Wrigley 1965:247). European farmers were to some extent protected from catastrophe (though some did fail) by government aid programs. African subsistence farmers were hit hard by the natural disasters, but because their needs for cash were minor, the collapse of commodity markets had little effect on them. The hardest hit were the Africans involved in commodity production. Locusts and drought undermined their subsistence production, and the impact of these disasters was probably even more difficult to absorb because so much of their productive potential was already directed away from the subsistence sphere and into the commodity sphere. On the other hand, since cash cropping had already changed the lives of these commodity producers in a way that made cash essential to their domestic economies, they were very seriously affected by the inability to sell their crops at reasonable prices.

The seriousness of the Depression's effect on the African population demonstrates how thoroughly implanted the commoditization of resources had become by 1930. The response to the economic crisis of the 1930's resulted in African commodity producers becoming even more deeply committed to a cash economy. Prices of African-produced commodities dropped particularly sharply, as did wages, and laborers were for the first time unable to find work. As Wrigley explains (1965:250–51), "Although African producers were not burdened by debt, they were faced with the fixed obligation of tax payments, which now became a much heavier burden in real terms. The only solution was to increase production. Whether or not the Africans would have reached this conclusion for themselves, the government had reached it for them."

Government moves to encourage African production were also an attempt to fill the gap left by the decline in European production caused by lower prices. Increased African commodity production could keep up the level of exports of the colony as a whole. African production was especially promoted for crops like cotton that were not being produced by Europeans in significant quantities. Though political constraints still operated against opening such controversial crops as coffee to African producers, the export of maize, in particular, had become essential to the colony's balance of payments, and since it was already being grown by Africans for the internal market, no political constraints existed. Extensive government efforts were also directed to the further development of maize partly as a response to increasing pressure to keep Africans out of the cattle market. The restriction of squatters' grazing and the forced return of violators to the Reserves were a part of this policy. Quarantine regulations were another. During the late 1930's concern over "overgrazing" of the Reserves became intense. The Veterinary Department had made no great efforts to control disease among African stock, and almost perpetual quarantines (which prevented marketing African cattle outside the Reserves) reflected the fear that African-owned stock was diseased and would endanger European stock. Open cattle auctions within the Reserves could have created a sufficient off-take of animals to reduce the pressure on pasture resources substantially, but this could not be permitted because sale prices of European settlers' stock would thus be undercut.

The European view of the situation became fixed in the myth of pastoral conservatism: these people are ruining their own land by overgrazing it; they should destock voluntarily, culling their herds by killing off some of their animals if necessary; the only reason they won't do this is that they have an irrational attachment to cattle that makes them care only about absolute numbers and not quality. This view, of course, ignored the fact that the Africans were being kept from acquiring high-milk-producing cattle and were forced to depend on large herds of lower-yielding cows.

The solution to the overgrazing problem as the Europeans saw it was destocking not through economic incentive but by force if necessary. A Rhodesian concern, Liebigs, was allowed to construct a meat-packing plant at Athi River in Machakos. The government undertook to provide a minimum number of stock yearly at a fixed price. The price offered to Africans for their cattle was 15 shillings per head maximum, while at the same time European cattle were going for 60 to 100 shillings per head on the open market. Not surprisingly, Africans refused to sell very many cattle at this rate. In late 1937 and early 1938, the government, frustrated by the "irrational" refusal of pastoralists to cull their herds voluntarily, decided to make such culling compulsory. These events led to the Kamba Destocking Crisis of 1938. The "worst" Kamba cattle were branded and confiscated for sale to Liebigs. In some cases up to 80 percent of a single individual's herd was confiscated (Van Zwannenberg 1973: 101). The Kamba reacted with vehement political protest; Government House in Nairobi was the target of mass demonstrations and the matter came up in the British Parliament. The scheme had to be abandoned, but similar schemes on a smaller scale in other pastoral areas were already afoot when the Second World War intervened.

The war provided an important impetus to the development of the Kenyan economy. Under U.S. loans for essential wartime needs, mechanization of European agriculture proceeded apace. Government credit was offered to farmers, and crops important to the war effort were bulk purchased at fixed prices (Van Zwannenberg 1973:44). A decade-long upswing in world prices of primary products (fueled in part by American stockpiling during the Korean War) began in 1942, and this further contributed to the prosperity of European agriculture (Wrigley 1965:264).

African agriculture, though to some degree sharing in the wartime prosperity, was allowed to stagnate by comparison with European agriculture. Moreover, attempts to solve what colonial officials saw as the problems of African agriculture and land tenure were temporarily shelved during the war. At its conclusion, these problems began to receive attention again. The Worthington Plan of 1946 established the African Land Development Program (ALDEV). The policies promoted by ALDEV were, in summary, the following: Africans were to be limited to growing subsistence crops and discouraged from cash cropping, which tempted them to overuse the soil in an effort to maximize profits. Only subsistence crop surpluses should be sold, and traditional forms of land tenure and economic cooperation should be preserved (Van Zwannenberg 1973:47–48). ALDEV also promoted planned group-farming schemes. Over 11,000 people were settled on thirteen schemes, but only a few of these were very successful and their cooperative aspects lasted only a few years (Van Zwannenberg 1973:48). All these policies created great mistrust of the government, so great that people refused absolutely to adopt soil conservation measures voluntarily, which meant that labor on conservation schemes was put under police supervision. Dissatisfaction with such government policies and long-time unsettled grievances over alienated land combined with extreme land shortage in the Reserves, particularly in Kikuyu country, finally erupted in the well-known guerrilla activities of the so-called Mau Mau movement and the declaration of a State of Emergency in the colony in 1952.

The emergency forced the British government to take a long hard look at colonial policy in Kenya. It was clear that popular unrest had reached the point where something, and possibly something quite radical, must be done to defuse it. The steps to be taken were outlined in the Swynnerton Plan of 1954 (titled "A Plan to Intensify the Development of African Agricultural Policy in Kenya"), drawn up by R. J. M. Swynnerton, then Assistant Director of Agriculture. The Swynnerton Plan was designed to end the stagnation of African agriculture and put it on a sound course that could be followed by an independent nation. It was thus a radical departure from previous colonial policy.

The plan proceeded on the assumption that fragmentation of landholdings and the insecurity of land tenure were the major factors that made it impractical for African farmers to develop their holdings and engage in farming practices considered "sound" from the point of view of soil conservation. The plan therefore recommended that the preservation of traditional systems of land tenure pursued under the Worthington Plan should be summarily abandoned. All African land of "high agricultural potential" should be surveyed, fragmented holdings should be consolidated and registered, and secure legal title to such consolidated pieces of land should be granted to individual household heads. The land concerned included "all of Central Province including Embu and Meru, all of Nyanza Province and Kericho, Nandi, Elgeyo and West Suk and the Taita Hills" (Van Zwannenberg 1973: 49). Title deeds could be used as collateral by African farmers to obtain loans with which to improve their holdings. The plan also recommended that the development of African holdings should be encouraged along with cash-cropping, that agricultural extension and technical assistance efforts should be directed to Africans, and that restrictions on the marketing of African produce should be lifted. These recommendations were put into effect almost immediately, first in the Kikuyu districts and also in Meru, Embu, Nandi, and Baringo in the late 1950's (Leys 1974: 69). By 1962, a total of 2.4 million out of 5.7 million acres of "high potential" land had been consolidated and titled (Van Zwannenberg 1973: 52). The effect of the Swynnerton Plan, then, was to turn the colonial administration's former policy toward African cultivation completely on its head. The period following its implementation was one of drastic change for African peasant producers in Kenya.

One avowed aim of land consolidation was to establish plots large enough so that crop rotation and other soil conservation techniques could be carried on while growing cash as well as subsistence crops. The minimum size for such plots prescribed in the Swynnerton Plan was 7.5 acres. In practice, most holdings registered in areas of land shortage such as Central Province were below this minimum, and average holdings have been shrinking up to the present time (Van Zwannenberg 1973:53). Most people thus have holdings that are too small to grow cash crops in addition to subsistence crops. African cash crop production increased dramatically in the late 1950's and early 1960's in response to the opportunity to grow valuable commodities, but in the country as a whole, and particularly in areas of land shortage, the major cash crop producers today are not the majority of peasant cultivators (Van Zwannenberg 1973:54).

It was clear during the 1950's that policy in Kenya must be developed from the standpoint of the country's coming independence. Negotiations leading to self-rule began in 1960, and it was agreed that total independence would be granted in December of 1963.

During the period of transition to self-government and independence, laws guaranteeing privilege to Europeans on the basis of race had to be eliminated. In 1960, land in the former "White Highlands" was opened to ownership by Africans. Many European farmers, fearing post-Independence political developments, began leaving the country. It was arranged that the British government would make loans to the new government of Kenya so that it could buy out European farmers and sell their land to new Kenyan owners. The terms of sale and purchase were made favorable to Europeans, as it was considered essential to the new country's economic welfare that the Europeans keep farming and not allow their farms to "run down" in the transitional period.

Some of the land bought from European farmers was redistributed by sale to the landless or poor in the form of settlement schemes implemented during the 1960's, which became known collectively as the Million Acre Scheme. The settlement schemes occupied "a fifth of the old White Highlands, perhaps 4 percent of the total area of the country available for agriculture" (Leys 1974:75). Nevertheless, resettlement could have been workable and beneficial for the country on a larger scale. Under the settlement schemes, total productivity of the land increased, though export production declined somewhat.

The vast majority of land in the White Highlands, however, was transferred as intact large holdings to owners of Kenyan nationality, the assumption being that this would safeguard export production. Leys (1974: 36–40) has aptly argued that the importance of the contribution made by large-scale mixed farms to the colony's economy was a myth originally propounded to protect the way of life of the mass of politically powerful Kenyan European settlers. The farmers' position was protected by an elaborate system of monopolies. Access to a disproportionately large area of the best land was restricted to Europeans by law, but this was not the only issue. Roads and rail lines were sited near European land, transport of European crops was subsidized, and the vast majority of agricultural extension and veterinary services were directed at European farmers. Without these various supports, the mixed farms would never have been able to compete economically with either peasant production at the one extreme or plantation production at the other (Leys 1974: 36–37).* But the myth of their importance, once established, was extremely tenacious. By Independence, a great many Africans as well as Europeans had a vested interest in the status quo. The more prosperous and better educated Africans had been conditioned to aspire to the settlers' way of life and were understandably not enthusiastic about the prospect of eliminating it completely.

The new Kenya government views agricultural exports as the mainstay of the nation's economy and has put resources into agricultural extension programs and the development of cash crops. Peasant farmers have been encouraged to grow crops (e.g., coffee and tea) to which they were formerly denied access, and to raise dairy cattle. These measures are only significant, however, where land is plentiful enough to sustain cash cropping as well as subsistence cultivation. In much of the country, average holdings are too small for significant cash crop development to be a reasonable option for the majority of people. There has been a shift toward export production by ordinary peasants, but its extent is limited. Some, but not all, of the props that favored export production by large-scale rather than peasant

---

*Leys (1974: 36–37) makes a point-by-point demonstration of this contention, to which I refer the interested reader rather than reproducing it here in its entirety.

farmers have been removed. Nevertheless, as in the colonial era, various forces of monopoly described above (e.g., marketing policies) still operate to favor large-scale producers over peasants even though the former are now Africans rather than Europeans. What has happened in Kenya since Independence is that "there is developing a hierarchy of peasant farmers with a few rich men forming the core of rural capitalist class" (Van Zwannenberg 1973:54).

Colonialism and Economic Change in Nandi

The history of agricultural change in Kenya sets the stage for understanding economic change in colonial Nandi, particularly the processes by which the relative economic positions of Nandi men and women have shifted over time. Throughout most of the colonial period, the Nandi and other pastoralists were viewed as "culturally conservative." Few "development" programs were directed toward them, and some that were (e.g., the attempt to upgrade local cattle with nondairy Sahiwal stock) were unenthusiastically received. The failure of such programs was then viewed as further evidence of the people's "cultural conservatism," resulting in even fewer attempts at relevant development programs—a vicious circle. At the same time, beginning in the 1930's, maize cash-cropping became a significant part of the economy, gradually resulting in growing dependence upon cash.

The adoption of the Swynnerton Plan in 1954 paved the way for the implementation of a different policy toward African production. Land was registered and titled to individuals, and by 1960 highly lucrative cash crops such as tea and coffee (though the latter was not very important in Nandi) as well as high-producing exotic dairy cattle came into African hands. The result was a period of extremely rapid social change. The changes brought about by the Swynnerton Plan had a significant impact on the situation of women relative to men. In the first place, women's economic rights were undermined by land consolidation, as a system of use-rights that included women was converted to almost exclusively male private ownership. Further, control of the most profitable cash crops, maize and tea, and of high-producing dairy cattle, came to be concentrated in male hands. The high profitability of these activities led to men controlling much greater cash incomes than women, thus widening the economic gap between the sexes.

In the Nandi precolonial economy the basic unit of both production and consumption was a nuclear family, which might be a subset of a larger polygynous family. Except for newly married wives who worked under the supervision of their mothers-in-law, each adult woman had her own fields and granary. However, there was a great deal of economic cooperation among members of a local extended family homestead. In each local community, the homesteads and fields were located in proximity to one another. The bulk of a local community's herds, though owned by individual families, were grazed together in a communal pasture at some distance from the homesteads, and supervised by young men and boys. It was a woman's responsibility to supply all but the animal food for her family, but older married men were also responsible to help their wives with cultivation (Gold 1977). A husband and wife divided their harvest between them.* The wife's share was for family subsistence; the husband's share was to be used by his wife for brewing beer for him and his guests to drink at parties given for male household heads of a neighborhood. These parties were not simply convivial: the beer was in fact a commodity that was indirectly converted to labor, because members of the households of guests at such a party were obligated to participate in the host household's annual planting or harvesting or whatever special work project (e.g., housebuilding) might be going on.

Grain shortages were common during some periods, and in such cases it was the women who went to trade sheep or goats for grain in lowland areas occupied by the neighboring Luo, Luhyia, and Terik. It can be argued that such shortages could have been avoided, but that there was an element of choice in the decision to satisfy the need for grain through trade rather

*I was told by informants that husband and wife typically had two granaries, one for each. Huntingford (1950:63) says that only millet and the small quantities of maize grown before the colonial era were stored in granaries; eleusine was stored in the ceiling of the house. Peristiany (1939:136) says the same for the Kipsigis. Therefore, it seems possible to me that most wives did not have an actual granary, but stored their portions of the harvest inside the house.

than in investing more labor (as well as potential pasture) in cultivating larger areas. As noted above, it is probable that the ratio of cattle to people varied over time. It also seems likely that a complementary relationship existed between herd size and the amount of land put to cultivation. As herd size peaked, more land was put to pasture and the decision to trade stock for grain was made, consciously or unconsciously. As herd size waned, cultivation waxed.

In the beginning of the colonial era, the Nandi became famous for the tenacity with which they resisted the imposition of British rule. The first concern of the Nandi with the new economic forces set in train by the establishment of the European colonial presence was to keep their impact in Nandi at a minimum. Swahili traders did not begin operating in Nandi until the 1850's. After two confrontations involving the violation of Nandi mores, as a result of which a large number of Swahili were killed by parties of Nandi, the Swahili presence was withdrawn (Matson 1972:44–49). For the next forty years, outsiders including Europeans generally regarded Nandi territory as impenetrable. Nandi warriors frequently attacked trading caravans and railway crews. In 1896 the building of Sclater's Road, which passed through central Nandi, and the establishment of a government fort in Nandi to guard the road brought Nandi country, in the view of the British, under British hegemony. The Nandi saw things differently and continued behaving as an independent people. The British officers assigned to the fort had little contact with the Nandi leaders or populace; taxes were not collected; there was no effective administration (Ng'eny 1970:105). The peace at this time was always uneasy. Punitive expeditions against the Nandi that ended inconclusively were mounted in 1895 and 1897 (Matson 1972:262–65) and in 1899 and 1900 (Ng'eny 1970:110–11). The stalemate persisted until 1905 when R. Meinertzhagen, the British military-administrative officer for Nandi, assassinated the Nandi *Orkoiyot* (ritual-political leader) during ostensible peace negotiations. In the ensuing confusion, the British mounted a massive punitive expedition in 1905–6, as the result of which the Nandi were finally subdued, though resistance was not totally crushed.

The impact of the 1905–6 punitive expedition on Nandi society and economy was devastating. According to official figures, 1,117 Nandi, over 2 percent of the total population, were killed (Ellis 1976:558). In addition, 16,213 cattle (estimated at half the cattle population) and 36,205 sheep and goats were seized and 4,956 huts and granaries were burned. (These figures are taken from Mungeam 1966:156.)

The punitive expedition also resulted in considerable loss of land for the Nandi. The Nandi were situated in a fertile area, near lands that were already allotted to European settlement and hence near key road and rail routes, and the colonial government thus considered it essential to confine and control them. The Nandi-controlled territory adjacent to the railway, below the southern escarpment, was alienated for European settlement and the inhabitants of this area were resettled in what is now northern Nandi District. The boundaries of the Nandi Reserve, comprising 1,890 sq. km. (730 sq. mi.), were gazetted in 1906— one of the earliest reserves to be gazetted. The economic impact of the 1906 land alienation went beyond increase of population density in a bounded space. For those Nandi living in the south and not resettled, it meant loss of critical grazing and access to salt licks. Ellis argues, further (1976:558): "Those Nandi resettled in the north found themselves in a marginal climatic area with less rainfall and unsuitable to the crops formerly grown in the south. This resulted in periods of food shortage, which in years of very low rainfall resulted in famine."

Nor did land alienation end after 1906. A government treaty of 1907 promised the Nandi that the land within the Reserve boundaries was theirs forever, but an additional 31 sq. km. was taken in 1912, and in 1919–20 the government alienated 336 sq. km., one-seventh of the remaining Nandi territory, for farms for British war veterans under the Soldier Settlement Scheme (Van Zwannenberg 1973:94). Thus, even though Nandi population density had traditionally been low, population pressure on land became a serious matter in the early days of colonialism, especially as the Nandi strived to return the numbers of their cattle to a level sufficient to semipastoral subsistence.

Though the economic difficulties precipitated in Nandi by colonial policies set the stage for later developments, in the years immediately following 1906 the Nandi remained aloof from government attempts to administer them, and the government, leaving well enough alone, did not try to do much beyond keeping military control and collecting taxes.

For the most part, the demand for taxes was met by selling sheep and goats. During the First World War a large number of young men from the newly initiated Nyongi age-set were recruited to the King's African Rifles for a campaign in Tanganyika. This brought some cash into the Reserve, which was quickly converted to livestock. Greenstein (1975) has studied this period in Nandi history and argues that KAR veterans by and large returned to their traditional way of life, that aside from the introduction of malaria and venereal disease the Nandi participation in the First World War produced very little socioeconomic change. Ellis (1976) sees the KAR veterans as the most significant vector of change in Nandi prior to the 1920's. She reports that "the spokesman for the ex-KAR in 1923, Arap Tarno, requested that they be allowed to form a separate location so as not to be subject to the collective fines, and requested a government school in Nandi" (Ellis 1976: 562).

Because livestock was usually converted to cash for tax payments, taxation as a form of pressure to engage in labor for European farmers did not fall so heavily upon the Nandi as upon peoples who were exclusively cultivators. Nandi were free to choose the capacity in which they would work for settlers, and most Nandi men would accept positions only as herdsmen or drivers on European farms. This is not to imply that there were not a lot of Nandi technically in European employ. Nandi began moving to European farms as "squatters" in 1913, and the number of people involved greatly increased from 1916 onward (Ellis 1976: 561). Middleton (1965: 346) estimates that by 1933 Nandi squatters "amounted to about one-quarter of the entire tribe." However, the wage labor participation of the Nandi was very different from that of other ethnic groups, with quite different implications for social change and sex roles. Nandi never saw a pattern of male labor migration to cities or tea estates, leaving women to manage the subsistence economy: insofar as Nandi entered the labor market it was primarily as squatters, which meant that whole families moved together. Its effect on the social fabric was thus more like that of real migration than like that of migratory wage labor. Many of the squatters did no work at all, but paid for the right to squat with milk or other produce (though this was technically illegal after 1918). Further, the motivation for squatting was as much the search for additional grazing and the desire to return to live on alienated Nandi land without the constraints of government administration within the Reserve as it was the need for cash to meet tax demands.* Ellis (1976:561–62) believes that squatting had conservative, not disruptive, effects on the Nandi. This system helped create conditions that allowed traditional relations of production to be maintained more or less intact until a later point in time.

In the early 1920's, a number of forces contributed to what Ellis (1976:573) has called an "organized campaign of non-cooperation" with government. One factor was the land alienation of 1920; another was increased taxation. Taxation tripled between 1909 and 1920, and in 1921, because of a change in collection date, two taxes were collected in one year. The Nandi and Kipsigis refused to pay, and collection was deferred to 1922 (Ellis 1976:564). To make matters worse, cash was in short supply in Nandi after fears that rinderpest might spread in the wake of an epidemic caused a stock quarantine to be imposed on the Reserve from 1921 to 1923. The Nandi, prevented from selling stock outside the Reserve, had no cash, and taxes had to go unpaid.

Normally, grain shortages in Nandi were met by selling stock and buying grain. The quarantine made this impossible. An additional reason for bitterness against the colonial government was the labor conscription that took place under the Northey Circulars (Ellis 1976:565). All these things contributed to a buildup of unrest and antagonism toward the government between 1920 and 1923. In 1923, the *saget ab eito* (sacrifice of the ox) ceremony, which marked the status transition of the age-sets to new age-grades, was scheduled to take place. This ceremony had always been followed by an increased rate of cattle raiding as the now formally recognized warrior age-set sought to prove its prowess. Its approach was therefore accompanied by expressions of mili-

*Food shortage caused by a rinderpest epidemic and drought was also a reason.

tary fervor, and it was an occasion on which all adult Nandi men gathered in one place. Further, alarmed because there was also at that time organized political protest among the Kikuyu and Luo (Magut 1969: 105), the colonial government came to believe (whether correctly or not will probably never be known) that the Orkoiyot was planning to use the occasion of the saget ab eito as a cover under which to gather forces for a massive military uprising. On October 16, 1923, several days before the projected date for the saget ab eito, the Orkoiyot Barserion arap Manyei and four other elders were arrested and deported to Meru in central Kenya (they were detained there for six years; Magut 1969: 106). Permission to hold the ceremony was withdrawn, and it did not take place (nor did it ever take place again). This episode went down in the colonial literature as the "Nandi Uprising of 1923."

The "Nandi Uprising" and other unrest in the Colony at about the same time followed shortly upon the change in personnel and policy in the Colonial Office. At the end of 1922, Coryndon had replaced Northey as governor, and the new administration appeared willing to try and correct some Nandi grievances. The events of October 1923 served as a catalyst for governmental action. Ellis (1976: 573) summarizes the changes in government policy toward the Nandi:

The protest prompted almost immediate changes in government policy toward the Nandi . . . immediate removal of the quarantine, the return of alienated land not yet occupied, reduction of the hut tax pending removal of the quarantine, immediate . . . access to the Kiboiin salt lick . . . the closing of the collective fine case of 1922, the return of cattle still held by the Government, and the appointment of *kiptaienik* as paid government headmen. Nearly all these suggestions were implemented. . . . Equally important, the government made plans to set up a government school in Nandi, one of the first in the country.*

The changes in the Colonial Office in 1922 also brought about a period of support for African cultivation of maize as a cash crop. In Nandi, the initial efforts to promote maize cash crop-

---

*Very little alienated land was actually returned. The alienation issue remained a point of contention between the Nandi and the administration throughout the colonial era as the Nandi petitioned repeatedly for the return of the Kipkarren and Kaimosi farms.

ping coincided with the stock quarantine and heavier tax demands, and also with the growth of tea plantations adjacent to the Nandi and Kipsigis reserves, which employed African workers who had to buy maize for food (Van Zwannenberg 1973:94). Increasingly in the 1920's, maize became an important Nandi cash crop.

The burden of taxation, and thus the need for cash, fell primarily upon men. Female household heads were not taxed until 1934 (District Commissioner for Nandi, Annual Report, 1934). During the 1920's eleusine was still the staple subsistence crop, maize being promoted at that time as a cash crop rather than as a combination cash-subsistence crop. Seed distribution and such extension services as existed were oriented toward men.* This led to a situation in which women contributed the major portion of labor for the cultivation of eleusine for subsistence, while the cultivation of maize was in the hands of men and profits therefrom were viewed as a man's personal property. Gradually maize came to be accepted as a subsistence crop as well, but the distinction between household fields and fields cultivated and owned exclusively by men remained at least during the 1930's. The situation has been described by Peristiany for the Kipsigis, but Nandi informants state that a very similar system existed in Nandi. Kipsigis (and Nandi) fields were of three types: (*a*) the *kapungut*, a vegetable plot controlled exclusively by a woman; (*b*) the *imbaret a' mossop*, which Peristiany calls the "field of the house,"† a field of eleusine and occasionally maize cultivated primarily by a married woman with the assistance of her husband, the crop of which was to be used exclusively for household subsistence; and (*c*) the *imbaret ab soi* (of which *kapande*, a plowed maize field, was the most common type), a cash-crop field cultivated and controlled exclusively by a man (Peristiany

---

*This pattern has continued to the present. One Nandi informant, who pioneered land in a little-populated area during the 1950's, described the indifference shown to her by colonial agricultural extension officers. Independence has not changed this. The pattern of systematic neglect of government services to female farm managers in Kakamega is analyzed by Staudt (1975, 1978).

†*Mossop* actually means a well-watered, easily cultivated area as opposed to *soi* or *soiin*, which means a low, hot, relatively dry area more suitable for grazing. These distinctions within the local community are not very important now in the northern part of Nandi District, though they may be more important elsewhere.

1939:129–30). Over time, maize became the staple crop; eleusine, which is less productive, was replaced (Miracle 1966:140; Brown 1968:62).

A second government push toward the cultivation of maize by Africans occurred during the 1930's when the government began showing some interest in developing African agriculture. A major development plan for Nandi Reserve that was drawn up in 1934 called for further development of maize cultivation and also for encouragement of the cultivation of potatoes, white runner beans, marrow fat peas, and linseed, and the planting of wattle and eucalyptus (Report: Nandi Reserve Development Programme, 1934).

Plows had been introduced in Nandi in 1925 but had not been at all widely used: in 1927 there were only four in the district, whereas there were 249 in the Kipsigis Reserve in 1929 (Manners 1967:288), used for plowing maize fields. The Nandi did not have that many until ten years later (Huntingford 1950:61). I infer, therefore, that the Nandi were about ten years behind the Kipsigis in adopting maize as the staple crop. From Peristiany's evidence that as late as the late 1930's eleusine was still the primary staple crop among the Kipsigis, it seems fair to postulate that the shift to maize as the staple crop took place in Nandi no earlier than the late 1930's and more likely during the 1940's. The move toward maize was probably encouraged by a failure of the eleusine crop in 1939, while maize prospered (D.C. for Nandi, Annual Report, 1939:2). In 1943, P. F. Foster, then District Commissioner, wrote: "There was a large increase in the land under cultivation. Most of it was put under maize" (D.C. for Nandi, Annual Report, 1943:7).

Once the shift to maize as the staple was relatively complete, it became easier to use plowing to break the ground for *all* planting, not merely the planting of that field exclusively controlled by a man. This set the stage for the combination of the household maize and the cash-crop maize into one large field—which we find today. The husband does the plowing and both the husband and wife do the weeding and harvesting. The crop is split into two portions. One portion, called the "wife's portion," is put into the granary and used to feed the household until the next harvest. From this purpose, as Peristiany (1939:130) says about the crop of the *imbaret a' mossop,* no member of the household can divert it; in this sense, it does not actually belong to the wife any more than to the husband. The other portion, the "husband's portion," like the crop of the *kapande,* is sold for cash, which the man (at least normatively) controls completely. Since weeding maize takes much less time than weeding eleusine—except for very large maize acreages (where hired labor is employed in any case)—this gradual shift has probably not meant a real increase in the amount of labor women expend in cultivation. What *has* come about, however, is a very gradual shift from a situation in which women, though they had little access to cash and few options as to the disposition of their product, were at least autonomous producers, to a situation in which women help to produce a surplus that their husbands can divert to their own purposes.

The 1930's were the period when the integration of Africans into the cash economy was solidified in many areas of Kenya. Nandi was one of these areas. F. C. Hislop observed: "In 1934 for the first time known, the Nandi had a real surplus of maize and sold an appreciable quantity" (D.C. for Nandi, Annual Report, 1934:42). During the 1930's consumer demand in Nandi for such items as cloth, blankets, tea, and sugar began to be important. This was thus the period during which commoditization of the Nandi economy became firmly implanted. Access to cash fueled the demand for consumer goods, and the goods stimulated dependence upon sources of cash.

The year of the Carter Commission report, 1934, was the point when "development activities" began to intensify in Nandi. Following a recommendation of the report, along with the return of a small amount of alienated land, the Nandi Local Native Council treasury received £5,000 as compensation for land alienated from the Reserve.* A large portion, £3,000, of that sum was used by the L.N.C. to build a thirty-bed hospital at Kapsabet (Report: Nandi Reserve Development Programme, 1936). Some

---

*It should be noted that though there was compensation paid, the Nandi still did not relinquish their claim on the alienated land and continued to petition for its return throughout the colonial period, especially after the Second World War, when it was proposed that this land should be used for a Soldier Settlement Scheme for Nandi veterans.

also was used for building roads and several new schools in out-lying areas. For the farmers, the most significant benefit was the sum that was voted as a yearly contribution to the budget of the government Veterinary Training Program at Baraton.

Even though cash-crop cultivation had rapidly gained ground during the 1930's, the administration believed that the future of the Nandi economy lay in cattle. By developing agriculture suffi-ciently to bring the people to rely more on grain than on milk for subsistence, more animal products would be made available for export. "The main line of economic development must be in ani-mal products, especially dairying" (Acting Provincial Commis-sioner's Report to the Director of Agriculture, 1934). The Vet-erinary station at Baraton was established in 1932, and in 1934 there were twenty students in the training program, working with the demonstration herd and dairy. In 1936 an insemination program was started in which people were encouraged to bring their heifers for insemination by a Sahiwal bull at the Station. Field dairies were set up to buy any local surplus of milk. By 1939 there were six such dairies throughout the Reserve, and bulls were available for breeding at two locations in the extreme south and north of the Reserve as well as at Baraton (D.C. for Nandi, Annual Report, 1939).

The activities of the Veterinary Department were in the main not enthusiastically received. There was a basic contradiction in the policy of cattle development that held the seeds of economic stagnation and led to the rise of the notion that the Nandi were yet another example of the cultural conservatism of pastoralists. The idea behind the government development plan was that the Nandi should become producers of milk for purchase by a gov-ernment marketing system to be converted to dairy products for the national and international markets. In order for this plan to work, either milk production had to be greatly increased, or home consumption of milk had to be greatly reduced. The gov-ernment evidently had no clear policy about which course it ought to emphasize. Some officers seemed to realize that the second course was actually being promoted, and that this was an important reason to encourage increased production of maize (e.g., Acting P.C.'s Report to the Director of Agriculture, 1934). Yet official talk about the activities of the Veterinary Department very often made it appear that they were intended to promote increased dairy production. The plans of the Veterinary Department called for "upgrading" cattle through breeding with supposedly superior stock, combating disease by inoculations and dipping, and controlling overgrazing through placing limits upon herd size.

Stock inoculation seems to have been the one innovation of the Veterinary Department to which the Nandi were receptive. In a 1937 report, the D.C. speaks of "an increasing demand in the Reserve for [rinderpest] inoculations" (D.C. for Nandi, Annual Report 1937: 26). Increased numbers of inoculations are reported in 1940 (D.C. for Nandi, Annual Report 1940: 9), and in 1943 the Local Native Council passed a resolution making inoculation for rinderpest compulsory, a measure to which there seems to have been no resistance.

"Upgrading" cattle was a different matter. The stock chosen for upgrading was Sahiwal, a breed that is superior for its beef and for draught purposes but is not much better as a milk producer than indigenous cattle (Manners 1967: 302). Cross breeding with exotic high-producing dairy cattle was not encouraged, because the government wanted to maintain a visible distinction between native and settler cattle as a way of combating stock thefts. Even an author whose work is not notable for an appreciation of the African point of view on colonial agricultural policy is critical of the government on this point:

[The] dismal picture of bad management and poor quality stock-keeping would have been reversed in some districts, notably Kikuyuland, Elgeyo, Nandi and Kericho (Kipsigis), if government policy had permitted it. Farmers in these districts were anxious to keep good quality European breeds of dairy cattle, but the policy of the Veterinary Department was to improve the local zebu stock by the introduction of Sahiwal bulls or the use of Sahiwal semen and to discourage the introduction of European dairy breeds except under very strict control in optimum conditions. African farmers were generally not interested in Sahiwals, which they regarded (with some reason) as very little better than what they had. [Brown 1968: 39.]

Thus, though the government stock development plan could hardly result in increased milk production per cow, government officials wanted the Africans to behave as though it did. They were expected to follow the example of European stock raisers in voluntarily reducing the size of their herds; it was not taken into account that Europeans could cut down the numbers of their animals and keep up milk production, whereas indigenous pastoralists could not.* District Commissioners and other government officials during the 1930's and 1940's constantly marveled at the lack of interest the Nandi showed in upgrading their stock and their unwillingness to reduce the size of their herds. For example, in 1934 the District Commissioner wrote of Baraton: "The Nandi are frequent visitors, especially the leading men, and they see results with a purely native herd which astonish them. So far, however, there is no sign of any Nandi endeavoring to model his methods on Baraton practice" (D.C. for Nandi, Annual Report 1934: 46). In 1942, on a visit to Nandi District, the governor of the colony had a similar impression: "The wealth and well-being of the Nandi mainly depended on their cattle, and as Government and the Local Native Council, every year, were spending large sums of money on the Training Centre at Baraton, he was surprised to see what little interest the Nandi appeared to be taking in veterinary education" (D.C. for Nandi, Report to the Information Officer on the Governor's Visit to Kapsabet, February 1942). In the Annual Report of 1944, the District Commissioner said: "Quality in cattle is appreciated, but quantity in numbers still takes first place in the mind of any Nandi. At sales, a man will still buy two bad cows rather than one good cow" (D.C. for Nandi, Annual Report 1944: 8). And the 1945 report commented: "Limitation of cattle numbers is definitely beyond the understanding of all except a few of the most sophisticated Nandi. The fact that successful demonstration of animal husbandry has been carried out now for thirteen years in their midst by the Senior Stock Inspector at Baraton, and no results worth mentioning have been achieved, proves this" (D.C. for Nandi, Annual Report 1945: 3).

*In fairness, it must be noted that the Veterinary department depended in its planning on the not entirely fallacious premise that reducing cattle numbers would lead to more grazing per animal and thus to generally better nourished animals that should produce more milk. The fallacy was that there was a limit beyond which the milk production of a single animal could not be increased, and in the case of indigenous and Sahiwal stock, this limit never approached the amount of milk given by two cows, even poorly nourished ones.

The Nandi point of view was quite sensible, of course: if they were only given Sahiwal crossbreeds, hardly better than their old stock, why bother? And how could they be enthusiastic about reducing their herds, even with problems of overgrazing and soil erosion, when they needed sizable herds in order to survive? Nandi was not so badly overgrazed as many other areas of Kenya, but the government saw overgrazing and soil erosion as potentially serious problems, and policy was formulated accordingly. The government saw the solution as reduction of herd size and decreased dependence upon milk as a dietary staple, a solution rather at odds with the development plan's avowed goal of producing increased quantities of milk for the market. The Nandi, though perfectly amenable to marketing surplus milk, were not interested in consuming less. They needed more milk, not less, and this could be had only by (*a*) access to high-milk-producing cattle, or (*b*) continuing to maintain large herds of low-yielding cows. Since the first option had been completely cut off by the government, they took the second.

In 1931, the total number of cattle in the Reserve was recorded as 185,441. By 1945 this number had dropped to 172,865. In both cases, more than 30,000 additional cattle were estimated to be held by Nandi squatters outside the Reserve, bringing total numbers of Nandi cattle both inside and outside the Reserve to 215,441 in 1931 and 208,865 in 1945 (Huntingford 1950: 33). The ratio of cattle to people changed only slightly during this time, from 5 to one to 4.5 to one within the Reserve, and from 4.2 to one to 4.1 to one when estimated numbers of squatters and their families are included in the calculation. The really dramatic change in the cattle/people ratio did not occur until after land registration and enclosure. Between 1931 and 1945 there was, however, a dramatic decrease in the numbers of sheep and goats, from 159,993 to 59,916 in the Reserve and from approximately 28,000 to approximately 10,000 outside it (Huntingford 1950: 33). This reduction of small stock was probably the result of increased cultivation. Increased cultivation probably also cut into grazing land, so that the cattle population was not only nearly the same as before but also was getting less nourishment and overgrazing available pasture.

It may be that to some extent the people were trying to find a solution to the problem: it is noteworthy that as overgrazing became a threat within the Reserve, a larger proportion of the total numbers of cattle came to be held by squatters outside the Reserve. Still, although in the late 1930's and 1940's the threat of overstocking was a matter of some concern among planners, the situation never reached a critical level in Nandi. As late as 1936 the D.C. for Nandi asserted unequivocally that the Nandi Reserve was not overstocked and had ample grazing (F. D. Hislop, letter in reply to Huntingford, copy to P.C., File PC/RVP/6A/ 11/28/#18, Kenya National Archives). Because their Reserve was not viewed as critically overstocked, the Nandi did not experience the kind of extreme measures to enforce reduction of cattle numbers that led to the Kamba Destocking Crisis of 1938. But they were under constant government pressure to reduce cattle numbers, and during wartime years this reduction was enforced by requisitioning for the Meat Control Board. Further, in the late 1940's government stock policies led to some political protest and "disturbances" in Nandi.

The "conservative" Nandi were always willing to sell cattle at reasonable prices. During the 1930's, a brief gold rush (Wrigley 1965:248–49) created a thriving market for cattle among the butchers of Kakamega. The Nandi took advantage of this market—legally or otherwise, since the Nandi Reserve was under quarantine regulations at various times during this period—selling them oxen and sometimes trading oxen for heifers. In 1938, the Local Native Council was persuaded to pass a resolution that set up cattle markets at ten locations in Nandi District, set rates for these markets, and made it illegal to sell or barter cattle elsewhere (File PC/RVP/6A/1/11D/2/#15, Kenya National Archives).

A system of government purchase of cattle to supply the meat-packing industry was not begun in Nandi until 1940, after the Kamba Destocking Crisis, which had made officials somewhat sensitive to the possibility of disturbances if government policy was too severe. The increased wartime demand for cattle tended to mean more favorable prices at first—though this was variable. The D.C. for Nandi notes at the end of 1940 that voluntary cattle sales were able to continue when a buyer who offered fair prices replaced one who paid prices far below market value

(D.C. for Nandi, Annual Report 1940:2). But voluntary sale of cattle at the prices offered by the Meat Control Board was impossible to maintain. The D.C.'s Annual Report for 1941 mentions the probable need to requisition cattle in future. In 1942, the D.C. records that 2,650 cattle were purchased, but at lower than market prices. "It was not unnatural, therefore, that sales ceased to be voluntary and a system of individual requisitioning had to be adopted" (D.C. for Nandi, Annual Report 1942:2). In 1944, a flourishing black market trade in Kakamega is reported (D.C. for Nandi, Annual Report 1944:8). The system of requisitioning continued until 1946, when it was felt that sufficient off-take could be achieved through other sorts of inducements to sell cattle. One of these methods was a flat-rate tax on owners of more than nine head of cattle, which the Local Native Council was persuaded to enact in 1945. A cattle census was taken the same year and a large-scale program of constructing cattle dips was also begun. It was unfortunate that measures to reduce herd size, the tax on large herds, cattle census, and dipping were thus connected in people's minds. Dipping seemed a surreptitious way of conducting a cattle census, and thus was unpopular. The tax, too, proved very difficult to administer. In 1946, the Local Native Council decided to lift the excess cattle tax for 1947 but to reinstate it in 1948 (D.C. for Nandi, Annual Report 1946:9). The D.C. in 1947 refers to a "conservative opposition party" that was active in Nandi, "spreading propaganda" against government schemes involving land and cattle (D.C. for Nandi, Annual Report 1947:2).

All this was the background to the "dipping disturbances" that took place in late 1947 in Kabiyet Location. I have little information on this incident, beyond the facts that there was opposition among the Nandi to the building of dips at Kiringan and Kaiboi, and that this opposition was sufficiently serious that it was ended only by the threat of government military intervention (D.C. for Nandi, Annual Report 1947:6). The government then understood that the Nandi were not prepared to accept the excess cattle tax, and it was never reinstated. By 1950, dipping had become "universally popular," possibly because its effectiveness in combating tick-borne diseases was demonstrable (D.C. for Nandi, Confidential Report, 1950).

The events cited above show that the Nandi were not quiescent during the 1930's and 1940's. The same kinds of pressures and tensions that affected pastoralists elsewhere in Kenya were present in Nandi. The contradictions inherent in colonial policy toward pastoralism were kept from becoming too explosive in Nandi. This was partly because these contradictions came to a head later in Nandi than elsewhere, when the government had already experienced popular response to its policies and some of the most extreme among them had been changed. It was also, in part, because ecological conditions in Nandi were more favorable than elsewhere. Meanwhile, the groundwork was being laid for a dramatic socioeconomic transition. By the 1940's and early 1950's the question of the reduction of herd size had not been resolved but was beginning to take a different form. Pressure to reduce numbers of cattle became internal as well as external as the cultivation of maize came to compete more and more with grazing for available land. Further, with the partitioning of land, this issue shifted to a large extent from a community to an individual concern.

The government's official position was that cattle should take the major role in development plans for Nandi, but because ownership of high-milk-yielding dairy cattle was forbidden to Africans and prices for beef cattle for slaughter were rigidly controlled, cattle had only a limited cash-generating potential. Thus, from the late 1930's onward, the Nandi turned increasingly toward the cultivation of maize for cash.

An unexpected influx of cash came during the Second World War in the form of remittances paid by the government to dependents of Nandi soldiers in the King's African Rifles. The Nandi contingent was one of the largest ethnic contingents, and as a result there was suddenly an abundance of cash. In 1940 the D.C. wrote: "Cash has never been so plentiful. As the Nandi have little use for money, it is quickly converted into cattle and the purchase of ploughs" (D.C. for Nandi, Annual Report 1940:2). It was ironic that though the colonial government had wanted the Nandi to become cultivators, colonial officials now became concerned about the scale on which this change was taking place. In 1941, the D.C. for Nandi suggested to the Provincial Commissioner that the Local Native Council be urged to set aside certain areas for grazing that it would be an offense for any person to cultivate. "Owing to the increasing number of ploughs in this District," the D.C. wrote, "the grazing areas in Mosop are in danger of being destroyed unless properly controlled. The practice today is for any Nandi with a plough to cut up large portions of virgin land wherever he desires."

In May 1941 such a resolution was passed (File PC/RVP/6A/1/ 11D/2, nos. 115, 126, Kenya National Archives), but in 1943, there was a sudden dramatic increase in the amount of land plowed and cultivated in maize, apparently following food shortages caused by the buying up of all available surpluses to feed troops. The inconsistency of the government's attitude toward the competition between cultivation and grazing is illustrated by the approval with which the same D.C. whose communiqué is quoted above writes about the increase in maize cultivation: "The tribe has never been self-sufficient as regards its food supplies, being used to purchasing large amounts of maize and wimbi from its neighbors. In 1943 they found that neither money nor cattle could purchase food and they went through a very lean period. . . . The shortage taught the Nandi a lesson, and there was a large increase in the area under cultivation" (D.C. for Nandi, Annual Report 1943:2). In 1944, Nandi exported 20,000 bags of maize in response to wartime demand. The D.C. commented:

The administration in Nandi for many years have been impressing upon the Nandi the need to grow enough foodstuffs for their own consumption. For years they have failed to do so and the Nandi women have been seen toiling up the escarpment under heavy loads of maize bought at the market in North and Central Kavirondo. Now the Nandi have taken to cultivation to such an extent as to require a control on the extent of shamba cultivation. [D.C. for Nandi, Annual Report 1944:7.]

Controls on the extent of cultivation, as well as a decline in demand from the wartime peak, resulted in a decrease in the amount of exportable maize cultivated in 1946. In the same year, in order to limit the expansion of maize cultivation, a policy of allowing new plows to be purchased only with a government permit was begun. Two permits per year were allotted to each location (D.C. for Nandi, Annual Report 1946:15).

Manners (1967:291–95) describes very well the process by which certain Kipsigis in the 1930's used customary land tenure and cultivation rights to sanction their enclosure and conversion to individual property of large tracts of land—a process against which others could protect themselves only by following suit until all land in Kipsigis was individually claimed. It is not demonstrable that the exact same process occurred in Nandi, but it seems likely that the process was at least very similar. It was probably not as early in Nandi as in Kipsigis, however. Nandi informants told me that land enclosure in Nandi began in the early 1940's. The process intensified in the late 1940's, abetted by policies of the colonial government. According to Magut (1969:106) those who benefited most were "Chiefs, headmen, and Protestant church leaders." In 1946 the Worthington Plan established ALDEV, the African Land Development Program. One of the programs undertaken by ALDEV was the settling of Africans in cooperative group-farming schemes that were to be farmed in accordance with what was viewed as good soil conservation practice. The schemes were also to serve as demonstration farms for government-approved soil conservation techniques. One such demonstration farming scheme was established in Nandi at Ndalat. The techniques demonstrated included fencing of harvested fields as cattle paddocks, which were later rotated back to cultivation. People outside the scheme who would follow the same program were permitted to claim and enclose land. Land enclosure became so popular toward the end of the decade that measures to control it were deemed necessary. In 1949, the Local Native Council passed a resolution that prohibited any fencing except with the permission of the Chief or *kokwet* elder. The latter individuals were to ascertain before approving any fence that it would not interfere with anyone else's grazing or cultivation rights and that the fencer would practice soil conservation measures and rotation within the fenced area (LNC Resolution 1/49, File PC/RVP/6A/1/11D/2, no. 299, Kenya National Archives). Thus, the 1940's saw the beginnings of land enclosure and the commoditization of land.

Though the process began gradually, during the 1930's and 1940's the Nandi became thoroughly enmeshed in the colonial cash economy—chiefly through the commoditization of cattle and the development of maize as a cash crop. The acquisition, disposal, and exchange of cattle other than those forming the core of the herd of a woman's house had traditionally been the prerogative of men. The commoditization of cattle did not change this. The process by which a household's marketable maize surplus came to be under male control, and by which female autonomy in staple production was undermined, has been described above.

The two major processes of incorporation into the cash economy thus brought cash into the hands of Nandi men almost to the exclusion of women. At the same time, other developments gave women access to limited amounts of cash. Women still had exclusive charge of the cultivation of vegetables, and they could grow vegetables in excess of their household needs and sell them. The presence of tea estates, mission compounds, and a growing number of boarding schools created a small new market for them. Chickens, too—the only other form of property that was traditionally regarded as the domain of women—were a minor source of profit. A part of the money that the Local Native Council contributed to the Veterinary Training Program at Baraton was earmarked for the upgrading of poultry. According to the District Commissioner's annual report for 1940, "84 Rhode Island Red cockerels and 61 sittings of eggs were issued from Baraton Poultry Farm" (D.C. for Nandi, Annual Report 1940: 9). The Baraton Poultry Scheme was abandoned in 1945, however, "following the withdrawal of LNC contributions toward its maintenance" (D.C. for Nandi, Annual Report 1945: 13). The cash-generating potential of upgraded chickens was no doubt limited by the small demand for eggs; and probably, also, the L.N.C. was reluctant to make an investment in an economic resource that was of little consequence in the traditional Nandi value system. Certainly, however, there was no interest, on the part either of the all-male L.N.C. or of the colonial government, in trying to develop cash sources that would primarily benefit women.

Throughout this period, women continued to cultivate on their own patches of eleusine, adjacent to or as part of the *kapungut* (vegetable garden). After the shift to maize as the staple, eleusine was used primarily in brewing beer. Exactly when beer became commoditized is not clear, but it is likely that it was not long after cash became commonplace in the Reserve. As the cultivation of eleusine had come to be largely conducted by women, and as the brewing of beer had traditionally been women's work, the beer industry came to be the one profitable cash venture that was primarily controlled by women. This control was not complete, of course, and the situation developed in such a way that large parts of the profits of brewing went to male entrepreneurs, men who owned buildings in trading centers from which beer could be sold. These men either supplied the space, equipment, and ingredients for brewing and hired women to do the actual labor, or charged rent for use of their space and sometimes equipment to women who brewed and sold their product independently. Even so, not inconsiderable profit went to women, and legal brewing was, throughout the colonial era and until recently during the postcolonial era, one of the few ways in which women could make a significant amount of money. Under the widening influence of fundamentalist Protestant denominations, which forbid the consumption or purveying of alcohol, brewing is no longer a possibility for very many women.

The other major avenue to the accumulation of cash open to women during this period was prostitution. Prostitution occurred traditionally in Nandi, as women who went into lowland areas to trade for grain were known to trade sexual favors as well as stock (Huntingford 1950:65, and personal reports of informants). During the 1930's and 1940's, Nandi women made their way into most of Kenya's cities as prostitutes. Their numbers were seemingly large, compared with the numbers of prostitutes from other ethnic groups in western Kenya.* In 1948, in a

---

*Just why so many Nandi women became prostitutes is still not clear to me. It is a question I should very much like to study further. I interviewed a number of old women who had formerly been prostitutes. The reasons they gave for entering the profession were so highly individualistic that they did not add up to an explanation, but the fact of childlessness was usually prominent. During the late 1930's and early 1940's there was an unusual amount of venereal disease in Nandi, probably because of returned soldiers and the presence of a camp for Italian POW's in Eldoret. One hypothesis is that an unusually high number of Nandi women were made barren because of VD. On the other hand, several former prostitutes I interviewed returned home with children, so it may have been Nandi men (returned soldiers) who were infertile. The trend to women going out as prostitutes appears to predate the war, however, so infertility due to VD would only be part of the explanation, if it is an explanation at all.

memo to the Provincial Commissioner, J. K. R. Thorp, the D.C. for Nandi, noted: "The presence of large numbers of Nandi prostitutes in all the big towns of Kenya has been the cause of much concern for many years" (File PC/RVP/6A/1/11D/2, no. 295, Kenya National Archives). Many prostitutes returned to Nandi with their earnings, bought land and cattle, and resettled in Nandi as independent householders. In 1950, Huntingford noted this trend and described a typical case (Huntingford 1950:87). The apparent attractiveness of this potentially economically profitable option led to concern among Nandi men over loss of control over women. In 1948, the Local Native Council passed the so-called Lost Women Ordinance, which stipulated:

(I) No Nandi woman or girl over the age of 12 years shall travel from the Nandi District to any place outside the Nandi District without the written permission of the Chief. (II) No African driver of any vehicle shall convey in any such vehicle any woman or girl from the Nandi District to any place outside the Nandi District unless such woman or girl is in possession of a valid permit to travel issued by her Chief. [L.N.C. Resolution 4/48, File PC/RVP/6A/1/11D/2, nos. 293,294, Kenya National Archives.]

This ordinance was of limited effectiveness. It is still true that there were few opportunities available to women during this period to gain independent status within the cash economy. Further, there were forces—whether lack of markets, lack of government financial support, the attitude of the missions, or the outright edict of the Local Native Council—that worked in each case to ensure that the availability of these opportunities was severely restricted.

Education for girls, on the other hand, had become popular by the late 1940's. The first Government African School was sited in Kapsabet in 1925, but all the students were male. By 1935, there were two central schools and eleven "outschools" in Nandi, including mission schools; these numbers increased gradually over the next ten years. One District Commissioner commented that the Nandi were extremely uninterested in education, as they were rich and the elders didn't see how it would be of much benefit to them (D.C. for Nandi, Annual Report 1935:39). By 1940, the government schools accepted female students, the

African Inland Mission was running a central school for girls at Kapsabet, and the Roman Catholic mission station at Chepterit was about to embark on a girls' program (D.C. for Nandi, Annual Report 1940:7). In 1942, an Elementary Teachers' Training Course for Nandi was begun (D.C. for Nandi, Annual Report 1942:5; 1943:6). In 1944, the District Commissioner reported a great increase in school attendance and applications to the Local Native Council to open more schools, and wrote of "a turn of public opinion in Nandi in favor of education" (D.C. for Nandi, Annual Report 1944:5).

Though interest in education in general, and in the education of girls in particular, had been growing gradually, 1945 seems to be the year in which a major change took place: "All school supervisors report much larger attendance at the outschools and a noticeable feature is the increase in the number of girls attending school. . . . The girls' school at the Africa Inland Mission in Kapsabet is growing rapidly. . . . The Catholic Mission also has a flourishing female section in the Headquarters Mission School at Chepterit" (D.C. for Nandi, Annual Report 1945:8). In 1946, steps were first taken to train female teachers for Nandi (File PC/RVP/6A/12/3, no. 17, Kenya National Archives). Interest in female education thus came late in Nandi, but by 1969, in a comparative educational profile of women aged twelve and over by ethnic group, the Nandi compared conspicuously unfavorably with only the Kikuyu, Embu, and Luhyia (Smock 1977:25). The education of girls was not always immediately relevant to the enhancement of opportunities within the modern economy. Programs designed specifically for girls, for example, might emphasize Western-oriented domestic science rather than agriculture. However, they also included Swahili and basic literacy, and the chance for education at least opened to women the option of skilled white-collar employment. Because of that option, a small number of women have been able to achieve real economic autonomy in the modern era. But the existence of an employed, literate female elite in no way transforms the lives of the mass of Nandi women. Moreover, education as a means of entry to elite status is a path that is still far more available to men than to women.

By the end of the 1940's Nandi had experienced a number of

significant, though gradual, socioeconomic changes. The sudden and dramatic transformation came in the 1950's, when the adoption of the Swynnerton Plan turned government policy away from the old posture of slow, gradual change and toward one of encouragement of rapid change in the agricultural economy.

The major provision of the Swynnerton Plan was the allotment and titling of individual plots of land in areas of "high agricultural potential." Nandi was one of these areas. In many parts of Kenya, the land registration program included the consolidation of a person's rights in many tiny pieces of cultivable land into one larger equivalent package (Brown 1968:77). In Nandi, where there was no traditional ownership of land, land in each Location was subdivided and allotted among adult males (and in some cases, female household heads with minor sons). Parcels of land thus allocated were of not less than ten acres and in many areas averaged twenty acres (D.C. for Nandi, Confidential Handing-Over Notes, 1958). Persons who had already been permitted to enclose large tracts of land were allowed to register these same tracts, which in many cases were larger than average holdings. As part of the program of land registration, alienated land in Kaimosi and Kipkarren (Sarora) was returned to the Reserve and people from more crowded locations could claim plots in those areas. Squatters on European farms were also allowed to return to Nandi District to make land claims. The demarcation of plot boundaries took place in Nandi during 1954–55, and the surveying of boundaries began in 1956. In 1958, Ndalat and Mutwot became the first areas in which the registration of land titles was actually completed (D.C. for Nandi, Confidential Handing-Over Notes, 1958). Land registration apparently had only slight popularity in Nandi at first, but accelerated in the early 1960's (Brown 1968:78).

Once plots were allocated, title holders were required to cull their herds to numbers in accord with government determinations of the carrying capacity of individual plots. Cattle could be brought into the Reserve only if bound for particular plots not yet filled to their determined carrying capacity. The culling of cattle was less a hardship to the Nandi at this time than formerly because stock policy was changing to a certain extent. From 1955 on, upgrading of indigenous cattle through artificial insemination with semen from Guernsey bulls was encouraged, though ownership of purebred European dairy stock was still denied to Africans until after 1960 (Brown 1968:49). The new stock policy was well received in Nandi:

It is planned to open an A. I. Centre at Kabiyet immediately and bull camps are being encouraged wherever there is a demand. Baraton stock is being pushed out as fast as possible and there is a definite feeling of revival over stock matters. . . . Destocking has been pressed with the utmost vigour but to a great extent our efforts have been met by those of the Nandi themselves in proportion to their realization that with enclosure stock holding must be correlated to available grazing. [D.C. for Nandi, Confidential Handing-Over Notes, 1958.]

In the late 1950's, following the demarcation of individual plots, Africans were for the first time allowed to plant profitable cash crops that had heretofore been forbidden to them: pyrethrum, coffee, and tea. The first two crops have turned out not to be well suited to Nandi District, and have never gained much popularity there. Tea, however, has come to be a cash crop of tremendous importance for the Nandi. At first, only a few demonstration farmers in each area were allowed to plant tea. By 1958, the number of farmers in Nandi District growing tea was still less than fifty (D.C. for Nandi, Confidential Handing-Over Notes, 1958). During the 1960's, tea rapidly gained in significance. Today, it is grown by most households in areas where its cultivation, which is restricted on the basis of soil type, is authorized by the Kenya Tea Development Authority.

All these changes had far-reaching implications. The change in the system of land tenure, in particular, could only result in the widening of the economic gap between individuals with differential access to resources. Though differences in wealth had already been emerging, this was the turning point in the movement toward real stratification.

Small inequities in the distribution of land gave rise to increasingly large inequities in the distribution of other resources, through credit. For the larger a piece of land an individual held title to, the more he could borrow as a result, and thus the more he was able to develop his holding and increase the resources he controlled. Moreover, the resources available for loans and their administration were not sufficient to cover all comers. Preference was given to persons with more collateral or with something other than land to offer as collateral. This process is perceptively analyzed by Colin Leys (1974:98–114), a scathing critic of the inequities of colonialism and neocolonialism. However, even Leys fails to appreciate a major, basic inequity: "The long-term social and economic effects of individualized tenure and the differential provision of credit . . . would be far-reaching. In the short run, however, most people with some customary title to land got a new title under registration and it was only the landless in the overcrowded parts of the former reserves who found themselves worse off" (Leys 1974:73). It is not true that in areas that were not overcrowded, such as Nandi, most people got land titles. Even such an astute critic as Leys ignores one extremely important class of people: women. What is true is that most *males* got titles. The traditional rights of women were virtually ignored as a complex system of use-rights that included women was converted into a system of Western-style "ownership" from which women were for the most part excluded. Further, since lack of collateral in the form of a land title made it impossible to get credit, it followed that women had no access to credit for the development of their own enterprises.

On the national level, after Independence, African large-scale farmers replaced European large-scale farmers on policy, marketing, and pricing boards and in other agencies concerned with the administration of agriculture. Thus, the protected position of large farms at the expense of peasants was maintained. Some of the advantages of the large farmers, with regard to credit, for example, were extended to middle-level farmers (Leys 1974: 105). For Nandi, which had relatively large average landholdings, the extension of the advantages of the large landholders to middle-level landholders contributed to general affluence. Under the new system, differences in access to credit widened the gap between large and small landholders, between men and women, and also between sparsely and densely populated ethnic groups and regions. In this process, because of traditionally low population density, the Nandi occupied a favored position.

Since Independence, through the development of dairy farming and tea planting as major sources of cash income, the Nandi have in fact experienced a great measure of affluence, and because of it they have become involved in what Leys (1974:105) calls the "process of co-optation into the large-farm interest." But if the Nandi as a group have been coopted to the interests of Kenya's landed elite, Nandi women as an interest group have also been coopted by the general affluence. Though Nandi women's relative economic position vis-à-vis that of men has declined, in the midst of affluence it is hardly noticed. In other parts of the country, women have become conscious of their situation as women, and have organized themselves into interest groups such as self-help organizations, cooperatives, and rotating credit associations (Pala 1975b). Such associations are conspicuously weak or absent among Nandi women. Maendeleo ya Wanawake, the government-sponsored organization that began in the 1950's to organize women and teach them "modern" techniques of housekeeping, child care, and so on, was not a success in Nandi. This was partly because the women did not view some of the skills in which they were instructed (for example, embroidery and baking) as highly relevant to the improvement of their lives. But neither were they interested in using the Maendeleo organization to seek other, more relevant, ends. Possibly the revitalized version of Maendeleo that was getting started in 1977 in the community in which I worked will do more to stimulate women's interest, since it has the goal of building a village polytechnic and sponsoring vocational training for women in trades such as tailoring. I have also heard that several women's vegetable-growing cooperatives, which existed almost in name only when I was in the field, have become active and are seeking loans and other sources of funds to expand the scope of their operations. What will become of these attempts to organize women in their common interest remains to be seen.

Thus, in a very short time from the mid-1950's to the mid-1960's, drastic and far-reaching changes took place in the Nandi economy. The land-tenure system was turned upside down. Having passed only a decade of fully individualized land titles as of the mid-1970's, the Nandi were still in the process of making an accommodation between the extremely fluid traditional land-tenure system and the new legal situation. Between the mid-1950's and the mid-1960's, the milk-production potential of cattle greatly improved, and consequently their numbers were greatly reduced. This resulted in changes in the social meaning and value of cattle and in a need to redefine some principles governing rights in them. Cash suddenly became plentiful in the wake of increased milk production and profitable cash crops. Differentials in landholdings and in access to such resources as credit gave impetus to a developing class structure.

Though the Nandi as of 1977 enjoyed the fruits of a high level of general affluence, tensions inherent in the new economic situation were beginning to make themselves felt. These tensions reflected the different interests of small landholders vs. larger landholders whose holdings continued to grow; of agricultural laborers vs. large landholders who are employers of labor (and at the same time frequently neighbors and/or kin); of Nandi landlords vs. Luhyia worker/tenants; and of men vs. women.

A Nandi house and granary near Kitale, northwest of Nandi District.
The landscape and scattered settlement pattern are typical of this area.

Women going home from market.

An elderly couple pose in front of their house.

A man and woman from neighboring compounds converse on a pathway.

A women's dance group in "traditional" dress entertains at a fund-raising event.

A prominent community leader and his wife, mother, and son.

A young woman hugs a cow she has just milked, illustrating a Nandi saying, *Toroch tich* (embrace cattle).

As part of a cooperative work group, a grandmother instructs her granddaughters in weeding maize and planting beans.

Boys bring their families' cattle to the river for a drink.

Cattle being driven into a community dip in order to combat tick-borne diseases.

A young wife milks a cow.

Two young men pick tea leaves.

A little girl helps her mother transport foodstuffs.

A man, accompanied by his young son, oversees his cattle herd.

A man prepares his tea seedlings for planting.

A child nurse carries her infant sister.

Girls thresh beans in a family compound while other family members watch.

A woman fastens a token around the neck of a boy
about to be initiated.

A girl being costumed for her initiation.

A group of men pass time by
playing a game in the
sublocation center.

Elders drink beer prior to an initiation ceremony.

SIX

Production of the Family Estate

THE FULL MEASURE of the shift that has taken place in the sexual division of labor in production in Nandi over the past several decades is difficult to assess because we lack complete and reliable data on the traditional division of labor. Probably, the shift to a cash economy has increased the workloads of both sexes, so that the gap between women's and men's labor input in cultivation has not widened appreciably. Yet when all forms of labor affected by participation in the cash economy are considered, the total workload of women would appear to have increased somewhat more than that of men. Certainly, to the extent that men have seen a higher return for their increased labor in terms of the amount of resources they are able to control, women have been the losers; and the economic gap between the sexes can be said to have widened.

The Family Estate

In Nandi, as in most other African societies, the basic unit of production and consumption is the household, a (usually) small coresidential unit whose core is a nuclear or extended family. The economic resources held and exploited by such a unit form what Gray and Gulliver (1964:5) refer to as the *family estate*. Viewing a household's economic resources as an estate helps to focus attention on their heritability, that is, the transfer of rights in them from one set of individuals to another over time. Such an approach concentrates attention on the system of rules that defines the various rights in such resources held by each of the members of a household or family group. The volume edited by. Gray and Gulliver (1964) exemplifies the view of social organization as embedded in a system of relations to property, a view that I believe is essential to a fruitful historical analysis of social organization.

The term "family estate" does have certain problems. For example, it, and the approach it denotes, imply that all economic resources are property. For Nandi, this obscures the fact that one of the most significant changes that took place during the colonial era was the transformation into property of some resources, particularly land, that were not traditionally viewed as such. Nevertheless, I shall continue to use this term because it has an established place in the ethnographic literature, and because better than any other established term it sums up the view that I wish to take of social organization as a system that defines and distributes the rights of various parties in resources.

The boundaries of the Nandi family group sharing an estate are not always specific and easy to define. A compound is a visible unit. Sometimes, though not always, the houses in a compound are grouped fairly close together. But even when the houses are widely separated, they still seem to be a unit: the doorways face toward a central area, connected by well-used pathways, and usually they are not separated from one another by hedges or permanent fencing. The smallest unit that holds its own property is a house made up of a married woman and her minor children.* If there are several such houses in a compound, each married woman usually cooks for herself and her husband and children (in which house the men and children actually eat is not fixed—it may be wherever they happen to be).

Traditionally, the Nandi family estate consisted of livestock (cattle, sheep, goats, and perhaps some chickens) and their products, houses and granaries, a number of household items such as cooking utensils and a few furnishings, crops stored in granaries and growing in cultivated fields, and rights to continue cultivating previously cleared and cultivated fields. In modern Nandi, the picture is much more complicated. Besides these tra-

---

*Nandi contains no terminological distinction between "house" and "compound." A compound is referred to as "Gab ——," using a man's name; houses within the compound are called "Gab ——," using the names of the women to whom they belong.

ditional items, the family estate also includes title to land, cash crops as well as subsistence crops, cash and bank accounts, items of material culture of vastly increased value such as cars, tractors, iron plows, radios, and also individual skills and knowledge that can be translated into cash through wage labor, and the cash potential of salable material goods. The system of rights in the traditional family estate is now being reworked to include these additional resources. This redefinition of rights in the family estate is the subject of Chapter 7. The present chapter analyzes the roles of various members of a household in producing and/or bringing under the control of the household the resources that make up the family estate. This analysis must begin with a description of the nature of the household unit itself.

Household Composition

Nandi define the sexual division of labor in terms of the responsibilities of husbands and wives. This view, which implies that the nuclear family is the primary unit of production, has a practical basis. The nuclear family *is* the basic coresidential and productive unit. Table 11 shows, for the random sample census of one sublocation, the numbers of compounds that display various types of family structure. In the table, "Single" means an individual man with independent land title who lives and farms completely by himself; presumably the younger ones of these few cases will in time become nuclear family compounds. "Simple nuclear family" compounds are those in which a man, his wife, and all or some of their children are the only residents. A "one-parent nuclear family" compound is the same, except that in these cases either the husband or (in one case) the wife is deceased. A "nuclear extended family" compound is one in which a nuclear family forms the core membership of the compound but one or more (up to 7) other (usually) related individuals are also residents. In most cases, at least one of these additional residents is the widowed mother of the male head of the compound. In 27 of the thirty-eight cases in this category, one of the attached relatives is the mother of the compound head. In 11 cases, the compound consists of the nuclear family, the husband's mother, and no one else. In 9 cases, at least some of the

TABLE 11
Distribution of Core Family Types by Age-Set of Compound Head for a
Random Sample of 115 Compounds

| | | Age-set of compound head | | | | |
| | | Kipkoimet age 14–30 | Sawe age 28–45 | Chuma age 42–59 | Maina age 57–74 | Nyongi age 72–90 |
Family type	NA[a]					
Single man		2	1	1		
Simple nuclear		4	10	18	4	
Nuclear extended		9	23	6		
Complete extended			1	2	10	1
Nuclear-polygynous			1	8	4	
1-parent nuclear	5				1	
Other	4					
TOTAL	9	15	36	35	19	1

[a]NA = not applicable (female-headed households).

attached kin are unmarried siblings of the household head. In only 13 cases are more distant kin attached to nuclear family compounds, and in only a handful are the relatives living with the family kin of the wife rather than of the husband. Normally, only one or two relatives more distant than siblings are attached to a compound. The highest number for any household head is four. A substantial number of cases of attached kin are explained by the practice of fostering children who help with household chores in exchange for board and school fees. The basic nuclear family structure of the typical Nandi compound is thus even more pronounced than these figures make it appear at first glance.

A "complete extended family" compound is one in which the compound is shared by members of three generations, including grandchildren and grandparents both of whom are living and active. Typically, such a compound is composed of the male head of household, his wife or wives, and at least one married son with his wife and children. (In Table 11, two of the "complete extended family" compounds are polygynous families.) The household may also include unmarried children of the household head and other attached kin. Among households in this survey, the one with the most complicated structure consisted of a Maina man, his two wives, four married sons with wives and children, a never-married daughter with her children, and the son of his wife's brother—a total of thirty-five individuals. There were in the survey a few unusual cases, including compounds such as this one having unmarried daughters with children, another in which the son was deceased but his widow and her children shared the compound with her parents-in-law, and one in which a man with a married son also shared his compound with his sister's son, whom he had "adopted," and the latter's wife and children. This was the only case in the sample of matrilateral attachment and inheritance by an adult male (though I personally knew of a few others).

A "nuclear polygynous family" compound is one in which a polygynous husband coresides with more than one wife and their unmarried children. (In one of these cases, the polygynist actually maintained two separate compounds in the same community, which cooperated economically to some extent but not as much as is typical of the houses of co-wives sharing the same compound).

The category "Other" consists of four households with female heads that were difficult to categorize. One is a female husband with her wife and child. Another is an old woman, her married daughter, the daughter's daughter (separated from her husband) and unmarried son, and the son of the granddaughter. In another case, two widows live with the unmarried children of one, along with her brother's daughter and father's sister's son. The last is a widow with her teen-age son, her mother's brother's son, and an unrelated teen-age girl. (Two other cases of woman-woman marriage occurred in this sample. One is one of the single-parent families, headed by the widow of a woman. Another is subsumed in one of the complete extended family cases).

Economic cooperation within compounds is considerable. Widows may cultivate on their own, or pool their labor with the wives of their sons and receive a share of the harvest. In any case, a widow normally maintains a separate granary. Though each married woman has fields and granaries that are designated as belonging to her house, there is still a lot of informal sharing of labor in cultivation among the members of a compound. In many compounds, all members take turns in working together on all the fields belonging to the compound. Attached kin pitch in to contribute their labor wherever it is most needed. Compound members help each other with both subsistence and cash crops. Tea, for example, though it is controlled by the male compound head, will benefit the entire household indirectly from the profit it brings, and therefore all members participate in cultivating it, as convenient. Normally, too, all a household's cattle are herded together, and though each woman may cultivate her own plot of vegetables, these are shared freely with other compound members. Other foodstuffs may also be shared with no formal obligation to make a return.

Land title is usually not divided within the lifetime of a compound head and frequently not for some time after his death.

Table 11 clearly reveals the typical developmental cycle of Nandi family compounds (Goody 1958). A couple ordinarily begins married life in a complete extended family situation in which the male head of the compound is the husband's father. The compound probably also includes other married brothers of the husband, with their wives and children, as well as their unmarried siblings. Table 11 shows that by far the largest number of complete extended families are headed by men of the next-to-oldest age-set, and that there are few compound heads among men of the youngest circumcised age-set. It is possible, of course, for a young man to set up an independent household immediately upon marriage (or even before), and this does happen. Another fairly common pattern is for older brothers to set up independent compounds some time after marriage but before the father's death. The customary large age discrepancy between husband and wife means that the male compound head will probably die before his wife or wives—most often after the age-set of his older married sons has reached the age-grade above that of the most recent initiates. With the death of their father, brothers normally establish their own independent compounds. (In only two cases in the sample did adult brothers with families continue to coreside in one compound and cooperate economically for more than a few years after their father's death.) When the brothers establish separate compounds, their mother attaches herself to one of these compounds, usually that of the youngest married son. In this way a complete extended family compound breaks up into a nuclear extended family compound (with the widowed mother) and one or more simple nuclear family compounds. Nuclear extended families can therefore be expected to occur most commonly among households headed by men of the age-grade immediately above new initiates, as can be seen in Table 11. Further passage of time brings the death of the widowed mother, as well as the adulthood and departure of fostered children, shifting the nuclear extended family over into the category of simple nuclear families. Table 11 shows that simple nuclear families are most commonly headed by men of the age-grade two steps above that of the most recent initiates. It is at this point, also, that a man is most likely to take a second wife, so that a simple nuclear family may change into a nuclear polygynous family. Further, the death of a spouse may change a simple nuclear family into a one-parent nuclear family. A man who survives to reach the age-grade three steps above new initiates, however, can expect to see his family and compound evolve into a complete extended family compound. Thus, the beginning point of the developmental cycle is again reached.

At any given point in time, most compounds are likely to be occupied by either a nuclear family only or by a group with a nuclear family as its core. At the time this census was taken (1976), 63.5 percent of compounds in the random sample had this structure. But *most* compounds can expect to have a nuclear family–based structure during the longest part of their developmental cycle.

The nuclear family of husband, wife, children, and, commonly, grandmother, is thus not only the smallest unit of economic cooperation in Nandi but also the typical one. This has probably always been the case: informants say that in the past it was not uncommon for elder sons to be given their cattle inheritance during their father's lifetime, move away, and establish independent households. In a situation of ample available land, men were not bound to their fathers' homesteads by land rights, as may be the case in horticultural societies under conditions of land scarcity. Also, it was possible for even a young man who had not been given his cattle inheritance to acquire wealth independently, by raiding. To some extent, these factors still operate in the modern setting. Though land is no longer free for the taking, it is still plentiful compared with the situation in other parts of Kenya. This fact, together with the individualization of land titles and the ready availability of cash resulting from the penetration of cash cropping and wage labor, creates a situation in which it is easy for a landless person to buy land. Since the ready availability of cash also makes it easy to buy cattle, young men do not have to overcome great barriers to gain independence from their elders, and thus the already present tendency toward nuclear family homesteads is strengthened.

The Conceptual Division of Labor

From this basic unit of production in Nandi, the nuclear family, the most common conceptual schema of the division of labor, that of husband and wife together, arises naturally. My Nandi informants' accounts of the sexual division of labor centered on the husband-wife relationship and the tasks deemed appropriate for each spouse. They were less specific about the appropriate participation of other household members in the domestic division of labor (except for vague assertions that boys should herd cattle and girls should care for babies). It should be noted, too, that Nandi informants tend to conflate the categories "man" and "woman" with "husband" and "wife," so that statements about "what men should do" and "what women should do" often refer to the ideal division of labor between husband and wife rather than between men and women.

I interviewed large numbers of people in Nandi informally on the division of labor within households and between the sexes. In order to give data on the conceptual division of labor a more formal structure, I used a set procedure. Together with four key informants, I developed a list of tasks that are essential to the functioning of most Nandi homesteads and are generally defined as "work" (*boisiet*).* I then read this list out to fifteen informants, eight women and seven men, and asked them to indicate for each item whether it was a task done mainly or exclusively by members of one sex or the other (by husbands or wives) or whether it was one in which both sexes (both husbands and wives) participated more or less equally. I also asked my in-

---

*Later I came to question whether most informants viewed a few of these items as "work," even though my key informants so defined them. These items relate to interactions with children, for example, playing with them, teaching them, and helping them with schoolwork.

formants to suggest any more tasks, not on the list, that they thought should be included. The responses are summarized in Table 12, listed separately for women and for men.

It can be seen from the table that there is a solid core of agreement among most informants of both sexes about the sex assignment of most tasks. There is little ambiguity in the conceptual division of labor by sex. Qualitative interviewing reveals that there are few tasks actually forbidden to one or the other sex by rules the violation of which could result in any type of sanction. There are a few exceptions. If a woman slaughters a cow, sheep, or goat, or if she thatches a house or climbs on the roof of a house for any purpose, she can be cursed. Other activities (not part of the daily division of labor) that invoke this sanction are using male weapons, wearing a man's helmet, or blowing the war trumpet (*igondit*). It is also considered extremely inappropriate (though not curseable) for a woman to build any structures, especially houses. How seriously are these prohibitions taken? One old woman (a widow) thatches her house. She is not a person who has absorbed a Western ideology and is flouting community norms; she is a Nandi traditionalist, a leader of women's rituals. When asked if she might not be cursed for this activity she replied, somewhat ambiguously, "Nonsense. Who would curse me?" I know of one instance in which a woman set the posts for a house. However, this information, when related to other informants, was greeted with derision and disbelief.

For men, the case is slightly different. It is not so much that men are forbidden to do certain types of work on pain of any sanction as that they *refuse* categorically because such work is beneath the dignity of a man. There are a few cases in which some type of traditional sanction was operative. For example, male participation in child care was precluded by beliefs in feminine-child pollution (see Chapter 3). In precolonial Nandi it was also considered extremely bad for a man to cut grass for thatching. Grass as food for cattle was sacred to men, who have a close association with cattle. It is not clear whether there was any sanction to enforce this prohibition (e.g., a curse). Today, young men will cut grass if they are paid for their labor, but cutting grass on the family's own property for its own use is still a woman's job.

Informants agree that under no circumstances will a man wash

TABLE 12

Women's responses	Men's responses

Tasks assigned exclusively to women:

Washing dishes	Washing dishes
Making beds	Making beds
Sweeping	Sweeping
Carrying water	Carrying water
Regular house plastering	Regular house plastering
Taking maize to mill	Taking maize to mill
Winnowing	Winnowing
Shelling and drying beans	Shelling and drying beans
Collecting and chopping firewood	Collecting and chopping firewood
Laundry	Laundry
Mending and pressing clothes	Mending and pressing clothes
Bathing and dressing children	Bathing and dressing children
Cutting thatching grass	Cutting thatching grass
Brewing	Brewing
Maintaining and operating lamps	Maintaining and operating lamps
Cleaning storage gourds	Cleaning storage gourds
Building inside fire	Building inside fire
Cooking	
Feeding chickens	
Spreading natural fertilizer	
Harvesting vegetables	
Weeding vegetables	
Buying kitchen utensils	

Tasks assigned exclusively to men:

Building house frame	Building house frame
Thatching	Thatching
Building fences	Building fences
Building outbuildings	Building outbuildings
Clearing land for cultivation	Clearing land for cultivation
Making and repairing tools	Making and repairing tools
Slaughtering (except chickens)	Slaughtering (except chickens)
Driving tractor	Driving tractor
Buying farm supplies	Buying farm supplies
	Plowing
	Cutting maize at harvest
	Hauling
	Breaking rocks
	Buying furniture
	Making kitchen utensils
	Trimming hedges

Tasks usually done by women, but not forbidden to men:

Milking	Milking
Collecting eggs	Collecting eggs
Selling vegetables	Selling vegetables
Welcoming visitors	Welcoming visitors

Conceptual Division of Labor by Sex

Women's responses	Men's responses

Tasks usually done by women, but not forbidden to men (*cont'd*):

Slaughtering chickens	Cooking
Making kitchen utensils	Feeding chickens
Carrying heavy loads[a]	Weeding vegetables
	Harvesting vegetables
	Buying food

Tasks usually done by men, but not forbidden to women:

Initial rough mudding of house	Initial rough mudding of house
Building outdoor fire	Building outdoor fire
Cattle health care	Giving salt to cattle
Plowing	Breaking ground with a hoe
Cutting maize at harvest	Buying household items
Trimming hedges	
Helping children with schoolwork	

Tasks assigned to both sexes equally:

Planting	Planting
Weeding with hoe (maize)	Weeding with hoe (maize)
Husking maize at harvest	Husking maize at harvest
Picking tea	Picking tea
Spreading chemical fertilizer	Sorting maize cobs
Buying clothes	

Tasks where informants disagree about sex assignment:[b]

Herding cattle	Herding cattle
Teaching children	Teaching children
Disciplining children	Disciplining children
Playing with children[c]	Playing with children[c] (bias → women)
Drawing water for cattle	Spreading fertilizer
Giving salt to cattle	Slaughtering chickens
Breaking ground with a hoe	Buying clothes
Buying food	Helping children with schoolwork
Sorting maize cobs (bias → women)	Carrying heavy loads
Buying furniture (bias → men)	Loading (bias → men)
Loading and hauling (bias → men)	Cleaning sand (bias → men)
Breaking rocks (bias → men)	
Cleaning sand for building (bias → men)	

[a]Most informants specified that men do this only when using a bicycle.

[b]This usually means disagreement on which sex more frequently performs the task, but it may be disagreement on whether the task is sex-specific or is performed by both sexes. Where a bias toward either sex is noted, it means that most informants interviewed assigned the task to that sex.

[c]Several informants remarked spontaneously that this is not done by adults at all, but by other children. This was the only task any informants assigned primarily to children, though they were given the option of doing so.

the clothing of women and children. The only exception to this rule I have ever heard of was the case of a young man (of an early Christian convert family) washing the clothing of his sick, elderly mother because there was no one else, no woman, to do it. Informants insist that no man will carry water, and it is a certainty that no man will carry anything on his head. Most informants state that a man will not gather firewood (and I have observed only one instance of a man doing so). One man, separated from his wife, tore out the rafters of the house he was sleeping in and burned them rather than be seen collecting firewood. No man will sweep or plaster a house. Most informants admit that a man may cook for himself or wash his own dishes if the alternative (most unlikely) is going hungry. Brewing, in the opinion of almost all informants, is by rights the exclusive work of women. Still, I occasionally observed men participating in almost every step of the process.

For the sex assignment of one task, herding cattle, my informants showed a great deal of disagreement. There are several factors that may be involved in this confusion. First, in the traditional ideology, cattle are the sole concern of men, as symbolized by the fact that only men can slaughter them; a woman who does so can be cursed. Whether there was ever actually a time when men were the exclusive herders of cattle is moot. To an extent, pastoral ideology (and not merely anthropological ideology about pastoralists) connects the care of cattle with men. Second, it is possible that male participation in herding was at one time greater than it is at present. Female involvement in cattle care has increased in recent times as men have moved increasingly into cash-generating activities. Third, confusion about whether the bulk of herding is done by men or women stems in part from the fact that it actually is done by *neither* men nor women but by children (Oboler 1977a:21). It is interesting that neither male nor female informants mentioned this fact (though the option of assigning tasks to children was available to them) during interviews. There appears to be a tendency among adults to ignore or undervalue children's extremely important contribution to subsistence. The "homemade model" of the division of labor held by Nandi adults of both sexes emphasizes the division of labor by sex and largely dismisses as unimportant the division of labor by age.

To summarize, in the Nandi conceptual definition of the division of labor by sex, more tasks are seen as sex-segregated than as the mutual responsibility of both sexes. Men and women, for the most part, share the same conceptual categorization of tasks. In the case of a small but significant number of activities, the sexual segregation of tasks was traditionally ensured by belief in the possibility of supernatural sanctions. In Bacdayan's terms, the Nandi division of labor (at least as it is conceptualized) is characterized by a low degree of mechanistic cooperation between the sexes, defined as a combination of the "rate of interchangeability of tasks" and the "rate of tasks done together" by members of both sexes (Bacdayan 1977:281). Bacdayan links mechanistic cooperation in the sexual division of labor with sexual egalitarianism in social life. If this hypothesis is correct, the inegalitarian nature of the interaction between women and men in Nandi, especially as husbands and wives, is related to the low level of mechanistic cooperation between the sexes in the division of labor.

Time Allocation and the Division of Labor

The Nandi conceptualize the division of labor as sex-segregated. Is this true in practice as well? Do men and women spend their time in substantially different or similar types of activities?

Detailed data on the allocation of time by Nandi women and men were gathered in a time allocation study of eleven households during the course of nine months (April–December 1977), which covered the period from planting to harvest in one agricultural cycle. The Nandi Time Allocation Study used the so-called "random visits" method, which was pioneered by Barker and Wright (1955) in socialization studies of American children and has recently been popularized in social anthropological research by Allen Johnson (Johnson 1975). This method involves visiting certain households at times selected entirely at random and recording the activities of all household members (preferably before they become aware of the observer's presence). Statistically, if the total number of observations is large, the random observations should approximate the actual activity pattern of the group under study. In the Nandi Time Allocation Study, the daylight hours of the week were divided into 175 equal time periods, and each time period was assigned a three-digit number, using digits between one and six. The time periods for observations were chosen by a random sampling procedure. Each household was visited four times weekly, on different days, for two weeks out of each month. The activities of each household member were recorded on mimeographed forms. The purpose and procedure were explained to members of the study households, who agreed to participate. Eleven households (a total of 117 individuals: 20 circumcised males, 29 females aged 16 or older, and 68 children) were chosen as the study group. (These are the figures for regular household members who were present for most of the observations. When other short-term household members and long-term visitors are included, the numbers rise to 26 men, 40 women, and 97 children.) Selecting a random sample for the whole of the sublocation or even for one *kokwet* (neighborhood) would have made observations impossibly difficult in terms of travel time. Instead, it was decided to select a sample of households approximately matched to the characteristics of the total population, and within easy walking distance (up to half an hour) of the compound in which I resided. Time Allocation data on the activities of adult men and women are summarized in Tables 13 through 16.

It is clearly impossible to present data on the incidence of every particular chore or activity people may perform. For example, in subsistence production, what these tables reveal is the amount of time various categories of people spend working on particular *crops*, not the extent to which they carry out particular activities (such as plowing or weeding) in connection with the cultivation of these crops. Thus the full extent to which the Nandi allocation of tasks is sex-segregated is not displayed here. What can be seen are broad patterns of differences by sex in the allocation of time to various types of activities.

One category, "General farm and household," presents a particular problem to the analysis of the division of labor by sex because it includes under one heading a number of activities that are almost exclusively the province of women (carrying wood and water, laundry, mending, dishwashing, etc.) under the same heading with others that are almost the exclusive province of men (fencing, repairing tools and furniture, and destroying animal nuisances such as rats) and one activity (carrying cash produce such as tea leaves and milk to the pickup points of market-ing cooperatives or agencies) that is performed with almost equal frequency by members of both sexes. The category "House-work" includes three distinct categories: housecleaning and weekly plastering, food preparation, and preparing harvested food for storage. Originally the category "General farm and household" was meant to contain other tasks peripheral to basic production that were left over after these several large categories of activity were accounted for. This distribution of categories re-sulted from an attempt to avoid the Euro-American concept "housework" as an a priori construct in the data analysis, in the hope of constructing a set of categories that could be used cross-culturally.* From the point of view of the Nandi material, how-ever, this particular division is unfortunate because "housework" (*boisiet ab got*) is a salient category for modern Nandi-speakers, and means very much the same thing that it means in Euro-American culture.

The Time Allocation of Women and Men

When one adds together the first thirteen categories in Tables 13–16, one arrives at a figure for the percentage of time allocated to activities that might reasonably be considered "work" by most commonly used definitions of that term. It will be seen that adult males spend 37.8 percent of their time, while adult females spend 60.0 percent of their time, in work activities (Table 13). When only active, married adults are considered, the gap is nar-rowed somewhat: 47.7 percent for men, 67.8 percent for women. If we stretch the definition of "work" to include religious activi-ties, civic activities, and events and ceremonies, married men still spend only 55 percent of their time "working" as opposed to 70.1 percent for married women. The data presented in the tables are conclusive for this point: women work more hours than men.

Housework accounts for a larger proportion of women's time than any other single activity. This is true regardless of the

*The categories were devised together by me and Lorraine Dusak Sexton, who used the same categories in the analysis of time allocation data gathered among the Yamiyufa of the Daulo Pass region of Highland Papua New Guinea (Sexton 1980).

TABLE 13
Activities of Adults by Sex
(Circumcised Males and Females over Age 15)

Activity	Men (N=26)		Women (N=40)		Total	
	No. of observations	Pct. of all observations	No. of observations	Pct. of all observations	No. of observations	Pct. of all observations
Maize	74	5.0%	106	5.1%	180	5.1%
Vegetables/eleusine	25	1.7	62	3.0	87	2.4
Crop unknown	7	0.5	1	—	8	0.2
Tea	20	1.4	23	1.1	43	1.2
Animal husbandry	65	4.4	161	7.7	226	6.3
Farm business	16	1.1	3	0.1	19	0.5
FIRST SIX CATEGORIES		(14.1%)		(17.0%)		
Self-employment	79	5.4	62	3.0	141	4.0
Wage labor	159	10.8	9	0.4	168	4.7
Housebuilding	18	1.2	50	2.4	68	1.9
General farm/household	59	4.0	311	14.9	370	10.4
Housework	9	0.6	320	15.3	329	9.2
Child care	10	0.7	125	6.0	135	3.8
Shopping	15	1.0	22	1.0	37	1.0
FIRST THIRTEEN CATEGORIES		(37.8%)		(60.0%)		
Religious activities	22	1.4	19	0.9	41	1.2
Civic activities	35	2.4	4	0.2	39	1.1
Events and ceremonies	19	1.3	26	1.2	45	1.3
Study	99	6.7	59	2.8	158	4.4
Leisure	611	41.6	634	30.3	1,245	34.9
Sick/medical care	8	0.5	31	1.5	39	1.1
Whereabouts unknown	104	7.1	28	1.3	132	3.7
Other	18	1.2	37	1.8	55	1.6
TOTAL	1,472	100.0%	2,093	100.0%	3,565	100.0%

TABLE 14
Activities of Ever-Married, Active Adults

Activity	Men (N=15)[a]		Women (N=29)		Total	
	No. of observations	Pct. of all observations	No. of observations	Pct. of all observations	No. of observations	Pct. of all observations
Maize	58	6.0%	94	5.3%	152	5.5%
Vegetables/eleusine	22	2.3	58	3.2	80	2.9
Crop unknown	6	0.6	1	0.1	7	0.3
Tea	12	1.2	18	1.0	30	1.1
Animal husbandry	45	4.6	147	8.2	192	6.9
Farm business	15	1.5	3	0.2	18	0.6
FIRST SIX CATEGORIES		(16.2%)		(18.0%)		
Self-employment	73	7.5	61	3.4	134	4.8
Wage labor	140	14.4	3	0.2	143	5.2
Housebuilding	14	1.4	46	2.6	60	2.2
General farm/household	38	3.9	270	15.1	308	11.2
Housework	3	0.3	286	16.0	289	10.4
Child care	10	1.0	100	5.6	110	4.0
Shopping	10	1.0	18	1.0	28	1.0
FIRST THIRTEEN CATEGORIES		(45.7%)		(61.9%)		
Religious activities	22	2.3	13	0.7	35	1.3
Civic activities	31	3.2	4	0.2	35	1.3
Events and ceremonies	15	1.5	19	1.1	34	1.2
Study	2	0.2	3	0.2	5	0.2
Leisure	382	39.2	579	32.3	961	34.8
Sick/medical care	7	0.7	25	1.4	32	1.2
Whereabouts unknown	60	6.2	24	1.3	84	3.0
Other	9	0.9	17	0.9	26	0.9
TOTAL	974	100.0%	1,789	100.0%	2,763	100.0%

[a]Does not include men of the oldest age-set, chronological ages over 75.

TABLE 15
Women's Activities by Marital Status

Activity	Never married		Monogamous wives		Polygynous wives		Widows		Divorced/separated		Temporarily separated		Total	
	No. of obs.	Pct. of obs.	No. of obs.	Pct. of obs.	No. of obs.	Pct. of obs.	No. of obs.	Pct. of obs.	No. of obs.	Pct. of obs.	No. of obs.	Pct. of obs.	No. of obs.	Pct. of obs.
Maize	12	4.0%	53	6.1%	8	3.6%	24	5.1%	8	5.1%	1	1.3%	106	5.1%
Vegetables/eleusine	4	1.3	44	5.0	4	1.8	8	1.7	2	1.3	—	—	62	3.0
Crop unknown	—	—	1	0.1	—	—	—	—	—	—	—	—	1	—
Tea	5	1.7	13	1.5	1	0.5	2	0.4	2	1.3	—	—	23	1.1
Animal husbandry	14	4.7	75	8.6	21	9.5	46	9.8	4	2.6	1	1.3	161	7.7
Farm business	—	—	—	—	1	0.5	2	0.4	—	—	—	—	3	0.1
Self-employment	1	0.3	36	4.1	4	1.8	5	1.1	15	9.6	1	1.3	62	3.0
Wage labor	6	2.0	2	0.2	—	—	1	0.2	—	—	—	—	9	0.4
Housebuilding	4	1.3	21	2.4	3	1.4	14	3.0	7	4.5	1	1.3	50	2.4
General farm/household	41	13.8	150	17.2	32	14.4	56	12.0	22	14.0	10	13.3	311	14.9
Housework	34	11.4	144	16.4	43	19.6	58	12.4	24	15.1	17	22.7	320	15.3
Child care	25	8.4	71	8.1	—	—	9	1.9	5	3.2	15	20.0	125	6.0
Shopping	4	1.3	12	1.4	2	0.9	4	0.9	—	—	—	—	22	1.0
Religious activities	6	2.0	12	1.4	1	0.5	4	0.9	—	—	—	—	19	0.9
Civic activities	—	—	3	0.3	—	—	—	—	1	0.6	—	—	4	0.2
Events and ceremonies	7	2.3	7	0.8	2	0.9	9	1.9	1	0.6	—	—	26	1.2
Study	56	18.8	2	0.2	1	0.5	—	—	—	—	—	—	59	2.8
Leisure	55	18.4	195	22.4	88	40.0	209	44.7	62	39.5	25	33.4	634	30.3
Sick/medical care	6	2.0	11	1.3	1	0.5	11	2.4	—	—	2	2.7	31	1.5
Whereabouts unknown	4	1.3	7	0.8	6	2.7	9	1.9	2	1.3	—	—	28	1.3
Other	15	5.0	15	1.7	2	0.9	1	0.2	2	1.3	2	2.7	37	1.8
TOTAL	299	100.0%	874	100.0%	220	100.0%	468	100.0%	157	100.0%	75	100.0%	2,093	100.0%

TABLE 16
Active Men's Activities by Marital Status

Activity	Never married		Monogamous husbands		Polygynous husbands		Divorced/ separated		Total	
	No. of obs.	Pct. of obs.	No. of obs.	Pct. of obs.	No. of obs.	Pct. of obs.	No. of obs.	Pct. of obs.	No. of obs.	Pct. of obs.
Maize	15	3.6%	47	5.9%	6	5.1%	5	7.8%	73	5.2%
Vegetables/eleusine	3	0.7	18	2.3	3	2.5	1	1.6	25	1.8
Crop unknown	1	0.2	6	0.8	—	—	—	—	7	0.5
Tea	8	1.9	12	1.4	—	—	—	—	20	1.4
Animal husbandry	20	4.8	31	3.9	14	11.9	—	—	65	4.6
Farm business	1	0.2	15	1.9	—	—	—	—	16	1.1
Self-employment	6	1.4	70	8.8	1	0.9	2	3.1	79	5.6
Wage labor	19	4.5	140	17.6	—	—	—	—	159	11.4
Housebuilding	4	1.0	14	0.7	—	—	—	—	18	1.3
General farm/household	20	4.8	35	4.4	3	2.5	—	—	58	4.1
Housework	6	1.4	1	0.1	2	1.7	—	—	9	0.6
Child care	—	—	9	1.1	—	—	1	1.6	10	0.7
Shopping	5	1.3	10	1.2	1	0.9	—	—	15	1.1
Religious activities	—	—	21	2.6	2	1.7	—	—	22	1.6
Civic activities	4	1.0	29	3.6	3	2.5	—	—	35	2.5
Events and ceremonies	4	1.0	11	1.4	—	—	1	1.6	19	1.4
Study	97	23.2	2	0.2	—	—	—	—	99	7.1
Leisure	159	37.9	272	34.1	66	55.9	44	68.7	541	38.7
Sick/medical care	1	0.2	4	0.5	3	2.5	—	—	8	0.6
Whereabouts unknown	43	10.3	40	5.0	12	10.2	8	12.5	103	7.4
Other	3	0.7	11	1.4	2	1.7	2	3.1	18	1.3
TOTAL	419	100.0%	798	100.0%	118	100.0%	64	100.0%	1,399	100.0%

NOTE: Data for one man in the study, who was blind, senile, and almost totally inactive, are excluded. Data shown here are for the four youngest male age-sets only.

woman's status. Housework and child care are definitely *not* the province of adult men: only 1.3 percent of men's time is spent in these activities. Even if the activities included in "General farm and household" are counted, men spend only 5.3 percent of their time in such activities. Instances of men performing domestic tasks or child care include several observations of young men holding or carrying their infant children, one observation of a man washing his own clothes, one of a man sewing a button on his own shirt, another of an old man spreading his bed-clothes in the sun to dry, and a handful of other observations that I am unable to recall in specific detail. The point is that they are rare enough to be memorable. By contrast, 36.2 percent of women's time (40.1 percent of married women's time) is spent in these activities. This is far more than the amount of time either sex devotes to basic production.

Wage labor and self-employment (contract labor or cash-generating entrepreneurial activities) account for the largest single category of time for adult men. This is especially true in the case of married men (21.9 percent), and markedly so for monogamists (26.4 percent). Among the married men regularly surveyed there were three full-time wage laborers (a primary teacher, the accounts clerk for the local secondary school, and a lorry driver for the Kenya Ministry of Works) and one part-time wage-laborer (a tractor driver). One of the never-married men was also employed part time as a tractor driver.

The relatively high level of self-employment and contract labor reflects a pattern typical of the young men of this community. Crosschecking some of the census data by observation reveals that this category is frequently underreported. People either forget about some of their money-making activities when asked directly, or don't consider them significant enough to mention. It is true to a greater extent than is commonly realized that most men have some cash-getting activity other than farming, and that they spend considerable amounts of time at such activities. The most usual form of contract labor is plowing and weeding for large landholders, but fencing and other general work around farm compounds have also been observed. One man in the study group was occasionally employed as a passenger vehicle conductor. Entrepreneurial activities of the men in the study group include cattle trading, buying and selling vegetables and eggs, dredging sand from rivers and cleaning it to sell for making concrete, and making charcoal for sale. Of the ten regularly surveyed Sawe and Kipkoimet men, only two were not observed doing work for cash, and one of these is known to do so at other times. One Chuma man in the study group was the proprietor of a beerhall and was occasionally observed supervising its operation.

Thus men as a group, particularly young men, have access, through regular participation in either wage labor or petty entrepreneurship, to significant amounts of cash. Women (wives) do not have any well-defined rights in men's (husbands') personal earnings. Women also sometimes engage in petty entrepreneurship, but the amounts of money they control thereby are small compared with those controlled by men.

Adult women as a group spend a small but significant portion of their time (3 percent) in cash-generating activities. It might be supposed that divorced and separated women, with no man to provide them with cash, would spend significantly more of their time at such activities, but this is not the case. Though one of the permanently separated women in the study was a very active businesswoman who made a not unconsiderable profit from brewing, the others were less active on the average in cash-generating activities than were married women. These women were contributors to the household economies of the compounds in which they lived, and were supported by them. Eleven of the seventeen married women in the study, on the other hand, engaged at some time in work for cash, giving an average figure of 3.7 percent for married women's time spent in such activities. The nature of entrepreneurship varied with the women's ages. The three from the oldest groups brewed. Since most of the younger women are Christians belonging to fundamentalist denominations, brewing for them is not a cash-getting option. Three women between the ages of 25 and 35 were engaged in selling their own produce. Two of these women sold so little as to be almost insignificant, but the third, toward the end of my field stay, was using her profits to embark on the venture of buying and selling eleusine. In the youngest age group, one woman engaged in the business of buying and selling beans, and four did weeding of the crops of large landholders on a contract basis.

Although there are some women wage laborers in this community (a few teachers, a typist for the local secondary school, a cook/waitress/dishwasher at the local café), they are an exception to the norm, and except for one unmarried woman who worked briefly at the café, none was regularly included in the study group. In fact, female wage laborers are so few that it is probably better that they be left out of consideration entirely, from the standpoint of having the study group represent the community as a whole. The figures presented here relate to the activities of typical rural women who are not wage laborers.

Women spend more time in basic production than men do, but the difference is only slight. All adult men spend 13 percent of their time in cultivation and animal husbandry, compared with 16.9 percent for all adult women. Among married people the figures are 15 percent for men and 20.2 percent for women. In cultivation alone, women's and men's contributions in terms of time are roughly equal: 8.6 percent as against 9.2 percent for all men and women, 10.1 percent to 11.4 percent for married men and women. These comparisons live up to the expressed ideal that men and women should spend approximately equal hours in the fields. Women spend slightly more time than do men in cultivating crops that are not major cash crops (i.e. vegetables/eleusine), but again the differences are too small to be significant. Women and men spend approximately equal amounts of time in cultivating maize and tea, the main cash crops.

Adults of both sexes have relatively short agricultural work weeks. In the context of other studies of production in African societies (e.g., those cited by Boserup 1970 and Pala 1975*b*), it may seem surprising that married women spent only 11.4 percent of total observation time engaged in cultivation. This percentage of time amounts to an average of only 1.5 hours a day for a seven-day week, or 2.1 hours a day for a five-day week. People usually report that it is their habit to go to the fields by 8:00 A.M. and not to return before noon. However, this refers only to those days on which they go to the fields at all, and there are many reasons for a woman to stay home from her fields on a given day. The hardest-working woman in the study group (as acknowledged by other women) customarily went to the fields five days a week during the peak agricultural season (which for her included a vegetable-growing season after the weeding of maize had been finished). The sixth day she stayed home to do laundry, and the seventh was the Sabbath. Nevertheless, this woman did *not* work in the fields five days a week, every week; various special events (shopping, business trips, visits, etc.) sometimes intervened. When all these factors are taken into account, it is clear that her typical agricultural work week was rarely more (and often less) than 20 hours a week, or an average of three hours a day.

For other, less active women, other things interfere with agricultural work more often. Women have the responsibility of herding cattle while children are in school, or at all times in families where there is no child old enough for this work. It is also frequently women who take the cattle to be dipped, for innoculations, or to be served by the government artificial insemination service. This is especially true in families where the husband is a wage laborer or spends substantial amounts of time in some form of self-employment. Women may stay home on various days to do domestic chores and leave their afternoon free for some other purpose. A trip to the local dispensary (in the next sublocation), either to be treated oneself or to take a child for treatment, takes up a full day. Therefore, when all is considered, the low number of observations of agricultural labor is not so very surprising. The average married woman's agricultural work week (in cultivation alone) is 10.5 hours. When the care of animals (herding, milking, taking them to the dip, etc.) as well as of crops is taken into account, married women are engaged in farm production almost 18 hours a week. Married men's average agricultural work week, in cultivation alone, is 8.8 hours. If the care of animals is included, married men spend an average of 13 hours per week in basic farm production.

Adult men are much more active than adult women in civic activities (2.4 percent of observations vs. 0.2 percent). In the case of married adults, this difference is even clearer (3.4 percent vs. 0.3 percent). This category includes participation in public meetings, participation in meetings of committees directing community projects, and work on projects such as the building of a piped water system. None of the women regularly surveyed in this study was a member of a Harambee project committee. In the sublocation as a whole, a handful of women are members of such committees, usually school committees. Women in general attend larger community meetings only as observers, and in a year and a half of residence in the community I never once saw or heard of a woman participating in a community work project. The nonparticipation of Nandi women in community work projects stands in marked contrast to reports of women's frequent participation in such projects in other parts of Kenya (Pala 1975*b*).

Both married women and married men have less leisure time than average for all adult women and men. However, in both the cases of all adults and of married persons only, men have significantly more leisure than women. Adult men spend 41.6 percent of their time in leisure activities, compared with 30.3 percent for adult women. Married men spend 36.9 percent of their time in leisure, compared with 25.9 percent for married women. Men also have more observations in the "Whereabouts unknown" category. Doubtless in some of these cases the men whose whereabouts were unknown were actually engaged in some form of work somewhere unknown to members of their households, but I suspect that they were more frequently engaged in a leisure activity, such as visiting at the home of an age-mate.

Two points, that women spend more time than do men caring for animals and the small amount of time (6.5 percent of observations) spent by married women in child care, may seem surprising. The ethnographic literature contains a widespread assumption that among pastoralist/cultivators it is usually the women who do the cultivating while men are responsible for herding. This type of division of labor has also been presented as characteristic of the "traditional" Nandi (Huntingford 1950:39). It is also commonly assumed that almost everywhere women have primary responsibility for child care, which is a time-consuming task. The way in which observations were counted in this study, precedence in coding being given to productive activities other than child care when they were combined with child care, leads to an underestimation of the amount of time women actually spend in child care.* But even if all cases in which child care was taking place were counted as primarily cases of child care, the figure for the percentage of time women spend in child care would, I think, still be surprisingly small.

The very important, though undervalued, contribution of children to subsistence explains these two unexpected aspects of the data. Although this chapter is devoted to the differing contributions of men and women to the production of the family estate, it would be incomplete if it did not consider the productive role of children. As I have suggested earlier, the contribution of children to the family welfare is overlooked by the adult Nandi people whom I interviewed. Yet as Tables 3 and 4 (Chapter 3), showing the preliminary results obtained in the first nine weeks of the Nandi Time Allocation Study, indicate, from the age of seven and up to the age of eighteen in the case of girls and fifteen in the case of boys, children bear an average workload comparable to that of married men. Indeed, many of the categories of children shown in these tables spend *longer* hours in "work" activities than do married men. Moreover, this participation in production and activities supportive of production is entirely aside from and greatly exceeds the time these children spend at school or doing schoolwork. Only in the case of boarding students do hours spent in school exceed those spent in production and domestic labor.

The work of herding cattle, sheep, and goats is overwhelmingly performed by children. During the first five months of the time allocation study, children between the ages of seven and fifteen accounted for 122 of a total 210 observations of cattle herding; 82 of these observations were accounted for by boys and 40 by girls (Oboler 1977a:21). Girls between the ages of seven and nine account for over half the total observations of shepherding (22 of 40), and children between the ages of four and six account for eight more (Oboler 1977a:21).

Child care is another category of work that is performed pri-

---

*If a person was holding a child while engaged in another "work" activity, the observation was counted as an example of the other activity (though the presence of the child was noted). If child care accompanied a "leisure" activity, such as conversation, the observation was counted as child care rather than as leisure.

marily by children—though in this case it is almost exclusively girls who are involved. During the first five months of the time allocation study, girls between the ages of four and twelve accounted for 76 of 124 observations of child care. Girls between the ages of seven and nine were particularly engaged in this task, accounting for 43 of these observations. Adult women were the next most active group (27 of 124), followed by girls between the ages of thirteen and eighteen (17 of 124). Only 4 of the 124 observations of child care were of males of any age (Oboler 1977*a*:21). (It is of course true that an adult woman usually supervises the care of infants and toddlers by older children, in the sense of being within calling distance should an emergency arise. Thus, women may be regarded as ultimately responsible for child care, though not immediately involved in it.)

The labor of children, then, is extremely important in the Nandi economy. However, adults of both sexes, in their willingness to describe all tasks as the primary preserve of either men or women, systematically undervalue the economic contribution of children.

The shortness of the average Nandi agricultural work week is a point that needs further elaboration. The average married woman in this data set spends about 10.5 hours a week in cultivation alone, or almost 18 hours a week in basic production if animal husbandry is included. The average married man spends 8.8 hours a week in cultivation alone, or 13 hours a week in agricultural production including animal husbandry. These hours seem remarkably short, in contrast to the work weeks of 15–20 or even 25 hours cited by Boserup (1970:20–22). Achola Pala cites women she studied in Kisumu district as budgeting between three and eight hours a day to agricultural labor (Pala 1975*b*:6). This would result in a minimum agricultural work week of 18 hours.

It may be that most of the studies cited by Boserup deal with exclusively horticultural societies, where cattle are not part of the economy. Nandi women's 18 hour work week in cultivation plus animal care would then be comparable to the typical 15–20 hour work week Boserup cites for other societies. Yet there does seem to be a big difference between the workloads of Nandi women and those of the Luo women studied by Pala. The Luo women, who spent approximately 18 hours a week in cultivation, also estimated that they spent equal amounts of time looking after cattle (Pala 1975b:6). The combination of time spent in cultivation and time spent in animal husbandry thus results in an estimate of about 35 hours a week, *minimum*, spent by Luo women in basic production. It therefore appears to be the case that Luo women, at least, work much harder in basic production than do Nandi of either sex.

To some extent, this discrepancy between the Nandi and Luo data is, I believe, explained by regional economic inequalities.* According to Edgar Winans (1972) women's workloads have been found to be heavier primarily in areas of small landholdings and small-scale unproductive agriculture (quoted in Pala 1975b:2). Nandi is an area of general affluence, of low population density compared with neighboring areas, high-quality soil and plentiful rainfall, and, in general, of lack of need for intensive cultivation of the relatively large landholdings. It is also true that many of the larger Nandi landholders employ permanent and contract laborers from other ethnic groups for agricultural labor. Such laborers were not included in the time allocation study. It may be that general affluence, relatively nonintensive production, and the use of non-Nandi labor in combination account for the low average Nandi agricultural work week.

Time Allocation and Economic Inequality

The foregoing analysis implies that the general affluence of Nandi, and the fact that many Nandi households employ non-Nandi labor, partly account for differences in time allocation patterns between the Nandi and some neighboring ethnic groups. The importance of such factors can be assessed by looking at their effect *within* this data set. To what extent do the more affluent households in the time allocation sample differ from the less affluent households in terms of their members' use of time?

Originally, the time allocation study was designed to reveal something about the Nandi sexual division of labor. Data were

---

*Possibly, too, Luo women's estimates of their work time are slightly exaggerated by unconscious bias in self-reporting. But even if this is the case, it could hardly account for all of the wide discrepancy.

collected on the activities of all persons defined in household census responses as members of households, as well as long- and short-term visitors. Later, I became interested in comparing what these figures had to say about the typical Nandi household economy with similar figures collected in other societies. The problem with such comparisons is that in some of the households from which these figures are taken, major contributions to the household economy are made by persons *who are not defined as members of the household.* This fact naturally has an important impact upon the activities of those persons who *are* defined as household members. It is a not uncommon practice for Nandi landholders, who may be in control of larger tracts of land than can easily be put to full use by members of their own households, to have landless (usually Abaluhyia) tenants. In return for their labor in cultivating the landholder's cash crops, these tenants are allowed to cultivate some land for their own subsistence and are also usually paid a small wage. Once again, it is clear that it is impossible to assess the effects of social change on Nandi or any other ethnic group as though that group constituted a closed system.

Census figures (Table 17) show that the majority of households in the research community employ *some* nonhousehold labor, but in 35 cases this labor is only one or two persons used on a very occasional basis for jobs such as harvesting, breaking ground for vegetables or eleusine, or picking tea. One impact of the cash economy has been that to a certain extent cash has replaced reciprocal social obligations in the recruitment of larger than household work-groups for short-term tasks. The employment of such occasional helpers does not replace household labor and does not have a significant impact on the division of labor. But almost one-third of the households in the research community *do* employ amounts of labor that to some extent replace the labor of household members.

Because of the resident-laborer system it seemed that a more significant comparison would be gained by using time allocation figures only from the Nandi households that did not employ nonhousehold labor as the basis for comparison with figures on labor inputs from other societies. In households that do not employ nonhousehold labor, the average work week of married

TABLE 17
Hired Labor in 115 Random Sample Census Households

Type of labor	None or little	Significant
No non-household labor	44	
1–2 occasional contract laborers	35	
More than 2 contract laborers		12
1 full-time laborer only		4
1 full-time laborer plus some contract		13
More than 1 full-time laborer plus contract		7
TOTAL	79	36

women in basic production turns out to be 19.8 hours, a figure more in keeping with those presented by Boserup and Pala. Dividing the data set in this way, however, is at least equally interesting for the internal comparisons thus generated.

Households that do not employ labor other than that of their own members tend to be the poorest households. They tend to have fewer animals, smaller landholdings, and less income from cash cropping. Comparison of time allocation among members of such households with that of members of more affluent households reveals incipient class differences that have important implications for the relative positions of men and women. Table 18 presents comparative figures on activities of adult male and female household members in "elite" households (households that regularly employ nonhousehold labor in addition to that of household members) and in households that rely on the labor of household members only. The presence of nonhousehold labor, for this table and the subsequent discussion, is assumed to be an index of a household's general economic status.

The advent of the cash economy has meant, for women, a somewhat greater workload and less control over the product of their labor. It can be seen from the data presented in Table 18 that this trend is exacerbated in less affluent households. Where landholdings are smaller, there is less income from cash cropping. Husbands in these cases are likely to spend more time working in other ways for cash. Table 18 shows that in fact married men in the less affluent time allocation study households spent 24.1 percent of their time in cash-gaining activities, as compared with 15.6 percent of time for those in the more afflu-

TABLE 18

Activities of Married Adults by Household Status as Employer of Labor

| | Households with farm employees | | | | Households without farm employees | | | | Total | |
| | Married men | | Married women | | Married men | | Married women | | | |
Activity	No. of obs.	Pct. of obs.	No. of obs.	Pct. of obs.	No. of obs.	Pct. of obs.	No. of obs.	Pct. of obs.	No. of obs.	Pct. of obs.
Maize	14	4.7%	14	3.7%	39	5.8%	49	6.7%	116	5.6%
Vegetables/eleusine	2	0.7	12	3.2	19	2.8	36	4.9	69	3.3
Crop unknown	3	1.0	—	—	3	0.4	1	0.1	7	0.3
Tea	5	1.7	3	0.8	7	1.0	11	1.5	26	1.2
Animal husbandry	24	8.0	28	7.4	21	3.1	69	9.4	142	6.8
Farm business	9	3.0	1	0.3	6	0.9	—	—	16	0.8
Self-employment	22	7.3	6	1.6	49	7.2	34	4.6	111	5.3
Wage labor	25	8.3	—	—	115	16.9	2	0.3	142	6.8
Housebuilding	10	3.3	13	3.5	4	0.6	11	1.5	38	1.8
General farm/household	17	5.7	74	19.7	22	3.3	112	15.3	225	10.8
Housework	1	0.3	61	16.3	2	0.3	127	17.4	191	9.2
Child care	—	—	8	2.1	9	1.3	64	8.7	81	3.9
Shopping	3	1.0	9	2.4	7	1.0	6	0.8	25	1.2
Religious activities	7	2.3	6	1.6	15	2.2	7	1.0	35	1.7
Civic activities	9	3.0	3	0.8	22	3.2	—	—	34	1.6
Events and ceremonies	6	2.0	4	1.1	8	1.2	5	0.7	23	1.1
Study	2	0.7	2	0.6	—	—	—	—	4	0.2
Leisure	118	39.3	110	29.3	283	41.6	177	24.2	688	33.0
Sick/medical care	3	1.0	2	0.6	4	0.6	10	1.4	19	0.9
Whereabouts unknown	16	5.3	5	1.3	36	5.3	8	1.1	65	3.1
Other	4	1.3	14	3.7	9	1.3	3	0.4	30	1.4
TOTAL	300	100.0%	375	100.0%	680	100.0%	732	100.0%	2,087	100.0%

ent households. Wives in poorer households spent 22.6 percent of their time in basic production, as compared with 15.1 percent for wives in elite households.

Participation in a cash economy, and the need for cash that most households now feel, pushes men into cash-generating activities—petty entrepreneurship if not actual participation in the wage labor force. This is particularly true for men with small landholdings, for whom cash-cropping cannot produce large incomes. Men who devote much time to cash-gaining activities spend less time in basic production. In elite households, hired labor takes up the slack left by a husband's lowered participation in production. In poorer households this slack is taken up by the wife. In neither case do wives have substantial control of the resources their husbands' labor brings into the household, but in poorer households, unlike the more affluent ones, wives must work harder to enable their husbands to control more resources. The widening of the economic gap between the sexes produced by integration into the national cash economy is thus felt more strongly by women in less affluent Nandi households than by women in elite households.

The data in Table 18 also show that wives in elite households spend less time than their poorer counterparts in child care (2.1 percent vs. 8.7 percent). I believe this is because wealthier households are more likely to be able to support a *cheplakwet* (child nurse).

Colonialism and economic change have brought to Nandi, as to other parts of the Third World, the process of class formation. This process is accelerated as large landholders use surplus income from their cash crops to enlarge their holdings at the expense of their poorest neighbors, who frequently must sell land to meet immediate cash obligations. For some, particularly in land-poor areas, the ultimate outcome is landlessness and perhaps the status of tenant laborers to large landholders (as many landless Luhyia have become tenants to landed Nandi). And because the landlord can use the tenant's labor to increase his profits and further extend his holdings, the process is self-feeding.

Changes in Time Allocation

The process of class formation frequently leads to a widening of the gap not only between rich and poor but also between men and women. Though we lack detailed and reliable information about men's and women's activities in the precolonial period, oral history texts collected from elderly Nandi informants by Gold (1977) give some idea of how time was allocated:

> Young girls and boys worked around the homestead, the girls helping with the domestic duties, but not cooking, and the boys looking after sheep and goats. Teenage boys and girls cultivated, while girls did domestic work and milked cattle in the far pastures, and the boys herded livestock. . . . The tasks considered most male were herding, hunting, guarding, raiding and slaughtering. The tasks considered most female were child care, cooking and cleaning. But in normal times, both men and women cultivated and cared for the livestock. Women milked, cared for the calves, sheep and goats, kept close to home, and cleaned the animals' sleeping places. Both men and women ploughed, planted, weeded and harvested the crops. The men cleared virgin land and the women cleared the fields which had already been cultivated. [Gold 1977:9.]

Any assessment of the degree to which the division of labor or time allocation has changed depends on one's interpretation of what it formerly was. Unfortunately, there is no one clear and agreed-upon interpretation of the precolonial division of labor for Nandi.

G. W. B. Huntingford, the best known authority on Nandi, is highly committed in his published accounts to the accuracy for Nandi of the male herding–female farming model of the division of labor in semipastoral societies. He limits men's traditional participation in horticulture to clearing brush, planting, and harvesting (1950:61) and comments that adult men spent the bulk of their time watching their herds or supervising the care of their cattle, an activity that looked like "doing nothing" to a European observer (1950:39): "Men do the preliminary work of clearing bushes and trees, though most of the digging is done by the women, and though men do a good deal of agricultural work nowadays, agriculture is still held to be mainly women's work. Twenty-five years ago, Nandi men very seldom used a hoe; now many of them cultivate the ground, not only when working for Europeans, but in their own plots" (Huntingford 1950:61).

Gold and I, working in different parts of Nandi District in the mid-1970's, both got similar reports from elderly people that conflict with the account given by Huntingford. Informants in their late sixties to early eighties, questioned on the typical division of labor during their childhood and young adulthood (a period roughly between 1900 and 1925), reported that it was customary for husbands and wives to go to the fields together to weed.* Some of my informants, moreover, when asked whether husband or wife did more of the work of cultivation, said that the husband did, since the wife left early to prepare the midday meal. A few of my informants said that women who were under postpartum restrictions dictated by feminine-child pollution (see Chapter 3) were forbidden to work in the fields. These informants maintained that in this case the woman's husband did the bulk of the work of cultivation.

To what extent are Gold's and my informants idealizing past behavior in terms of present expectations? To what extent were Huntingford's early observations colored by what he expected to see in a "pastoral" society? These questions, of course, cannot be answered definitively, but some clues to the source of this discrepancy may be available.

Bonnie Kettel (1980) argues cogently that all the Kalenjin are essentially highland, cultivating people among whom pastoralism as a mode of production predominates only in peripheral settings. Gold (1978) has argued for Nandi that predominant pastoralism was a transient phenomenon characterizing a brief historical period. The tendency of East African peoples (particularly Kalenjin peoples) to define themselves as predominantly pastoralists in the face of overwhelming evidence to the contrary has been noted by several commentators (Sutton 1968; Conant 1974; Kettel 1980). Conant mentions that though Pokotland has 75,000 farmers and only 25,000 herders, all Pokot regard themselves as pastoralists (Conant 1974:266). Probably Huntingford's Nandi informants also drew an idealized picture of themselves as pastoralists and the extent to which pastoralism dominated

---

*A few of my informants—an extreme minority—said that men mainly cared for cattle and were not active in cultivation. I cannot really account for this discrepancy. It is possible that there was some regional variation in the division of labor. One elderly Kipsigis woman told me that Kipsigis, unlike Nandi men, did not cultivate. She viewed this as one characteristic differentiating the two ethnic groups.

their economy. As I have pointed out, a part of the "pastoral ideology" is that men are responsible for cattle. It should be made clear that Huntingford's statement that "agriculture is still held to be mainly women's work" (Huntingford 1950:61) is an assertion about ideology, not about the actual division of labor. Whether his statement that men formerly rarely used hoes reflects informants' reports or his own observations is not clear.

The importance of cattle in the Nandi economy is a source of considerable confusion in the existing literature. It has been shown that recorded Nandi cattle/people ratios varied between 0.5 to one and 4.3 to one, a range typical of East African semipastoralists. The low point in the cattle/people ratio followed a rinderpest epidemic of the late 1890's.* The 1932 high point was reached because new sources of cash income reaching the Reserve (e.g. army salaries, ex-soldiers' pensions, squatters' wages) were immediately translated into cattle. The acquisition of European cattle and land enclosure led to a dramatic reduction of herds, so that the cattle/people ratio is now approximately one to one. It is therefore clear that neither the precolonial cattle/people ratio nor the degree of Nandi former commitment to pastoralism as a way of life can be viewed as a steady state. Human society is a historical process, and ethnography that does not make a deliberate attempt to take a historical view frequently results in misinterpretation.

In the case of the Nandi division of labor, several points must be considered.

1. Huntingford's interpretation of the Nandi subsistence system is based upon observation at a time of peak herd size.

2. The 4.3-to-one cattle/people ratio probably represents a small proportion of extremely large herds, and a large proportion of smaller ones, rather than consistently large herds.

3. Even at this point, the cattle/people ratio was not unusually large, though it was in the high range for cultivating pastoralists.

4. Several authors have shown that East African semipastoralists typically overemphasize the importance of pastoralism in their economies.

---

*The cattle/people ratio actually plunged lower than this after the capture of Nandi cattle by the 1905 British punitive expedition.

5. In view of this, informants idealizing the past would be unlikely to underplay a subsistence system based on male herding.

6. The "chronic Nandi grain shortage" problem so entrenched in the colonial record may be taken as evidence that the Nandi were unused to depending upon cultivation. However, Ellis (1976:558) has interpreted this as a transient phenomenon resulting from the upheavals of resettling the Nandi into the Reserve. To what extent Nandi chronically failed to cultivate sufficient grain remains a moot point.

7. As a colonial officer and headmaster of the government school, Huntingford probably had only limited interaction with nonelite individuals. His conclusions may be based upon observations of the wealthier households, whose members were likely to be his chief associates.

The conclusion to which I am led by these points is that it is likely that Huntingford's interpretation of the division of labor around 1925 is biased against seeing the extent to which men participated in cultivation. He argues in several places that Nandi subsistence was formerly much like that of the Maasai (1950:49). I believe it is clear that this was never the case. But believing that it was so, Huntingford could not be expected to investigate thoroughly men's role in horticulture. His elite informants were probably large stock-owners, and it may have been they he observed "doing nothing" (1950:39). Further, their own view of themselves as predominantly pastoralists probably led them, in the course of interviews, to reinforce his interpretation.*

Gold's account of the precolonial Nandi division of labor is thus more convincing than Huntingford's. There has probably been no radical shift from a "pastoral" division of labor, in which men herd and women cultivate, to an "agricultural" one in which cultivation is done by both sexes. Gold's account, of course, does not answer the question of how much time various categories of persons spent in various activities. Comparison of present time allocation with that presumed to have characterized the precolonial period must for now be based on speculation.

Weeding is the most time-consuming task in the process of

---

*Could there be further confusion in interviews between the dual meanings of the term *murenik* (men/warriors), so that assertions about "the work of warriors" are taken as assertions about "the work of men"?

cultivation. If married men participated in this task during the precolonial period, there was probably no great difference between the amount of time husband and wife spent in cultivation. Then, as now, little of the herding was done by married adults of either sex, but I believe it is reasonable to assume that aside from milking, men were somewhat more active than women in the care of livestock. The pastoral ideology that associates the care of livestock with men may be an exaggeration, yet it probably has *some* basis in observable phenomena rather than being in direct contradiction to them. Today, adult women spend more time caring for livestock than do adult men, which reflects men's decreasing pastoral role.

Cattle herding nowadays is a very easy task that involves merely watching the animals and turning them aside if they begin grazing toward a cultivated plot, driving them to water when it is time to drink, and to the dip once or twice a week. It is a job that can be done by anyone over a certain minimum age. What was formerly the work of warriors has been delegated to little boys and girls. The "warriors" are left with much more time for pure socializing, plus marriage and the adoption of the economic roles of married men at a much younger age.

Women, too, are marrying at a much earlier age and often move directly to nuclear family situations, maintaining their own (relatively) separate dwellings and economic activities rather than participating in their mothers-in-laws' work forces. Where formerly there was a large female work force in the average homestead, with adolescent girls and young wives participating in domestic labor under the supervision of an older woman, there are now several small, relatively independent establishments. In the precolonial period, as now, females, rather than males, certainly did almost all the "housework," but since there was less to be done then, and there was also more help available from adolescent girls, married women did rather less in the house than they do now. Today there are more dishes and utensils to wash, more items in a house to be maintained, lamps to be cleaned, furniture to be moved for regular plastering, constant laundry, mending, ironing, and so on. It is true that some modern improvements, like piped water, grain mills, and the convenience of buying, rather than having to make, tools, clothing, eating utensils, may cut down the workload in some instances; but few family compounds have piped water as yet, and though it is more pleasant, it is doubtful that carrying grain to the mill and waiting to have it ground is much less time consuming than grinding it by hand. And in the old days, manufacturing was not really part of exclusively feminine domestic labor, as men were also involved in the making of tools, small items of furniture, and so on. On balance, work defined as "housework" and relegated almost exclusively to women and girls is more time consuming now than it was in the precolonial period.

The precolonial division of labor, in which men and women (husbands and wives) participated in cultivation and manufacture, though it meant that women spent less time on domestic work and men were more active than women in herding and the care of animals, was probably not dramatically favorable to men. It was certainly not equal; from informants' accounts, I infer that Nandi women have always worked harder (in terms of time allocated) than men. Men undoubtedly had more clear-cut leisure than did women. The gap between married women's labor and that of married men today is very wide, however: 67.8 percent as opposed to 47.7 percent of time devoted to clear-cut work activities. I believe that participation in the cash economy has increased the workloads of members of both sexes, but women's somewhat more than men's.

In the area of cultivating, there have been both gains and losses in time. The old staple crop, eleusine, is not planted in neat rows, as maize is, and weeding is slow and difficult, requiring more time per equivalent spatial unit (though the maize yield from each unit is also greater than the yield of eleusine). Furthermore, maize can be replanted in the same ground several years in succession, whereas a new plot must be cleared for each crop of eleusine. On the other hand, near-universal cash-cropping of maize means that each family cultivates far more maize than it needs for its own subsistence. Thus there has probably been a net increase in person-hours spent in cultivation of maize vs. eleusine. Not all these person-hours are contributed by members of a household, however. Much of the time formerly spent preparing ground has been eliminated for two-thirds of households by investing cash-crop profits in hiring tractors. Census figures reveal that only 31.3 percent of households in the research community prepared ground for planting without the use of a tractor and driver, and one-third of the households employed significant amounts of nonhousehold labor (see Table 18).

These factors, taken together, probably come close to canceling one another out. The average amount of time currently spent by members of both sexes in cultivation is 10.4 percent, or 9.1 hours per week (11.7 percent or 10.2 hours per week when only members of nonelite households are considered). It can hardly have been much less than this at any time in the past for a people who were even partly dependent upon cultivation for subsistence. Cash cropping has therefore probably not increased the amount of time married Nandi adults spend in cultivation of the major crop. For members of elite households, it has probably decreased the amount of time spent in cultivation.

Other factors stemming from integration into the national cash economy have had the effect of increasing workloads, however. As men move into cash-generating activities, women have to take up the slack left in areas where men's participation was formerly greater. In households where less income is from cash cropping and where men therefore spend most of their time in cash-generating activities (the nonelite cases), women spend more time than men in cultivation and far more in animal care. Furthermore, these same women are obliged, under the demands of modern lifestyles, to earn a certain (albeit small) amount of cash. In many families, particularly those in which money is in short supply, the mother is the one who is responsible for providing school fees for her children's primary education, while the father provides secondary fees. This was a reason female informants often cited for brewing. Further, as I have pointed out, "modern" housekeeping is more time consuming than was "traditional" housekeeping.

The various changes that have come about in the Nandi division of labor and time allocation between the precolonial period and the present may be summarized briefly.

1. Integration into the cash economy has brought with it a net increase in the workloads of both sexes.

2. This net increase is not accounted for simply by increased

labor demands of cash-cropping. Near-universal cash-cropping does bring cash into the community and creates a market for male labor in nonagricultural activities. Husbands' work for cash leaves slack in the household division of labor to be taken up by wives, who now also spend more time in housekeeping. The specific nature of the impact of cash cropping in Nandi depends upon the existence of a pool of cheap labor, the legacy of the colonial policies described in Chapter 5.

3. Women's workload has increased somewhat more than men's.

4. In spite of their increased workload, women's control over the product of their labor has decreased. Women spend far more of their time on maize, tea, and cattle—the products of which are theirs only as items of family consumption, and as commodities are controlled by men—than on crops in which they have rights of control. In fact, except in the case of the elite, women spend more time on male-controlled resources than men themselves do. Married women spend a few hours a week in cash-generating activities, and they do control the money thus earned, but their earnings are minuscule compared with those of men.

5. All the above points characterize the two-thirds of households I have labeled "nonelite" to a greater degree than the one-third of "elite" households.

Thus both sexes are working harder (at least among the non-elite majority) as the result of entry into the cash economy. Men, however, see a far greater return for their increased labor, in terms of the resources they are thereby enabled to control, than women ever do. The discrepancy between the cash resources controlled by men and women is detailed in the following section.

Men's and Women's Incomes

Men usually control their own cash incomes, and male household heads control income from major cash crops. Women control any cash gained by the sale of produce from their vegetable gardens, but since there are few outlets for vegetables (unless a woman is a very large producer with a contract to supply an institution or a retailer in Eldoret or Kisumu), the income is small. Women also keep chickens, mainly for domestic consumption, and they can sell eggs and chickens when they need extra cash. But the local market for poultry and eggs is even more limited than the market for vegetables, and since other markets are difficult to reach and hardly worth the bother for the amount of profit that can be made, chickens and eggs are not at all a good source of income for women.* Brewing, as I have mentioned earlier, was historically a good source of income for women, but is reported to have diminished greatly because of the disapproval of the Moi government.†

The incomes that can be derived from male-controlled resources (maize, milk, and tea) are far greater than those from female-controlled resources (vegetables, chickens, sale of a part of the household milk, and brewing). The returns indicated here are rough approximations. Though reliable figures on returns to producers are given in the Ministry of Agriculture Annual Reports for some districts, they are not given for Nandi. The figures I use, then, are based on published information for districts other than Nandi and for years other than 1977. In all cases, I use figures that underestimate rather than overestimate the returns that can be realized in Nandi, and minimize rather than maximize income differences between men and women. I make no claims for the accuracy of specific figures, though I do consider that they reveal accurately the gender-differential in income. Elsewhere (Oboler 1982:334–36) I explain in detail how my estimates for returns per acre for various crops were derived. The estimated returns for various crops are shown in Table 19.

It seems, as a conservative estimate, that 0.14 acre of maize is

*The story of a short-lived poultry upgrading program run by the Veterinary Department in the 1940's has been told in Chapter 5. The program could perhaps have led to the development of a transport and marketing infrastructure through governmental agencies, as in the case of milk and tea, but there was no commitment on the part of either the colonial administration or the Local Native Council to the development of a resource traditionally viewed as unimportant and controlled by women.

†I have been told by several informants that since my field stay it has become illegal to brew and sell traditional beer. I have been unable to confirm this in conversations with researchers recently returned from Kenya, so it is not clear whether my informants' reports refer to a national law or a local regulation, nor can I say what the extent of compliance with the law is. But as I noted earlier, the growing influence of the fundamentalist, anti-liquor church, to which many of the younger Nandi women belong, will no doubt eventually mean the end of brewing as a sideline for many energetic Nandi women.

TABLE 19
Estimated Yearly Cash Returns from Agricultural Products
(Shillings)

Product	Estimated return
Maize	1,000 / acre
Milk	960 / milking cow
Tea	2,500 / acre
Vegetables	1,000 / acre

needed for a year's subsistence for each member of a household. Using this formula, I calculated for each census household how much of its total maize crop was used for consumption and how much was surplus.* The surplus figure was multiplied by the income estimate of 1,000 shillings per acre to get estimated yearly income from surplus maize. The absolute mean for estimated maize income (number of acres at 1,000 shillings per acre) is 3,268 shillings per year, but this is heavily skewed by the few cases of enormous maize crops. The figure of 1,851 shillings per year derived by disregarding the six highest and six lowest figures is a truer mean, but the most useful figure for giving a picture of the "typical" case is probably the median income, 1,200 shillings per year.

The number of milking cows held by compounds in the community census ranges from none (seven compounds) to twelve (one compound); 80 percent of compounds have one to five milk cows. The cash-generating potential of a milk cow is estimated at 960 shillings per year. The mean number of milk cows is 3.3 (an average yearly income of 3,168 sh.); the median is 3 (2,880 sh.).

Over 75 percent of male-headed compounds in the census grow some tea, but the numbers of acres involved are usually small. It was estimated that the yearly income produced by an acre of tea is about 2,500 shillings. The mean tea income for male compound heads, therefore, is 2,460 shillings. Again, however, because of a few extremely large holdings, the median is probably a more useful figure. The median number of acres of tea per compound is 0.5; thus, the median yearly tea income is estimated at 1,250 shillings.

If a typical male compound head in Kaptel has the median

*Of course, this calculation is rough. No attempt is made, for example, to distinguish between children and adults in terms of volume likely to be consumed.

available maize surplus, the median number of milk cows, and the median-size plot of tea, he controls a yearly income of about 5,330 shillings from these major cash-producing agricultural activities. Seven single men (in two cases living with their widowed mothers) have a median income of 4,680 shillings, while seven female-headed households have a median income of 3,875 shillings.*

The actual range of variation in estimated incomes from cash crops is extremely wide, from essentially none in two cases to over 60,000 shillings in two cases. Seven men in the census have estimated cash-crop incomes of over 20,000 shillings per year, and some of these seven also have other sources of income. The process of consolidation of *all* the most lucrative economic pursuits in the hands of a small male elite is very similar to the process well documented for a Tugen community by Kettel (1980).

Most women engage in a combination of economic activities that is less easy to predict than the combination of major cash crops. Some women depend on nothing but brewing for their income. Others may only grow vegetables, but grow a large quantity. Still others may combine two, three, or all four of these activities, with varying emphasis. Table 20 shows the numbers of wives of compound heads in the random sample census who engage in each of the four major female cash-generating activities.† Seventy-seven women (almost three-fourths) combined more than one activity; only seven reported no income from any of them. Seven had income from brewing only, seven from vegetables only, and nine from chickens only. In addition, one woman in the sample is a teacher, one is a tailor with a shop in a neighboring sublocation center, another runs a small shop, two engage in trading items other than their own agricultural produce

---

*It may be noticed that the numbers in these categories are not the same as those given in Table 11 at the beginning of this chapter. In that table, the two cases in which widows and unmarried sons live together were counted as female-headed households; in Table 19 they are reported with the single men because the son reports that he controls this income.

†The number of women for whom these data are available—107—is less than the total number of wives of male compound heads in the census. In some cases, accurate data were not collected for both wives of a polygynist, one of whom lived in another community. In a few cases, full accurate data were not collected for idiosyncratic reasons.

TABLE 20
Sources of Income Controlled by 107 Wives of Compound Heads

Activity and measure	No. of women	Activity and measure	No. of women
RAISING VEGETABLES FOR SALE		**RAISING CHICKENS FOR SALE**	
No. of acres:		No. of chickens:	
0	30	0	29
0.2	35	1–4	21
0.3–0.5	18	5–9	24
0.5–0.7	21	10–14	20
1.0	3	15–19	4
		20–29	5
BREWING		30+	4
No. of times a year:			
0	70	**DAILY SALE OF MILK**	
1	3	No. of liters:	
3	1	0	87
4	1	1.0	8
6	1	1.5	2
12	13	2.0	3
24	12	3.0	2
36	5	5.0	4
72	1	7.5	1

(e.g., buying a sack of oranges or large bunch of bananas in a town and selling them in rural markets), and three reported that they do occasional agricultural contract labor. It is my impression that this last category is grossly underreported, possibly because the income usually derived from it is very small.

Informants say that an enterprising woman can make 1,000 shillings a year from an acre of vegetables. Figures from other districts (see Oboler 1982:335) would lead one to expect a higher figure. The lower figure results from the use of much of the vegetable crop for home consumption and the lack of a formal marketing procedure, which forces women to sell vegetables at lower than standard rates.

Eggs, in 1977, sold for half a shilling apiece, chickens for 12– 15 shillings (sometimes more). Some women regularly sell small numbers of eggs through (usually male) petty entrepreneurs who buy in the country and resell in town. Some make a business of keeping chickens in large numbers, with regular outlets. I estimate the cash-generating potential of a chicken at 30 shillings yearly (Oboler 1982:342). This estimate probably considerably overestimates the value of most chickens.

Most women do not sell milk, but a few do—to households with insufficient supply, secondary school students, and in a few cases to the government marketing cooperative. The rate is at least the government standard (for 1977), that is, 1.32 shillings per liter.

The expense and profit involved in brewing on three particular occasions were collected from different informants (Oboler 1982:343). On the basis of these figures, brewing income averages 60 shillings per instance.

What sorts of incomes do women's major cash-generating activities add up to? My estimate assumes that a woman's yearly income is 100 shillings per 0.1 acre of vegetables, 482 shillings per liter of milk sold daily, 30 shillings for each chicken, and 60 shillings for each instance of brewing. On the basis of the distribution of activities shown in Table 20, a picture of the economic activities of a "typical" woman in Kaptel may be drawn: she has five chickens, grows 0.2 acres of vegetables, sells 0.5 liters of milk daily (on the basis of the mean; most women actually sell none), and does not brew. These activities would result in an income of 641 shillings a year. Using these figures to make estimates from the activities women actually reported results in estimated incomes ranging from zero to 5,120 shillings a year, with a mean of 996 shillings a year and a median of 700 shillings a year. The highest income (5,120 shillings) was that of a woman who grew vegetables and kept chickens at moderate levels, and brewed more often than once a week. The second-highest income (4,310 shillings) was for a woman who never brewed but grew an acre of vegetables, kept 30 chickens, and sold a gallon of milk daily to a local boarding school. Other high incomes reflect many varied combinations of activities: there is no single pattern that yields maximum economic returns.

Comparing the estimated on-farm incomes of men and women (including brewing in the case of women because it is such a ubiquitous home industry) reveals a great disparity (see Table 21). Men's median income is more than seven times as great as that of women, men's mean income is almost nine times as great as that of women, the highest income controlled by a man is

TABLE 21
Estimated On-Farm Incomes of Men and Women
(Shillings)

Category	Range of income	Mean income	Median income
Male compound heads	0–68,800	8,896	5,330
Wives of compound heads	0–5,120	996	700

thirteen times that controlled by a woman, and the highest income among the women is not as great as the median income for the men.

Moreover, it must be remembered that it is common for men but rare for women to engage in other, non-farm-related income-generating activities. Though women in Kaptel typically control small but significant independent incomes, these do not begin to compare in magnitude with those controlled by men. It is clear that one important impact of incorporation into the cash economy is a growing economic gap between the sexes, shown in the disparity between the value of resources controlled by men and those controlled by women.

The foregoing analysis has demonstrated that the process of production in modern Nandi is marked by economic inequality beween the sexes in two ways: women contribute more hours of labor than men do to the process of production, and they have substantially less control over the product. Further, forces that have their origin in the colonial situation and incorporation into the cash economy exacerbate this situation. Resources controlled by men have developed into major cash crops whereas those controlled by women have not. Men frequently do work or petty business for cash, but women are too involved in domestic work supportive of the process of production (housework, food preparation, child care) to spend much time in this way; and they have no direct control over the cash incomes their husbands gain through these activities. The on-going processes of commoditization and class formation intensify this differential control of cash. Rich men acquire ever larger landholdings, use them to produce male-controlled crops (maize, milk, and tea), and thereby increase the economic gap between themselves and their wives. In poorer households, it is less and less possible to meet cash needs by agricultural income alone, and men move into wage or contract labor or entrepreneurial activities to earn cash (which they control), increasing the economic gap between them and their wives *as well as* increasing their wives' workloads in basic production. These processes thus put poor women at a greater disadvantage than elite women. In either case, however, the economic position of women vis-à-vis men worsens.

SEVEN

Rights in the Family Estate

IN NANDI SOCIETY, as has been shown, the domestic family group—usually a nuclear family—is the basic unit of production. Within this unit, certain structural tensions and oppositions exist between the productive roles of its various members and their rights in the product and the means of production. These oppositions, long implicit in norms surrounding access to resources, became explicit as the contradictions embodied in them were exacerbated by pressures created by the colonial situation. At the same time that these material changes in production and the division of labor were taking place, Nandi ideology was also in the process of adapting to altered circumstances. Old norms about the rights of various members of productive units in property, particularly, are in the process of being redefined in response to the new socioeconomic context. Ways in which this process of adaptation and redefinition threatens to erode women's traditional rights in property will be described in this chapter.

There is at present a substantial amount of disagreement about exactly who holds what rights in what property. Within the traditional system of definitions of rights in property there were certain norms that, though not in active conflict, held within them the seeds of contradiction. Under the new set of circumstances, these norms are now generating conflict—for example, between the norm that husbands ("men," since Nandi conflate these categories) should manage any household property of value (which today means anything with significant cash-generating potential), and the norm that wives ("women") have absolute rights to certain forms of property. Different norms can be appealed to by different parties attempting to maximize or protect their own interests.

Two Principles: Female House Property, Male Control

Two principles are fundamental to the Nandi system of relations of people to property and assure each member of the society rights in basic economic resources. They are: (1) the right of men to inherit and hold predominant control of the most important forms of property, which, in the precolonial period, meant livestock; and (2) the right of women to hold house property, with residual rights to control it, and to pass it on to their male heirs. A man acquires his major property rights through inheritance from the "house" of his mother, though cattle not assigned as house property can in theory be "willed" directly from father to son. A woman acquires her major property rights from her husband at marriage, though her house may also receive gifts from other relatives, acquire resources through her own efforts, or in some other way add to its fund of property. In a sense, though Nandi is a patrilineal society, most property is not transmitted from father to sons. Rather, wives gain property rights through husbands and sons gain property rights through mothers. Property rights are assured to every member of the society because every man is a woman's son and every woman is legally one and only one man's wife.

The house-property complex is characteristic of other Kalenjin societies besides Nandi (Kettel 1981:6; Peristiany 1939:211). The term was originated by Gluckman to describe the inheritance system of the Zulu, though he also noted its applicability to certain other southern and eastern African patrilineal societies (Gluckman 1950:197–98). In such an inheritance system, a man "allots land and cattle to each of his wives. Land and cattle thus allotted become irrevocably property of the house. . . . This property . . . is inherited by the sons of that wife against their half-brothers by their father's other wives" (Gluckman 1950: 195).

The house-property complex in Nandi operated primarily with regard to livestock. Land was traditionally plentiful, and its allotment and inheritance were not issues. Today the principle of house property has been extended to include land and other property. A new wife is assigned (at least in theory) certain animals from her husband's herds. These animals and their off-spring, together with those she receives as gifts at her initiation and/or marriage, those she acquires through her own efforts, and those received as bridewealth for her daughters, form her house property. Each wife in a polygynous marriage is supposed to receive from her husband the same share of house-property animals as every other wife. All cattle a man inherits are rightfully to be distributed as house property, an equal share to each of his wives. If a man acquires cattle by his independent efforts (e.g., in the past by raiding, today by wage labor) he has somewhat more freedom of choice in the allotment of them. At a husband's death, however, wives have a strong moral claim to have unallotted livestock inherited in equal numbers by each of their houses.

A woman's house property is inherited only by her own sons. It makes no difference if one wife has one son and another has ten—the husband has no right to redistribute his wives' house property. A woman's house property can revert to the sons of her co-wife or her husband's brother only if she dies without a male heir. The property of a woman who has no heir goes to the husband's closest patrilineal descendants: sons by other wives first, then brothers' sons, then father's brothers' sons, etc.

A man can marry only by using those cattle that have been received as bridewealth for his own full sister (along with cattle contributed by his father and sometimes by other relatives, particularly his mother's brother). He should not use his half-sister's bridewealth cattle, nor may his father allot him cattle from the herd of one of his mother's co-wives. If a woman has no full brother, her bridewealth cattle still cannot finance her half-brother's marriage but must remain in her mother's house. Her father may, however, use the cattle he acquires through wage labor or the sale of cash crops—which have not been assigned as house property—disproportionately for the marriages of sons in a house that lacks daughters.

The principles that bridewealth cattle cannot be transferred between the houses of co-wives and that house property should devolve continuously and never revert to collateral lines (though it can never be inherited by a female) together are the basis of the institution of woman-woman marriage. A sonless woman past childbearing age may use her house-property cattle or her daughter's bridewealth cattle to take a wife for herself (Oboler 1980). The wife conceives children through liaisons of her own choosing or liaisons that are arranged for her by her female husband, with the hope of bearing a male heir for her female husband's house property (which, of course, since marriage endows a wife with house property, is now her own as well). The female husband assumes male social status, and counts as legal and social father to the children borne by her wife. Two other alternatives, besides woman-woman marriage, for wives without heirs are the adoption of a son, or keeping the youngest daughter at home in lieu of a wife, to bear a male heir for the house. In the latter case, the daughter is said to be married to the house or its center-pole.

A woman's rights in her house property are (at least normatively) inalienable. Though divorce is extremely rare, separation occurs. A woman may leave her husband for a period of many years or even for life. She may have children by other men. All this does not alter her marriage and property rights. She remains the legal wife of the man who first married her, and her children remain his legal heirs. A separated woman always has the right to return to her husband's home and resume her rights in her house property, and her sons always have the right to inherit this property. I recorded a number of cases in which elderly women, long since separated from their husbands, returned to take up property rights in their husbands' homes. This could occur either while the husband was still living or after his death.* Such a woman can pick up her own property rights effectively as if she had never left.

It is normatively held that husband and wife have joint rights in house property. In practice, however, a wife has no right to take the initiative in disposing of house-property animals or in other aspects of herd management unless her husband is generally recognized as being incapable of administering the property adequately (e.g., because of chronic drunkenness).† Property

*In many cases, the woman was sought out and persuaded to return by an adult son she had left behind with his father.

†In the precolonial period, disposal of cattle was not a consideration except in the context of cattle-lending relationships.

management is considered a male prerogative; it is, in fact, an extremely important part of the cultural definition of male gender (see Oboler 1980). Though informants consistently say that a "good man" would not sell an animal from his wife's herd without consulting her, a wife's ability to prevent a "bad" husband from doing so is very limited.

The relation of husband and wife to property is conceptualized as essentially inegalitarian. Though the principle of the wife's right to her house property is extremely important, the husband is thought of as in some sense the ultimate "owner" of all family property. There is no verb in Nandi that can be translated into English as "to own." The word used to indicate proprietorship of property is *bou*, to control or rule. The noun derived from this verb is *boiyot*, which also means "elder" or "husband." A husband is viewed as gaining ultimate rights in his wife and all her endeavors through the payment of bridewealth. This ideology is held and stated more strongly by men, but it is not limited to them only. Informants encode it by such statements as: "You know, when a woman is married to a man, everything she owns belongs to the husband," or—an extreme case—"Always everything is mine, even that eleusine she plants. What do you think a woman/wife is when she is here? She is my servant. She is mine and all that she does is mine."

That female property rights are nested within those of males is dramatized by the way compounds and households are referred to in everyday speech. A whole compound and its members is referred to as *Gab X* (The House of X), using the name of the male elder who heads it (frequently even for some time after his death). Individual houses within the compound are always referred to as Gab A, Gab B, Gab C, using the names of the individual married women who inhabit them.

Thus, the basis of the Nandi system of relations to property is a form of the house-property complex in which a woman acquires the inalienable right to hold certain property, but not the right to manage and control that property. Property management, particularly the control of livestock, is the preserve of men, though they are supposed to take into account their wives' opinions where women's house property is concerned. House-property cattle cannot be said to be "owned," in a Western sense, by anyone, since no one person has an indisputable right to alienate them or holds the bulk of significant rights in them. Even though men in Nandi traditionally were associated ideologically with cattle and had predominant rights of control over them, they cannot be said to have been the "owners" of the means of production—the family herd—to the exclusion of women.

In Nandi, men rather than women have always dominated in controlling the major means of production, but their rights in most of the cattle in a herd were never absolute. The cattle that men gained by their own efforts (raiding, e.g.) were more or less theirs alone and under their complete control. There were no categories of cattle, sheep, or goats over which wives had anything approaching complete rights of control. All cattle or other livestock acquired by a woman became part of her house property and thus came under her husband's ultimate purview. In other words, men could hold *some* livestock as "private property" in a sense that married women could not. Though the Nandi property system gave significant rights in property to women as well as to men, the distribution of such rights on the basis of gender was always far from egalitarian. Nevertheless, as I shall argue below, the commoditization of the means of production, and other forces stemming from colonial policies and the advent of the cash economy, have increased the sexually inegalitarian nature of the distribution of rights in property.

Rights in Livestock

It is appropriate that the discussion of rights in property begin with rights in livestock, since in the precolonial period this was the most significant form of property, and therefore the one surrounded by the most complex structure of rights.* It is easy to delineate the principles governing the house-property complex, as I have done above. In practice, this system can become quite complicated.

In order to give an adequate account of rights in cattle, at least

---

* A reader familiar with the literature on Kalenjin peoples may note that this account diverges significantly from that given by Snell (1954:52–54), who virtually denies the significance of the house-property complex in Nandi cattle inheritance. The disparity between Snell's version and that presented by my informants is so great that I make no attempt to reconcile the accounts.

four categories of cattle that can accrue to a family must be distinguished.

1. Inherited cattle (sometimes called *tugab boiyot*, the elder's—meaning father's—cattle), which a man acquires from his father as his patrimony, either during the father's lifetime or upon the division of his estate following his death. Such cattle and their offspring are supposed to be distributed to a man's wives as house property, and the husband and wife share rights in them.

2. Cattle acquired by a couple as bridewealth for one of their daughters (which may be called *tugab koito*, engagement cattle). These cattle and their offspring join the family herd and come under the control of the bride's father, but the most significant rights in them really lie with the bride's mother and full brothers.

3. Cattle given to a woman as gifts at her marriage, usually by her father but sometimes by other relatives (called *chepsegut*, sing., from *segutiet*, the grass that is tied around the wrists of the couple during the marriage ceremony). These cattle, which I shall call "wedding" cattle, and their offspring also join the family herd, and though the wife cedes control of them to the husband, they are recognized as property in which the rights of the wife predominate.

4. Cattle that a man acquires through his own independent efforts (e.g., by raiding in the precolonial period, or at present by buying with money he earns through wage labor). These are the cattle that an individual man holds almost all significant rights to and may sell or otherwise allocate at his own discretion.

It is possible, though it is certainly not common, for women to acquire cattle through their independent efforts. At present, a woman who works for wages may buy cattle. If these go with her to her husband's home, they are usually treated as the equivalent of wedding cattle; however, because women who leave their husbands do not have the right to take their cattle with them, most female informants say that a woman should leave her own cattle behind in the care of a consanguine when she is married. Acquiring cattle was also rare for women in the precolonial period, though there were ways. Gold (1978:16) says that "when a man died and left no sons, the daughter could receive one cow; the woman who supplied firewood to the warriors to roast their meat before a raid was rewarded with a captured cow." I suspect that cattle acquired in these ways were also treated as equivalent to wedding cattle. Women could acquire small stock—that is, sheep and goats—through trade of their own produce, or in exchange for manufactured items, or for services such as feeding girls in seclusion following initiation (Gold 1978:16). It seems doubtful, however, that they could acquire cattle in these ways. Women's rights in sheep and goats will be discussed separately.

Talking in the abstract about the respective rights of husbands and wives in cattle is too indefinite to mean much because rights in particular cattle differ depending on how these cattle were acquired. Though inherited cattle are technically supposed to be distributed as house property, in practice the distinction between house-property cattle and other cattle is blurred. Elderly informants report that at an earlier historical period it was actually the practice to assign certain cows to each married woman to milk when she acquired an independent house within a compound, and these cows formed the core of her house property. But it must be remembered that it took several years for a married woman to achieve this independent status, and the person who actually assigned her the cows might well not be her husband but rather his father, probably in consultation with the husband's mother. The son of a young father might not actually be in control of all the cattle he ultimately would hold as inheritance cattle until he himself neared old age. I have said that a wife at marriage was endowed with house-property cattle, but this is an oversimplification. Actually, she was endowed with a small number of animals and the right for her house to share equally, with the houses of any other wives of her husband, cattle that her husband ultimately stood to control through inheritance. Cattle a man thus gained through inheritance formed the bulk of his wives' house property.

Today, when cattle have been largely commoditized and are bought and sold easily and frequently in accordance with the desire to balance the size of herds and the size of landholdings, indigenous, low-milk-producing cows that were originally assigned to wives as house property may be sold and replaced with smaller numbers of high-yielding European dairy cows. Thus a woman's house property may well consist more of her rights to a certain share of the family's cattle than of specific rights in individual animals. Particularly in monogamous marriages, the distinction between a household's various categories of cattle is becoming increasingly unclear.

In theory, a wife has the right to be consulted by her husband about the disposition of inherited cattle that are counted as her house property, but her rights in this matter are weak (unlike her rights in wedding or daughters' bridewealth cattle). In practice, because herd management is a male prerogative, a wife can do little to block her husband's decision to sell an inherited cow. However, a man has a strong moral obligation to use the profit from the sale of a cow for the benefit of the nuclear family of the wife whose house property the cow was. Thus, if a husband wants to sell a cow from his wife's house property to pay school fees for her children, and she favors some other means of acquiring the money for school fees, he can override her opinion and sell the cow. What he cannot do, without damage to his reputation, is use the money to benefit the house of another wife, or "consume" it himself, or use it for some purpose of his own that does not directly benefit his wife's house. If a husband does this, his wife will be considered by the community to be within her rights if she goes to the local elders to ask them to use any means they can to prevent her husband from selling her house-property animal the *next* time he proposes doing so.

Though I recorded only one case in which a woman actually successfully blocked her husband's proposed sale of a cow (see Chapter 4), the following case is illustrative of the sort of sanction a wife can invoke.

Kiplagat, a young wage laborer soon to be married, bought a heifer from Arap Mibei and paid him 400 shillings. When Kiplagat came to drive the heifer to his home, Arap Mibei was not at home and his wife would not allow it to be taken. She protested that she hadn't seen any money and had no way of knowing that her husband had really sold it. Kiplagat acknowledged that Arap Mibei had not consulted his wife about the sale and that she was within her rights in attempting to block it. Nevertheless, he had paid 400 shillings, so he sought out Arap Mibei and asked him to return the money. Arap Mibei said he no longer had the money, but that he would straighten things out with his wife and Kiplagat could come for the heifer in a week's time. When Kiplagat tried to take the heifer the second time, Arap Mibei's wife was adamant. She repeated that she had not seen the money, that the cattle do not belong to her husband alone, that since she also worked for her husband's wealth she should share the benefits, and that her husband had no right to sell cattle in order to consume ("eat") the money himself. Kiplagat finally got her to agree to let him take the heifer by playing on her sympathy and saying that he had named that very animal as part of his bridewealth, and would be greatly shamed before his future affines if he could not deliver it. The conflict between Arap Mibei and his wife over the heifer became a scandal in the local neighborhood, and some elders went to make peace between them. The wife was hostile to this attempt and said this was not the first such incident—that similar occurrences had been going on for some time. She said that if Arap Mibei wanted to marry again she could make no legitimate objection, but he takes the money and consumes it with his mistress [*chebaigeiyat*], and in this he is doing wrong. Arap Mibei received a warning from the elders that he should change his behavior in this matter.*

It should be noted that in this case everyone agreed that Arap Mibei was wrong, and his reputation in the community suffered. Nonetheless, though his wife acted within her rights, she could not keep him from selling the cow.

There is disagreement among informants about the degree to which a wife can exercise a veto over her husband's decision to sell a cow. The case just described illustrates some of the ambiguity that lies behind such disagreement. Though a wife may have a *right* to a veto under certain circumstances, she often has little power to use this right effectively. Men tend to downplay wives' rights to be consulted about the sale of cattle. They may frequently agree that they should consult their wives in this matter, but they justify their statements in terms that mask the wives' right to be consulted. A wise man will consult his wife, they say, because she is the one who milks the cows and therefore has the most informed opinion about which animal the household can best afford to do without.

Women have somewhat stronger rights in wedding or bridewealth cattle. The husband has no right to sell or dispose of a wedding cow (*chepsegut*) without his wife's consent. To attempt

---

*This case was related to me both by Kiplagat, one of the protagonists, and by one of the elders who was involved in the "resolution."

to do so would be considered a serious offense in the eyes of the community. Women point proudly to such animals as their own property. I heard of no cases of a man's even attempting to take his wife's wedding cattle. Though the wife does not own such an animal in the sense of having the right to dispose of it on her own, neither does the husband. To an outsider it may be indistinguishable from any other animal in the herd, but intimates know to whom it belongs. One informant says of such a cow: "If I own (or am given) a cow, after I am married it will not really be mine, but will belong to the family. It will be referred to as my husband's cow." Another informant, however, stresses the primacy of the wife's rights in the wedding cow: "The cow is referred to as belonging to the family [using the husband's name], but everyone knows it is mine. I will divide its offspring among my sons in my old age."

Ideally, cattle that are acquired as bridewealth for daughters of a house should be used as bridewealth to acquire wives for the same house. One cow from each daughter's bridewealth becomes the property of her mother, which the mother retains as her personal property in widowhood. (The mother's rights in this respect may, however, be sacrificed to ensure that all her sons are provided with bridewealth. It is primarily the male elders of a family who make such decisions during the division of a man's estate.) Where there are great disparities in family size and composition between wives, the principle that bridewealth cattle must not cross the boundaries between houses can create tremendous inequities and resentments within polygynous families. It happens fairly frequently that a husband/father wishes to use bridewealth cattle from a house with many daughters and few sons to pay bridewealth for sons in another house with few daughters. Technically, it is not his right to make such a transfer. In the words of one informant: "A woman's daughter's bridewealth cannot find a wife for the son of her co-wife. A woman can never allow that!" But because the husband/father is the ultimate manager of the property of all his wives' houses, it may be extremely difficult for his wife to prevent such a transfer if he decides to make it. This is particularly true if the family's resources are limited so that without the transfer the sons of the cattle-poor house will have difficulty procuring bridewealth. A husband cannot equalize bridewealth cattle between houses capriciously, but only if one house is in dire need. I was told that what usually happens is that such a transaction is viewed as a loan, which the sons of one house must ultimately repay to the sons of the other house.

In precolonial times the fourth category of cattle, those that men acquire through independent efforts, must have represented only a small fraction of a household's herd, but today the commoditization of cattle, near-universal cash-cropping, and general affluence and easy access to cash in Nandi have made it a very significant, if not the most significant, category. This gives rise to confusion about the respective rights of husband and wife in the bulk of the family herd. There is a feeling, derived from expectations that have their roots in the precolonial period, that husbands and wives should have joint rights in most family cattle as house property. Just as clearly, however, there are norms about cash-cropping that derive from the early twentieth century when it was practiced on a very small scale with little female participation: that a man has the right to plant and cultivate cash crops and use the profit to acquire cattle that he controls independently. Commoditization of cattle also leads to confusion as to which category individual animals belong to. A man may, for example, sell an indigenous cow that he inherited. He may then take the proceeds of the sale and add it to money he has earned through wage labor, or profits from his cash crops, and buy a European dairy cow. In some sense, the new animal is a replacement for the old one, but because cash has gone into its acquisition, his wife's rights in it are much less clear than were her rights in its predecessor.

Commoditization of cattle thus is increasing the relative numbers of cattle of the fourth category (male-owned cattle) at the expense of the first (inherited cattle). This process obviously benefits men and undermines women's rights in the bulk of the family herd. At the same time, however, there is a similar potential for increasing the relative numbers of cattle in the third category (wedding cattle). As cattle become commoditized, and cash more plentiful, the gift of a cow to a woman at her marriage represents a smaller investment than formerly and is therefore more likely to occur. This is especially true if the bride is a special favorite of a wage-earning kinsman. Further, in a few instances, a woman will work for wages before marriage and buy cattle, which she owns independently and in a sense continues to own when she marries. The possibility of women gaining independently owned cattle and/or large numbers of wedding cattle represents a threat to male power in the marriage.

The response to this threat has been the development of ideologies that combat trends toward greater female control of cattle. Christianity is sometimes used as a vehicle for such ideologies. Several informants told me that young Christian men have begun to refuse to allow their brides to accept wedding cattle during a Christian wedding ceremony (two informants reported having done this themselves). The rationale they use is that such a "heathen" custom has no place in a Christian event. At a modern Christian wedding I attended, the (Nandi) presiding minister's remarks included the following statement:

I have seen wives show visitors around their compounds when their husbands are not at home. They point to some cattle (presumably their wedding cattle) and say, "These are my cows." Or they say of the vegetable garden, "This is my field." But it is not like that. A good Christian wife will not say that she owns anything, but will say, "These are my husband's cows" or "This field is ours." Because a Christian wife does not own anything of her own, but everything belongs to both of them together.

A number of informants also told me that if a woman owns a cow before marriage she should not take it with her to her husband. Such animals, it is said, are bound to cause quarrels between husband and wife because property ownership makes a wife too "proud" (that is, she attempts to use the fact that she controls some economic resources to gain power in household decision making). In the words of one informant: "If the wife owns something, when she makes a mistake and you quarrel a bit, she refers to this tea or cow that she bought, and that everything which is here originated from that. In most cases, she does not stop talking about the tea or cow. So most men do not like their wives to own anything. They could own something small, maybe, but not something big."

It is impossible for a married woman to save money from her

own endeavors (e.g., vegetable gardening) and buy a cow in which she has the same kind of rights as she has in a wedding cow. On this point all informants are agreed. This is because a married woman does not have the right to hold and use independently as large an amount of money as would be needed for such a transaction. If a woman were to buy a cow independently, my informants (male and female) agree that her husband would be perfectly justified in selling it.

Some informants claim that in the same way it is impossible for a woman to own a sheep or goat. Most maintain, however, that independent female ownership and control of small stock are currently possible and were possible traditionally. Gold (1977:12) describes ways in which women in the precolonial period could control small stock: "An ambitious woman could cultivate extra grain on her own which she traded for a sheep or goat; when a girl married, she gave a goat or sheep to the woman who had fed her while she was in seclusion immediately following circumcision. . . . [Also] women performed a variety of services for which they were compensated with milk, grain or small livestock; they were curers, midwives, basketmakers, potters, female circumcisors, and they blessed the crops after the harvest."

Another way mentioned to me by informants for a woman to acquire a sheep or goat was as a gift from her son-in-law at her daughter's marriage. Basket and pottery making are rare skills today, and crops are no longer blessed by a female ritual expert (or by anyone). Otherwise, most of these avenues for acquisition of small stock are still open. More and more, however, services such as those mentioned by Gold are paid for in cash. The consensus among informants is that women *do* have the right to save small amounts of money from their independent cash-gaining endeavors and acquire small stock. Several of my female informants reported that they personally own sheep or goats. Stock bought for cash or acquired by a woman in any of the ways mentioned above is rightfully under her control. She can sell it or its progeny to get money for family needs, though many informants add that it is desirable that she discuss her plans for the animal with her husband before acting upon them. The husband, for his part, does not have the right to dispose of the animal without his wife's consent. However, as in the case of house-property cattle, a wife can do little if her husband chooses to ignore her rights. I heard from several different informants about a case in which a man slaughtered a goat his wife had acquired through her own efforts because, he said, she had become "too proud" about owning an animal. This case stood out, apparently, because of its rarity. The people who related it to me regarded the man's behavior as scandalous—mean, petty, and unworthy of a prominent community member. The man himself seemed embarrassed about the incident. Still, as in the case of Arap Mibei and his wife, though the man's reputation suffered, his wife had no power to prevent his action. Nevertheless, in general it is true that wives have a right to independent ownership of small stock that they do not have in the case of cattle.

Rights in Land

Land was not a scarce resource in precolonial Nandi and there were no formal rules governing access to and inheritance of rights in it.* Population density was always so low that land was not at a premium. Carrying capacity was determined by the size of the herds, and the limiting resource was pasture land rather than land available for cultivation. It seems, in any case, that herds were always small enough and area for territorial expansion was always great enough that natural resources were never placed under strain.

There were some rules surrounding possession and inheritance of land once it had been cleared for cultivation. Any community member could clear land, and this belonged to him or her as long as he or she continued to cultivate it. When the land was allowed to lie fallow and return to bush, rights in it lapsed. Cultivated land was inherited by the sons of the woman who cultivated it and their wives. No other land was inherited.

In precolonial Nandi, because a newly married couple lived in the husband's parents' compound, there was at least a tendency for residence to be patrilocal. However, men had the right to mi-

---

*Hollis (1909:86) notes proprietary rights in land held by families in one part of Nandi territory but says that "elsewhere in Nandi no proprietary rights are acknowledged."

grate to other communities, and exercise of this option was probably not infrequent. Genealogical ties were not long remembered. Local communities were and are not agnatically structured. They *are* predominantly endogamous and are cross-cut by a dense network of affinal ties. Certainly a wife was likely to be living with her husband's kinsmen and cultivating land adjacent to their homestead, but she was also likely to be living in a community that included her own relatives.* Insofar as land was held by the local community, then, it was held by a group of men who were likely to be natives, and their wives who might be strangers but were also more likely to be natives. This, together with the fact that land was ideologically associated with women's activities, prevented the development of a fully conscious idea that the land really "belonged" to men in the same sense as cattle.

Under the Swynnerton Plan of 1954, land was partitioned and titles were issued in the names of male heads of households. (In the case of widows, titles were issued to their minor sons.) The custom that has evolved regarding the inheritance of land title is similar to the traditional custom providing for the inheritance of cattle: land held by a deceased male should be divided equally among the "houses" of his wives, and each house's share should be divided equally among its male heirs.

The distribution of land title to men, and the inheritance of land by men, undermines women's position in two ways. First, the new concept that husband rather than wife owns the land the family cultivates gives husbands an added source of dominance over wives. Second, it is now possible for women, under certain circumstances, to be denied access to land, which formerly was available to anyone.

At present, it is extremely difficult for a man without land to marry. Either he must have land that he stands to inherit from his father, or he will acquire a piece of land through his own efforts before he even considers marrying. This results in a situa-

---

*Community endogamy is the statistical norm now and probably was in the late nineteenth century also. Lacking statistics, one cannot deduce the degree to which the composition of local communities has changed, but very likely the advent of patrilineal land inheritance increases the probability of groups of close agnates co-residing in the same neighborhood.

tion where virtually every newly married woman comes to stay with her husband on his or his family's property. There is now a very clearly expressed public sentiment that the land on which the family lives is that of the husband and not the wife. Informants note that the matter of ownership of land will often be the clinching factor in arguments. If a wife tries to have too much voice in farm management decisions, the husband can always say, "Whose land do we live on? Did you own a plot when you came here?" The fact that the land is the husband's is also commonly cited as the reason why the wife cannot unilaterally decide to grow profitable cash crops (such as tea) of her own on it.

Because land is still plentiful, the loss of access to land for some women is not so far a serious problem, but it could become serious as the population increases. Along with the principle of wives having access to land through their husbands, a clear understanding has been maintained that a widow has a perpetual right to cultivate crops on the land of her son, and that a daughter or sister has the right to support herself and her children on the land of her father or brother. Therefore (most) widows and separated women are not in danger of losing access to land. But if a widow does not have a son, her husband's land is inherited by her husband's nephew or by the son of her co-wife if her husband was a polygynist. A kinsman who inherits in this way may feel a moral obligation to allow the widow access to his land, but he is under no *legal* obligation to do so. The same rules apply in the case of a brotherless woman attempting to gain access to land that formerly belonged to her deceased father but may after his death be held by her half-brother or patrilateral parallel cousin. With increasing population density and land scarcity, distant male kin who may be heirs to a man's land in preference to closer female kin may also be land-needy and thus may feel their moral obligation to such women less keenly.

There is evidence that women are not content with a body of inheritance law that treats land as male property. Some current trends both in behavior and in public opinion can be seen as reactions that attempt to preserve women's rights of access to land. An apparent increase in the incidence of woman-woman marriage since land partitioning has the effect of ensuring rights in land to these sonless women who might otherwise stand in

danger of losing them. There is also a growing body of sentiment that daughters as well as sons should have rights to inherit
family land under certain circumstances. Widows with no sons
have been known to resist the idea of woman-woman marriage
on the grounds that rightfully their daughters should be permitted to inherit land. The right of separated women to live in the
compounds of their fathers and/or brothers and cultivate nearby
land is now usually extended to never-married women (of whom
there is a growing number). Several informants expressed the
feeling that the rights of unmarried women should be extended
still further—that such women should inherit land on an equal
footing with their brothers, so that their children will be provided with land rights.

Another aspect of the reaction against male ownership of land
titles is the pattern of informants' responses to questions about
wives' rights in land. In the case of cattle, which have traditionally been rather unambiguously classified as under male
control (though women have not insignificant rights in them),
women are willing to allow fairly clear-cut male control and
male-biased inheritance. This is less true in the case of land. Although men participated in cultivation, land has traditionally
been associated with women. Most informants agreed, as I have
discussed earlier, that though a man ideally should consult his
wife before selling a cow that is the property of her house, if he
decides to do so against her wishes it is questionable whether
she can stop him. But in the case of land, almost all female informants (particularly older women) agreed that a wife rightfully
can veto her husband's decision to sell it. Once a wife is married,
a share of her husband's land is conferred upon her house, and
it is not only her right but her duty to safeguard it. A husband
should always confer with his wife about land transactions. If he
decides against her wishes to go ahead and sell part of the plot,
it is a serious matter. She can block the sale through recourse to
the neighborhood elders. As one informant put it: "If he tries to
sell the land, I have to be harsh/fierce [*korom*]. If he is about to
sell it all, I call for help from people." Thus, in the women's view,
at least, men do not "own" land in the same sense that they
"own" cattle. In the abstract, men agree with this evaluation,
but male informants tend to justify the behavior of a hypotheti-

cal husband in such a case. A typical response is: "Well, he wouldn't want to sell the land if he didn't have some good plan for the money. Therefore, the wife should not try to stop him." I did not encounter any cases of husband and wife disputes over the alienation of land in my fieldwork. It may be that women, though they are viewed as having very firm rights in land, are in many cases nearly as powerless when it comes to land alienation as they are in the case of cattle.

Certainly modern inheritance law is disadvantageous to women in that it places limits on their rights of use in land that were never part of the traditional system. On the other hand, it is possible in the modern setting for an independent woman with an income to buy land and acquire title to it entirely in her own right. This option is open only to unmarried (or separated) women, and not to wives. It is almost unheard of for a married woman to hold title to land independently of her husband. In the few cases where I heard of this happening, it was the prelude to separation. It is perhaps true that some women have benefited from the commoditization of land in that owning land allows them a degree of independence heretofore impossible, but these women are certainly only a small minority.* For the majority of women, commoditization and individualized title holding by men mean that their access to land is insecure and depends on husbands, who use this fact as a source of leverage in family decision making.

The Property of Women

All Nandi informants agree that three things belong to (married) women (in Nandi, *ko bo chebiosok*), or that women own/control (*bou*) three things: a vegetable garden (*kapungut*), chickens, and the milk from the afternoon or evening milking.

In precolonial Nandi, the morning milk was set aside to be drunk by the men of a family, while the afternoon or evening milk was kept solely for consumption by the women and children. Something of this concept is carried through into the modern setting, in that the morning milk, which is sold to the

---

*I have no idea what percentage of women hold land titles, but the number, though small, is not so rare as to be a phenomenon.

Kenya Creameries Cooperative (the government-run marketing cooperative), is thought of as belonging to the husband. The afternoon milk is for consumption by the family, though it is said to belong to the wife. It does belong to the wife, in that if there is extra milk over and above what can be consumed by the family, she is free to sell it (e.g., to boarding school students) and use the money for her own or household needs. The right of the wife to control the afternoon milk may be negated, however, in the opinion of some informants, if there is a very large number of milk cows. In this case, afternoon milk must also be delivered to the KCC, and money coming from the sale of milk to the KCC is usually thought of as belonging to the husband.

Concern with chickens is considered beneath a man's dignity. Chickens were described by one informant as "*tuga che bo chebiosok*" and "*ng'ombe ya wanawake*" ("the cattle of women"). Most informants believe that chickens belong to women and are absolutely under their control no matter how much money the business makes. Some assert, however, that as in the case of the evening milk, if the chickens are very many and the profits are very great, control of this money can legitimately be taken over by the woman's husband. I heard of several cases of women making significant amounts of money from chickens, and of only one case of the husband intervening in such an operation. The discouragement by the Local Native Council of efforts to upgrade chickens and make poultry production more profitable has been described in Chapter 5.

Various subsidiary crops were grown by women in precolonial times for use by their households. Growing exotic vegetables and marketing them for cash dates from the 1930's or 1940's, and it was encouraged by the national women's organization Maendeleo ya Wanawake in the 1950's and 1960's. Because of this history of association with women, vegetables are usually considered to belong entirely to them. A woman is free to cultivate as large a plot of vegetables as she has time, energy, and ambition for, and to market them or use them at home as she sees fit. It is not uncommon for husbands to help their wives find markets for their vegetables, but most men would not think of interfering with their wives' profits from vegetables. The man has income from milk, maize, and tea, the three major cash crops, and as one informant put it, it would not be "polite" for a man to demand money from any of the typically feminine spheres as well. Only a minority of my informants (mostly young married men) said, as they said also of milk and chickens, that if the profits derived were large, a woman's husband could legitimately exert his right to control them.

In the case of vegetables, however, women are lately encountering competition from the youngest circumcised age-set (Kipkoimet), who are entering the vegetable business, often as "Young Men's Vegetable Cooperatives" organized by a group of age-mates as a joint business venture. Most of these young men I encountered were recently married. They did not have large plots or many animals as yet, and were impatient with tea, which cannot yield a cash income for several years. They viewed exotic vegetables as having the potential to yield a not inconsiderable income in a short time. Whether these men will abandon vegetables to their wives' control as they become more established, only time will tell. Even if they do, there is a possibility that markets for exotic vegetables will come to be dominated by successive age-cohorts of young married men, rather than by women. Young men's interest in vegetables contains the seeds of yet another form of erosion of women's economic position: male encroachment on a formerly feminine economic preserve.

In the precolonial period, women were free to control their three forms of property, though their options about how to dispose of them were limited. They could gain prestige in their communities through gift giving, and there is evidence that small stock—including chickens—could sometimes be traded for grain in times of shortage.* The unstated principle that underlies the Nandi property system is the right of men/husbands to control the means of production, or the most significant economic resources. The resources controlled by women were not equivalent to the means of production but rather were almost entirely intended to yield a product for home consumption only. The commoditization of these resources means that it can now

---

*Poultry keeping was not widespread in precolonial Nandi, however, and there was a belief that consumption of eggs by women caused infertility, miscarriages, stillbirths, and various gynecological ailments.

be profitable to produce surpluses of them, so that chickens and vegetable gardens are now in some cases almost comparable to the major means of production as sources of income. As long as female property remains in the category of product, or the profit produced from it is insignificant, virtually all informants acknowledge women's right to control it. Where women's property is profitable, and thus becomes equivalent to the major means of production, many informants believe a woman's husband should move in to control it. What almost all informants believe a woman does *not* have a right to do, except with express permission of her husband, is to reinvest her profits in her economic enterprises in an attempt to expand them to yield greater profits. A wife does not have the right to attempt to make economic spheres under her control competitive with those controlled by her husband. To do so would be to flout the important principle that a woman should never "try to be bigger than" her husband.

There are interesting demographic differences in informants' opinions about the degree to which chickens, vegetables, and the evening milk should be absolutely under women's control. Older, less Westernized informants—particularly women, but most men too—are likely to maintain that these things belong to women and men have no business interfering with them. Younger, more Westernized (highly educated and/or Christian) informants—particularly men, but also many women—are likely to take the position that the husband should control these ventures if they are profitable. They argue that, after all, *all* property actually belongs to the family, of which the husband is the head. One old woman noted that young husbands want such control of their wives' enterprises, adding "but our husbands don't ask for these things, these old ones." This potential loss of control by the younger generation of wives over economic resources that once unequivocally belonged to women is yet another way in which the economic position of women is deteriorating.

Rights in the Staple Crop

I have already described the way in which the eleusine crop was traditionally divided into two parts, one part stored in the wife's granary, to provide food for the family until the next harvest, and the other part—the husband's share—to be used for brewing so that the husband would have beer to entertain the male elders of the community. The field was planted jointly by husband and wife and they worked on it together (or in the case of polygynous marriages, each wife had a separate field and the husband was obliged to distribute his labor equally).

When maize began to be cultivated in significant amounts as a cash crop, men frequently had their own maize fields that were distinct from the staple crop of eleusine cultivated with the wife. Today, husband and wife cultivate maize together in the same field. Most of the couples who still maintain two granaries are older people; normally, there is only one granary. But the old principle of two shares still prevails. The wife's share of grain is for family consumption, and what is left over—the cash crop portion of the maize—is controlled by the husband. It is up to him to sell it and decide how the cash profit should be used. It would be wrong, however, for him to use it for his private consumption rather than for the benefit of his family. A man's reputation in the community would suffer from such a misuse of his cash-crop profits, but as in the case of the sale of cattle, if he chose in the face of community disapproval to use this money for his private ends, his wife would have no effective means to prevent him from doing so. It is the responsibility of the husband to pay for seeds, fertilizer, plowing, and any other expenses incurred in planting a crop of maize out of his profits from the sale of the previous year's crop.

It is also generally accepted that a man is free to decide to sell the bulk of the crop at harvest time, though it is up to him to provide maize when the wife's share runs short. If his behavior in the past has been such that the wife might reasonably suspect that he will neglect this responsibility, she can rightfully appeal to the elders of the neighborhood to prevent him from selling more than the surplus that remains after the household share has been set aside. Some informants maintain that the husband can under no circumstances sell all the maize—that the wife has an absolute right to a share.

Informants have different opinions on the question of who decides, under normal circumstances, how much maize constitutes the wife's share. Some say that the husband takes what he intends to sell, and that what is left is the wife's share. The wife may protest if she thinks her share is too small, but probably to no avail, since the final decision rests with the husband. Other informants say that it is the wife who decides how much will be needed for the household, and that the remainder is the husband's share—it is the wife, after all, who is in the best position to know how much maize the members of the household are likely to consume in a year. Still other informants take a middle position, which probably comes closest to the truth in most cases. They say that how much maize will be left and how much will be sold is hardly ever a matter for discussion and decision making—both parties know from experience how much is required for household consumption. In the one case where I actually witnessed the decision of how much maize to store for home consumption, the husband and wife agreed with hardly any discussion.

Another question on which there is lack of full agreement among informants is the extent to which the "wife's share" is truly a share that belongs to her and can be disposed of by her as she likes. Some informants say that this share is for household use only, that none is to be sold, and that any that is left over at the time of the next harvest must be used as food for the cattle. Others say that the woman may sell a few bags of the household maize to get money for her own needs, as long as there is still enough left so that the family doesn't run short of food. Still others report that not only can the wife sell a few bags of maize during the year but also she controls any portion of her share that is left over at the time of the next harvest. Like the husband, the wife does not have the right to use money from the sale of maize from her share for any personal wants; she can use it only for the benefit of the family. One woman explained that even though the wife controls the money from the sale of this maize, "it isn't actually yours. It goes for family expenses. It is only yours because the maize meant for food belongs to the woman." Another woman said, "The maize in my small granary is mine completely. I can sell it, or use it to brew some beer so as to make more money."

As in the case of the degree to which women have an absolute right to control women's property, there appears to be a connection between an informant's degree of traditional vs. Western orientation and his/her beliefs about wives' rights to control their share of the maize crop. Younger, more educated and/or Christianized informants—and young men more than young women—tend to report *less* right on the part of a wife to control her share of the crop independently. It is precisely these people who have had most opportunity to absorb the new "community property" ideology. Men are likely to absorb this ideology more easily than women because it serves their vested interests.

The husband is the one, in general, to decide how much maize will be planted. If the husband is less ambitious than the wife and plows only a small field, she is free to decide on her own to plant more maize, but she will not "own" or control the crop. Informants agree that any surplus produced over what is needed by the family for food belongs to the husband regardless of who planted it. I was told that a man would never object to his wife's planting more maize and cultivating it with her own labor, because it will be his anyway. Informants are unanimous that it is impossible for a married woman to grow maize of her own that is entirely hers to control. She may grow a small amount in her vegetable garden, but this is considered insignificant.

Informants uniformly hold that if co-wives cultivate one field jointly, at the time of harvest exactly equal maize portions must be put into each wife's granary. Most wives prefer to cultivate separate fields. Ideally, the fields plowed and paid for by the husband should be the same size, and the husband should provide equal labor (his own or contract) for each wife's crop. Informants agree, however, that one co-wife can rightfully have a larger field than the other as a result of her autonomous actions. She can use money from her other enterprises (e.g., chickens and vegetables) for this purpose. In the words of an informant: "At the time of plowing, one of the wives may think of giving some of her money to the husband so that he plows a bigger field for her." Each wife in a polygynous marriage must have her own granary, in which the maize from her field will be stored. The husband ideally should take an equal amount for sale from each wife's granary. Even if the harvest happens to be good in one field and poor in the other, the husband has no right to effect what might seem to be a more equitable distribution between the two wives. Nor is the number of children in each house relevant to the distribution of produce. As one informant (herself the wife of a polygynous husband) explained: "If the house with more children finishes its portion, the cow belonging to that house will be sold for them to buy more maize. If I get a poor yield, the cow belonging to my house will be sold. I will not go to share with the other wife. No. The cow from my *biut* [cattle pen] must be sold."

Although this kind of equality between wives' houses is the ideal, in practice the situation is rather more flexible. First, it is likely that if two co-wives have radically different numbers of children, the one with more children will have made an effort to cultivate a larger crop—probably using additional labor provided by her older children. Second, if co-wives are on good terms and the house of one has a surplus and that of the other is in need, the former will probably make a voluntary "loan" of grain to the latter. Third, it is recognized that husbands *do* sometimes take more maize for sale from the granary of one wife than from that of the other, even though theoretically they should not. Most men feel that a husband has the right to do this if his intentions are good. A man who forcibly effects a redistribution will probably not lose face in the (male) community if his action is judged to have been warranted by circumstances. Women, not surprisingly, tend to feel that a wife's right to control her share of the maize crop herself should be inviolable, and that when husbands effect a forcible redistribution of maize among their wives they are going beyond their rights.

There is complete agreement among my informants that it is impossible or unheard of for a wife to refuse to work on the maize crop in order to pursue some other activity (for example, growing vegetables) that will benefit her more directly. It is her duty to cultivate the maize, even if she suspects that her husband may squander the money from the sale of the surplus and not use it for family needs. Informants also point out that a wife would be stupid to refuse since she will surely get enough of the crop to feed the children. In thus arguing, these informants are making the implicit assumption that even the worst incorrigible will not attempt to abrogate his wife's right to a household share of maize. A wife's right to a share of the maize for household consumption, at least, is absolute.

The change in status of eleusine from the staple crop to a subsidiary crop has resulted in certain ill-defined changes in the distribution of rights over it. In the precolonial period, eleusine, the staple crop, was the joint product and property of husband and wife, but it was women, not men, who bartered grain for animals or animals for grain in times of shortage or surplus. Several female informants compared the degree of control women have over maize as the staple crop unfavorably with the control they formerly had over eleusine as the staple crop. What has happened is that with the commoditization of the staple crop, control over the surplus and the profit it generates has shifted to men.

Some informants stressed the idea that women can now control eleusine absolutely, and regarded this as a gain for women; they ignored the fact that increased control of eleusine by women has only occurred because its significance has diminished. Though eleusine is still considered somewhat similar to maize, its status is ambiguous; it is more like vegetables in that women have the same sort of right to control it. In the words of one informant: "Wimbi [eleusine] is more or less like maize. Once it is in the granary, the wife has got to ask permission from her husband to do what she likes with it. Nevertheless, in a Christian family, the wife can own wimbi completely. Wimbi is actually supposed to be a woman's property." According to another (non-Christian) informant: "Wimbi belongs to the woman who grew it, and the money is hers. She only gives her husband some if he has been sharing his money with her."

The most usual use for eleusine is in brewing. The consensus of informants is that if the woman uses for brewing (along with the eleusine) maize that she acquired independently of her husband (e.g., by being given it by her parents, or by buying it with profits from her vegetables), the money she gains from the venture will be hers to control. Opinion is divided on whether the money will still belong to her if she uses part of the household maize, or whether she will have to share control of it with her husband. In any case, the proviso is always that a married woman brews in order to get money to use for purposes within her own family, and she will normally have discussed her plan with her husband in advance.

It would appear that married women have more autonomous

control of eleusine at present than they had when it was the staple crop, but at the same time, they have lost ground so far as their control over the staple crop is concerned.

One could say that the portion of the staple crop (maize) that the husband now sells is more or less equivalent to what was formerly used for brewing. In the way that, in precolonial times, beer was exchangeable for labor, surplus maize is today converted to cash, which is used to hire (exchange for) labor. In the past, only a limited amount of surplus maize could reasonably be put to use as beer to recruit labor; there was no advantage to men in controlling a greater surplus than this. Wives, who were viewed as responsible for the provision of non-animal food, converted any surplus they controlled into chickens or small stock, which was reconverted to grain in times of shortage. In any case, grain surpluses were small, and their potential uses were limited. Wives had limited control over these surpluses as product. Commoditization of the staple crop means a market for large surpluses, and the potential, via cash, for the conversion of surplus product to the means of production. Husbands thus increasingly have a vested (though not expressed) interest in seeing that their wives control very little more maize than can be used for household consumption—so that economic resources that can be converted to the means of production do not slip into female control. In this way, control of the surplus product has gradually shifted almost completely to men.

Rights in Cash Crops

The three major cash-generating resources in Nandi are maize, milk, and tea. Two of these—maize and milk—are also the backbone of the subsistence economy. To understand some of the apparent ambiguities of the respective rights of husbands and wives in milk and maize, it is necessary to keep their subsistence and cash-generating aspects analytically separate. That tea is a pure commodity, introduced specifically as a cash crop, explains why it is unequivocally controlled by men, though women's labor goes into its production. The role of tea reinforces the point that men control products when they become commodities with significant cash-generating potential.

From what has been said above, it is clear that wives and husbands do share rights in milk and maize. Wives hold rights in these items as product only, however; it is the right of husbands to control them when they enter the commodity sphere. It is true that married women may sometimes have control of small amounts of money gained from the sale of maize or milk, but this is only from the sale of whatever small surpluses are left over from the wife's (family's) allotment for food.

Tea, the third major cash crop, is more clearly and totally under the control of men than is either maize or milk, though it is not uncommon for a man and wife to hold two tea numbers from the Kenya Tea Development Authority.* The usual explanation for this is that there was a time when a certain number of plants per account could be obtained on credit from the Authority, and men took out numbers in their wives' names in order to get twice as many plants on credit. Many informants were at great pains to explain that though a number might be in the wife's name, the money from that tea was not actually hers but came under the control of her husband. Nevertheless, there seem to be a few cases in which the money that comes from the tea held in the wife's name is kept by the wife and used for her own needs. A few women interviewed on this subject mentioned tea independently as something they own. Even so, such an arrangement, where it exists, is at the discretion of the husband. Probably it occurs only where the plot of tea held in the wife's name is quite small, and the husband has a significant income from alternative sources. Almost all informants agreed that a wife has no intrinsic right to own tea. A woman cannot independently use money she controls to buy tea seedlings and plant them on her husband's plot.

The reason usually presented for the wife's inability to plant and control tea independently is that the husband is the owner of the plot and that anything planted on it is therefore his. Here the fact that men and not women now hold land titles is used as a justification for further denying women's right to autonomous

---

*Tea is extremely important in the community where my fieldwork was conducted, as it is in a great many areas of Nandi District, but it is not grown everywhere in the district. It can legally be planted only in an area where it has been determined that typical soil conditions meet a specified minimum standard set by the Kenya Tea Development Authority, the semi-governmental agency that controls the production and marketing of tea and issues account numbers.

economic action. Yet a wife clearly can grow certain crops on her husband's land and have autonomous control of them. Some informants say that what makes tea different is that it is permanent. However, the same informants admit that the wife can plant and own a small number of fruit trees, which are equally permanent. I believe that what distinguishes tea from fruit trees in this context is that it is both self-perpetuating and an economically significant commodity. It is in this sense equivalent to the herd as a major means of production.

A few exceptional informants claim that a woman *does* have the right to plant and own her own tea. One of them, a Kenya Tea Development Authority agricultural extension instructor, related the following case:

> There is a woman called Dorcas who lives in [a neighboring community]. Her husband refused to give her money [to buy tea], so she went to her parents' home and was given it. She bought the tea with it. Now her tea is doing well. When the husband realized that the tea gave lots of money, he went to seize the disc [which must be presented to collect a payment for leaf] from her. When he wanted to go and get the money, the wife went to report him to the KTDA and that money was withheld. The man was warned that he would be taken to court if he insisted on keeping the disc. In the end, he gave the disc to his wife and his wife went to get the money. That woman is now getting on well with her work of taking care of the tea.

Husband, wife, and other household members participate in planting, weeding, and picking tea. Though men control the income from tea, I never heard of a case of a woman refusing to participate in cultivating the tea so as to have more time for pursuits that would yield income she could control independently (e.g., cultivating vegetables). My female informants denied that such action was even conceivable, and noted that the amount of effort involved in tea cultivation is not great and all family members benefit from the profits.

Rights in Income

Opportunities for wage labor mean that cash incomes have become economically significant, in some cases even capable of replacing the means of production in the household economy. It

follows from this, together with the fact that cash-crop production was originally the province of men, that cash has come to
be regarded as a resource that male heads of households have
the right to control.

Married women, most informants of both sexes agree, do not
have the right to independent control of large amounts of money.
Any significant household income, whatever its source, comes
under the husband's control. Male informants express the dangers of female control of money in the following terms: "If a
woman earns more money than her husband, she can easily
boast. Whenever a quarrel arises, she can say that she is the
master of the economy in the family. That way, she will seek to
be the head of the family. I have seen some women here in
Nandi who earned money. Eventually, they could not lead a
good life with their men. Therefore, some of them parted." Or:
"Our women are easily swayed by money. Once she has a lot of
money, a woman can break away from her husband."

In spite of such statements, most men (and women) do not
oppose the idea of a married woman working for wages, particularly in occupations that require a relatively high level of education (e.g., teaching). Most husbands welcome this additional income, as long as it is clearly understood that the woman will not
have autonomous control of it. Many informants regarded favor-
ably the idea of a joint bank account. They made clear that while
a husband is free to draw from such an account without consultation with the wife, she can only withdraw with permission of
her husband.

If a woman *does* control any money, she definitely does not
have the right to disperse it in any way that is not to the immediate benefit of her family of procreation without her husband's
consent. She cannot, for example, invest in a business venture
(though if her source of income is marketing or the operation of
a shop, it is considered all right for her to reinvest her profits on
a small scale), or use the money to help her own siblings with
school fees, or make gifts or loans to persons of her own choosing. But the husband definitely *does* have the right to use money
in these ways without consultation with his wife. It must be
borne in mind, however, that this is what informants say when
speaking normatively. I knew of a few cases where women who

had recently acquired fairly large amounts of money, from brewing, for example, or from the sale of several bags of vegetables, used this money to make loans apparently without consulting their husbands. One woman lent her own sister money to buy grain for brewing; another woman lent her husband's brother money to buy a bicycle.

A few informants pointed out that if a wife is educated and working for wages, it would be very bad for her husband to refuse her request to help her family of orientation: "He knows very well that my parents educated me and otherwise that money would not exist," one commented. Another said: "The wife can tell the husband, 'My parents educated me and that is why I have a job. I haven't done anything good for them, and so I would like to build a better house for my parents.' If her husband knows that he really married her before she did anything for her parents, he will not refuse to let her do something for them."

Though it is considered that wives do not have the right of access to or control over significant amounts of money, almost all informants believe that women should have small amounts of money that they can use as they like in ways that will be "of benefit to their families." Such money either may be given to the wife by the husband as an allowance (especially in households that have significant cash income from employment or large-scale cash-cropping), or may be the result of her own activities in economic spheres considered to be the province of women.

Rights of Widows in Property

When a woman's husband dies, her status with regard to property changes dramatically. Widows, unlike wives, can and do hold and manage property in their own right.

Though the bulk of a widow's house property is inherited by her adult sons at their father's death, or by minor sons when they reach maturity, certain categories of cattle become her personal property, and she maintains full cultivation rights in the family land. Snell (1954:53) says that "each of the deceased's widows, in order of seniority, received one or more cows, according to the number available." I was told that a widow has a right to retain as her own property one cow from the bridewealth paid for each of her daughters. She also has the right to control the distribution of the offspring of her wedding cattle (those she received as gifts at her initiation or marriage) among her sons.

If a woman dies without a son or a wife, her house property reverts to sons of her co-wife or of her husband's brother, but in her lifetime the widow maintains control of the disposition of her property, and can therefore circumvent inheritance by those people. In one case, a widow with a daughter but no sons sold her farm and gave the money to her son-in-law to pool with his own for the purchase of a large farm in another sublocation. She then moved with her cattle to live with her daughter and son-in-law.

Nearly always, an older widow with adult sons lives with one of them on his share of the family land. It is then the son, not the mother, who is held to be the head of the compound and owner of the land. (If the son is not yet married, the question of who is head of the compound may be somewhat blurred.) Most informants say that widows usually prefer to pool resources with this son and not take independent responsibility for the management of their property. They keep working as long as they are able, but usually in cooperation with the wife or wives of their sons, and are given their share of maize and milk from those of the family. They may maintain some sidelines of their own—chickens or a vegetable plot, for example—as a source of private cash. A number of widows I knew brewed and sold beer on a more or less regular basis. In a fairly typical case, the family had one maize field, but the widowed mother weeded only in the section immediately behind her own house. She referred to this section as "my field," though the son and daughter-in-law recognized no such distinction and maize from it was not separated from the rest of the maize at harvest time. This woman also kept a few chickens and brewed occasionally. A widow has her own house within the compound of her son and cooks for herself and her visitors separately from the rest of the family.

Though older widows may usually choose to pool resources with a son, informants unanimously agree that a widow is perfectly within her rights to insist upon cultivating her own separate plot of maize independently of her son. There is no limit to

the size of the area she may cultivate (provided the land is sufficient for the son to cultivate his own maize as well), and the produce belongs to her absolutely. Even if the son provides his
mother with seeds and fertilizer, and plows the field for her, he
has no legitimate claim on his mother's maize. In fact, it is considered his responsibility to provide his mother with such help,
without any reciprocal obligation. If the widowed mother grows
more maize than she needs for her own food, she may sell the
surplus and use the profit as she likes. She may own any type of
property whatsoever. If she can save enough money, she is perfectly free to buy a cow or even a piece of land. In one case, a
widow lived with her son and cultivated separately. He was a
poor property manager who had been forced to sell all his cattle.
The mother, however, owned a number of cows, including two
milk cows. She gave a small quantity of milk to her daughter-in-
law to feed the children, but sold the rest and used the money
for her own purposes. Though it may not be the most commonly chosen alternative, stories abound of widows who took
over the management of their property "as if they were men,"
and even became rich in their own right.

A widow with minor sons holds her sons' share of her house
property in trust for them and manages it in their names until
they come of age. She can sell animals if necessary, but the ideal
is to hold the property intact insofar as possible until the sons
reach their majority. Informants, especially men, say that it is
the duty of the dead man's brother (whether or not he is the
wife's levirate husband) to oversee the management of the property and make sure the wife does not "misuse" or "squander" it.
Thus, if a widow with minor sons wishes to sell a cow, and the
need to do so is not obvious, her husband's brother might successfully intervene. If she is administering the property capably,
however, his rights to intervene are very limited. Men sometimes claim (and other men may support their contention in
this) that they are in fact managing the property left by a
deceased brother, when it is clear to an outside observer, and
openly recognized among the women of the neighborhood, that
the widow is the actual property manager.

The role of widow, as opposed to that of wife, is marked
by the activation of the woman's residual right to manage her

house property. Widows, very much unlike wives, are free to assume economic rights and autonomy that closely approach those of men. In modern Nandi, the autonomy of widows is quite striking. As I have noted in Chapter 4 in relation to levirate marriage, it appears likely that the advent of the cash economy and commoditization of resources has actually increased this autonomy. Widows now enter into levirate marriage only very rarely, since they can use cash to hire male wage laborers to do any tasks the levir otherwise might perform. A widow, if she has sufficient economic resources, answers to no one. Thus, interestingly, though the effects of the cash economy have been largely detrimental to women as wives, the opposite appears true for women as widows.

Property Rights and Woman-Woman Marriage

Like widows, women who marry wives assume control of their house property. The difference is that in the case of female husbands, there are no sons with whom any portion of this property must be divided. The female husband thus assumes control of property in which her husband's rights heretofore dominated, as well as those (e.g., wedding cattle) in which her own rights were predominant. She assumes such control when she marries a wife even if, as sometimes happens, her male husband is still alive. I knew of one case where an elderly woman and her elderly husband married young brides almost simultaneously, divided their plot, and from then on lived side by side with their young wives at a level of amity and cooperation such as characterizes the relationships between the households of brothers who occupy adjacent plots. To avoid the ambiguity of a woman managing property that should rightfully remain under male control, the female husband is said to become a man (Oboler 1980).

Just how long a history woman-woman marriage has in Nandi is unclear, but it is my belief that it is not ancient. It occurred only rarely in precolonial Nandi, according to informants' accounts, and probably mainly in the case of sonless women whose houses held exceptionally large numbers of cattle. Informants who claim any knowledge of the origins of this institution hold that the Nandi acquired it from the Kipsigis. I believe it diffused to the Kipsigis from the neighboring Bantu Gusii (see Oboler 1980). However, much more research is clearly necessary to provide support for this belief. Woman-woman marriage is unknown among the more northern Kalenjin, though it has recently begun to occur among the Keiyo. I was told by Keiyo informants that the Keiyo acquired the idea of woman-woman marriage from the Nandi.

The case of woman-woman marriage in Nandi is an interesting instance of the type of response to socioeconomic change in which a traditional institution is used in an attempt to maintain the status quo in the face of changing circumstances. Woman-woman marriage is taken by many Nandi "progressives" as a hallmark of Nandi traditionalism. It is denounced in the preaching and teaching of missionaries and decried by educated and Christianized Nandi as an example of "backwardness." Yet despite this campaign against it, far from dying out in the modern setting, it has flourished. There are more such marriages now than there were in the precolonial period. In what way is the decision of increasing numbers of sonless postmenopausal women to marry wives a response to the current socioeconomic context?

My informants are in agreement that, though the possibility of woman-woman marriage has existed in Nandi for at least a hundred years, there was a sudden increase in the incidence of this institution about twenty-five years ago. Informants consistently told me that the women who first became female husbands in large numbers were "wives of Kimnyigei and Nyongi." I think it is not merely coincidental that women of these age categories were postmenopausal and thus eligible to take wives just around the time of and shortly after the partitioning of land under the Swynnerton Plan.

In the precolonial period, a widow without a male heir continued to live where she had always lived and to cultivate a plot in the same area where she had always cultivated. It is now possible for a sonless widow to be denied rights in land when land title passes at her husband's death to his nearest male heirs. The devolution of land title to other houses does not occur in the case of a female husband, however. If her wife has a son, he is considered a male heir of her husband. Even if her wife has not yet borne a son, it is assumed that she will. The property of the female husband's house is held in trust for future male heirs. Thus, a female husband, though sonless, *cannot* be denied rights in and access to land. She continues to control land that she holds in trust for future sons of her house, as a widow with minor sons controls land that she holds in trust for them.

Marrying a wife is a way in which a sonless widow can maintain control over land that would otherwise pass out of her house, and to which she might therefore be denied access. Before private land ownership was instituted, no such strategy was necessary. In some other East African societies the role of female husband is open to any woman who chooses to and can afford to adopt it (see Obbo 1976); in Nandi, only a relatively small number of women can make this choice. Nevertheless, an increasing incidence of woman-woman marriage must be viewed as one aspect of Nandi women's reaction against the diminution of their rights in land brought about by male inheritance of land title. The fact that private ownership of land and this increased incidence of woman-woman marriage are linked in time lends support to this interpretation.

The Case of Independent Women

Most of the women, aside from widows, who live independently of a man are separated from their husbands. If a woman decides that she can no longer live with her husband, she has the right to return to her own family. Except in the very rare instances of formal divorce with return of bridewealth, she cannot remarry. There must always be a place for her on the land of her father or one of her brothers (though her children have no rights in their grandfather's or uncle's property but must claim their inheritance from their mother's husband). A woman who has returned to her own family usually assists in the cultivation of the family's maize, and in return is provided with enough for her own maintenance and that of her children. Though she may sometimes cultivate a plot of maize of her own, she does not have the automatic right to cultivate maize independently or to own her own cattle and graze them on her father's or brother's land; but she may work as she likes in any of the economic activities reserved for women (vegetables, chickens, brewing, etc.). Brewing, on which a woman (in 1977) can make a profit of 200–300 shillings a month, is a fairly common sideline for separated women who are not under any religious strictures that forbid it. Separated women who are educated and can work for wages are, of course, in the best position. In the modern setting, once such women have saved enough money from their salaries, they are quite free to acquire land, cattle, or any other form of property, or to invest in their own businesses. Occasionally, even a separated woman who is not educated can acquire significant property; I was told of a case in which a young woman who had separated from her husband was given a plot of land by her parents as a gift.

Another category of independent women, one that is becoming increasingly common, is that of women who have never married. Despite the great prejudice among men against marrying women who already have children, premarital pregnancy among adolescent girls is common. These unmarried girls usually remain in their parents' homes and raise their children; or if they are educated, they can, like educated separated women, work, save money, acquire property, and become completely independent. Because of the increasing number of never-married women, the idea of inheritance of property by daughters is being talked of—though so far as I know it has not been carried out. Particularly in families with no sons, but also in some families with sons, I have heard discussions of the possibility of allowing unmarried daughters who have borne children at home to inherit on an equal basis with their brothers. Some forward-thinking people have told me that they definitely plan to make such provision for their daughters.

Independent women, though perhaps more common at present than in earlier times, are not a new phenomenon. An example is the case of a woman, now in her eighties or possibly nineties, who lives in the community in which this research was conducted. She migrated from the extreme south of Nandi, in the borderland with Terik, over forty years before the time of my fieldwork. She was then a young widow with three daughters. She homesteaded in the forested area in the research community and developed her farm entirely through her own efforts. Since there was no male in her household, at the time of land partitioning she received title to her farm. When her daughters reached adulthood, she divided the plot into three portions and gave each daughter one. Two of the daughters sold their portions and with their husbands used the money to add to the husbands' holdings. The third, a woman now in her forties, continues to live with her mother on her portion. She is periodically visited by her husband, who lives elsewhere.

It is possible, but certainly not typical, for an unmarried woman in Nandi, unlike a wife, to achieve a high level of economic independence. The partitioning of land has somewhat undermined the positions of separated women and the newer group of never-married women—particularly as the obligation of fathers, brothers, and their male heirs to support separated or never-married daughter/sister/aunts is a moral and not a legal one. Though a separated woman technically retains rights in her husband's property, if reconciliation is impossible her situation can be very tenuous unless she has left a son behind in her husband's home, in which case she usually returns to live with her son when he establishes an independent household.

Only a few independent women are in a position to take advantage of the opportunities offered by the cash economy—that is, the educated elite, who can earn wages sufficient to yield significant savings. A handful of elite women have attained considerable economic independence—indeed, a few educated women are beginning to make a conscious decision not to be married. The position of the majority of "independent" women has been undermined by the loss of automatic access to land.

Women, Men, and Changing Rights in Property

When questioned in the most general terms about the traditional property rights of wives, most informants stress their *lack* of rights. Typical informants' statements include:

A woman had no power over anything . . . as soon as she went to live with her husband, all that she possessed would belong to the husband.

There was no property for a woman, mainly because all women were considered to be junior and weak-willed. . . . Even all the items used in the house were claimed by men. Men thought they totally possessed their wives because the bridewealth had been paid.

The wife had absolutely nothing, and although she was the one who worked, the product belonged to the husband.

More direct questioning about the specifics of rights in and control over property reveals that wives have/had economic rights that are not insignificant. Clearly, the distribution of control of property between husband and wife is unequal; but just as clearly, it is not as unequal as informants' general ideological statements would lead one to believe.

Certain changes in ideology about land tenure that would seem likely to improve the economic position of women in general are actually only relevant to independent women. Legal ownership of land is now open to women as well as men, but it is almost impossible for a wife to take advantage of this. Further, among women who are separated from their husbands, land ownership is a real option only for a handful of educated elite women. Another possible change is the option, being considered (and perhaps only that) by certain families, of allowing daughters to inherit family land on an equal footing with sons; but this is being considered only for the minority of daughters who fail to marry and therefore need land to support themselves. Those who do marry—the majority—will be provided with land by their husbands.

At the same time, a number of recent developments threaten to erode the traditional economic rights of wives. Though it has been a basic Nandi axiom from precolonial times that men control the major means of production, such control traditionally did not amount to "ownership." In reality, land and the bulk of the family herd were "owned" by no one. Many people were involved in a complicated network of rights of various kinds in these forms of property, and no single individual had the right to alienate them. The cash economy and commoditization of these basic resources brought about real ownership of property—ownership that makes possible the alienation of property by a single person. It is now legal for a husband/father to sell a piece of the family land and consume the profit, ignoring the rights of both his wives and sons, who stand to inherit this land.

I know of several such cases. The distribution of land titles to males only under the Swynnerton Plan, with the assumption and consequent emergence of patrilineal land inheritance by males only, seriously undermined the rights of women in land. Women can now lose their access to land, and the assumption that family land is owned by the husband rather than by the wife strengthens the husband's authority in family politics.

The commoditization of cattle has also undermined wives' traditional rights. The common practice of selling off low-milk-yielding indigenous cattle and buying European dairy stock very often means that the wife loses her house-property cattle and has less definite rights in their replacements, which, having been bought with male-controlled cash, are usually regarded more as cattle independently acquired by men than as inherited house-property cattle. As the distinction between house-property cattle and other cattle becomes increasingly blurred, wives' rights in the bulk of the family herd become much less clear than they once were.

One significant aspect of women's economic rights has been the fact that several well-defined (albeit minor) spheres of economic activity have been reserved for them as beneath men's dignity. Modern young men, less constrained than were men of previous generations by concepts of male "dignity," have begun to encroach on formerly feminine spheres of economic activity that are capable of yielding large profits. This seems to be especially true in the case of exotic vegetables.

Young men, especially those of the educated and Christian elite, also give less cognizance to women's various specific traditional economic rights, preferring to emphasize instead the modern "community property" ideology. Whether or not the teaching of missions—particularly Protestant missions—is the origin of this ideology, it serves to reinforce it. Christian missionaries consciously teach "family life," including the ideas that husband and wife should reach joint decisions in love and harmony, should act as a corporate unit, and should not have separate, possibly conflicting, economic interests. The intent of such teaching is no doubt good. The model missionaries have in mind for husband-wife relations is a relatively egalitarian one (though they also teach that the husband is the head of the family as

Christ is the head of the Church). However, the notion of community property does not serve to enhance egalitarian relations between spouses in practice. What it usually means is that various categories of property are merged and that the husband assumes the dominant role in controlling everything. Commoditization aids this process because all resources are now translatable into cash and therefore can be regarded as essentially alike. In practice, the wives of the young, Christian, educated elite, when questioned intensively about the specifics of household economic decision making, do not report any more mutual decision making than do other wives—in fact, in many cases they report less. What "common ownership" actually means is greater rights of ownership for husbands. Wives are in fact losing their right to total control of female economic spheres without gaining more influence in other spheres.

Older and more traditional men are very reluctant to trespass on their wives' activities in female economic spheres. Young men seem to feel that they are within their rights in attempting to control their wives' profits from these spheres (because they see it as the husband's right to control *all* income). This is particularly the case whenever a large profit may be realized in one of these spheres. The theme is reiterated, especially by young, educated, Christian, "modern" informants: if there are a *lot* of chickens or cows, or a very large plot of vegetables, a man may have to take over financial control of his wife's venture.

A conflict of norms is generated here. On the one hand, that men (husbands) should control the means of production is axiomatic. On the other hand is the norm that women (wives) have the absolute right to certain forms of property. These forms of property are ones that formerly were economically insignificant. With commoditization, however, it can be profitable to step up the production of such resources—so that they are comparable to cattle in value. In this situation of competing norms, different actors can appeal to the norm that maximizes or best protects their own position: women—especially the older ones—are much more likely than men to hold out for women's absolute right to certain forms of property. This norm, however, is likely to fall by the wayside in time. What is happening is not really a change in ideology about women's rights in property but a redefinition of the more fundamental norm: that men control the means of production. It is where women's resources rival the means of production in economic significance that men step in to control them. This explains informants' statements such as: wives may not reinvest their profits without their husbands' consent; if a man's wife is a professional such as a teacher, he should control her income; husbands can take over forms of property technically reserved for women if their value becomes significant. The difference between the statements and behavior of young and old men should not be interpreted entirely as a shift in ideology. In a sense—though their position is bolstered by statements about communal ownership in Christian families—young men are merely ahead of the older men in realizing the implication of commoditization. This is that once all resources can be converted to cash, the issue in who controls them becomes their quantity rather than their type.

Perhaps, then, the general affluence of modern Nandi has an adverse effect on the economic status of wives vis-à-vis husbands. The expansion of cash-cropping increases the amount of income controlled by men much more rapidly than that controlled by women. This would be enough to lower women's economic status vis-à-vis that of men. However, not only do men already control much larger incomes than do their wives, but also they now seek to assume control of income from what were formerly wives' economic preserves. Still, it is important not to overstate the ubiquitousness of this trend. Many husbands do allow their wives autonomy where female economic spheres are concerned, and I know a number of women who control significant incomes from them.

This brings up another point of great importance in the assessment of Nandi women's economic rights: the degree to which such rights exist at the discretion of husbands. Though wives have a great many economic rights *in theory*, I have pointed out above how little power they have to prevent their husbands from violating or ignoring those rights. The main sanction that can be invoked against a husband who persistently violates his wife's rights is public opinion—the importance of a man's reputation for "polite" behavior within the local community. This sanction can be expected to be very powerful in a traditional community. If "modernization" brings about, as it so often does, larger communities, mobility, and increased impersonality of relations between neighbors, the sanction of damage to reputation and community opinion may become ineffective. I would surmise that this situation is a long way off in Nandi, but it still has potential for undermining women's position in the long run.

Though I argued above that affluence has increased the economic differential beween the sexes, there is a way in which affluence may have helped to maintain women's economic position. As long as community opinion is still a powerful sanction, affluence defers the *need* for men to risk damaging their reputations by violating their wives' rights. A man with a large herd or with a good income from cash-cropping does not have to sell land or a cow from his wife's house property—he can find some other source of needed cash. Bad economic times, however, could change this picture very quickly. It is important to acknowledge the tenuousness of the forces supporting an equilibrium in which women's economic rights, though eroded, are to some degree maintained.

Another threat to the economic status of wives is the refusal of young, educated men to allow their wives even the traditional limited ownership of livestock. This is epitomized by the refusal of the traditional wedding cow (*chepsegut*) during some Christian wedding ceremonies.

The transition from eleusine to maize as the staple crop has also possibly adversely affected the economic position of wives. Maize was first grown in Nandi as a male-controlled cash crop and was strongly encouraged for that purpose by the colonial government. Now that maize has replaced eleusine as the staple crop, it is not at all clear to people that wives should have the same relatively absolute rights over their share of maize as they once had over their share of eleusine.

Thus, a large number of factors are at work that adversely affect the position of women (especially as wives) vis-à-vis men with regard to economic rights. These factors mainly have their roots in the commoditization of resources and the advent of private ownership, together with the basic Nandi axiom that men are the appropriate controllers of the means of production. There are some elements of the current socioeconomic context, it must be granted, that have the potential of being ultimately beneficial to women's economic position. The cash economy has also helped bring about greater autonomy for widows, but widowhood does not occupy the largest part of the average woman's life cycle. Unfortunately, these positive elements are of little significance when compared with the numerous ways in which women's economic rights have been undermined. The net impact of the changes that have taken place in Nandi ideology about men's and women's property rights has been detrimental to the position of women.

EIGHT

Sexual Stratification and Socioeconomic Change

THE TERM "sexual stratification" is borrowed from Alice Schlegel, who defines it in terms of differential access, based on sex and gender, to rewards, prestige, or power (Schlegel 1976:3). Rewards is understood by Schlegel to refer to access to and/or control of material goods (Schlegel 1976:6).* Prestige is measured by deference. Schlegel makes clear that she distinguishes prestige from value. A person can be valued without necessarily receiving prestige or deference—for example, a slave may be valued as an economic producer (Schlegel 1976:7). For reasons that I shall elaborate upon later, I disagree with Schlegel's decision to use deference as a simple index of prestige. Prestige has to do with questions of whether one sex is considered to be in some sense "better" than the other, whether its activities are evaluated as "more important" than those of the other sex (by members of both sex and gender categories). These factors are not correlated with overt deference behavior in any simple way. Power is seen by Schlegel as intimately bound up with the concepts of authority and autonomy. "By power, I mean the ability to exert control, whatever the means of this control may be,

*In my description and analysis of differential male and female control of material goods in the Nandi case, I have made a distinction between control of product and control of the means of production. This distinction is important to understanding Nandi assertions about men, women, and property, and would be of value in the analysis of other ethnographic cases as well. I shall not try to follow through on it in my discussion of comparative material, however, because it is a distinction that most of the authors whose work I am discussing do not make.

within the domestic, political, economic or religious spheres. Authority is one form of power; it is the socially recognized and legitimated right to make decisions concerning others. . . . By autonomy, I mean freedom from control by others" (Schlegel 1976:8–9). In discussing sexual stratification, Schlegel is most concerned with the power dimension: she regards as sexually stratified any society in which men have greater power than women, in which men, as a general category or by differential access to particular roles, have much greater ability to control the behavior of women than women have to control the behavior of men.

More conventional definitions of stratification focus on the economic dimension. Fried (1967:186) defines stratification as "unequal access to the basic resources that sustain life." Fried and other stratification theorists do not intend such a definition to apply to differences between the sexes; rather, they are setting a framework for the analysis of social systems in which a group of people can be cut off from the possibility of sustaining their very existence, and this is never true of a gender category. This concept does not have to be stretched very far, however, before it becomes applicable to sex. Where private ownership of the means of production is found together with inheritance by males only, women's only access to basic resources is through men. Regardless of whether women are denied access to basic resources, they are denied the right to control them or to have the same degree of control over them that men have. I think it is reasonable to use the term sexual stratification for this less extreme case also.

Technically, the classic definition of stratification does not apply to relations between the sexes in pre-class societies. But this does not mean that the sexes are equal in such societies. There are important bases for sexual inequality besides differences in access to the means of production. Though the term "sexual stratification" may be somewhat ambiguous, it has a place in the anthropological literature on sex roles, and I continue to use it because it highlights the significant inequality that frequently exists between women and men.

Sexual Stratification, Power, and Male Dominance

A persistent problem that arises in the study of sex and gender* in anthropology is the difficulty of discussing substantive issues such as the proposition that certain types of societies are more sexually egalitarian than others without having a standard vocabulary of terms. We disagree on what certain basic terms mean, yet we continue to use them. A lexicon of terms from any ethnographic account of gender roles (including this one) would have to include, in the power dimension alone, such concepts as power, authority, influence, autonomy, deference, and dominance. All these terms are used and reused in the description of relations between the sexes that are said to be egalitarian or inegalitarian. Many times they are used without a great deal of clarity, even interchangeably. Although there are undoubtedly connections between the constructs these terms stand for, it is possible to separate one from the other. In fact, very little headway is going to be made in the cross-cultural study of gender inequality until we reach some basic agreements about what our terms denote so that we can then focus on how these phenomena are connected to one another. With the exception of "dominance," these power concepts can be sorted out fairly easily. In the prestige dimension things again become conceptually murky as we struggle with notions of value, evaluation, and esteem, and the significance of ritual power, authority and danger, purity and pollution, sexual segregation, and ideological differentiation by sex.

*Sex and gender are two analytically separable concepts. Sex is a biological phenomenon, a configuration of chromosomal pattern and internal and external genitalia, on the basis of which an individual plays a particular role in the process of biological reproduction. Despite the existence of numerous types of "intersex" individuals, most mammals belong to one of two biological sexes. Gender is a cultural-social phenomenon. Gender categories are sets of ideas and behaviors that distinguish (at least) most members of one sex from most members of the other in a given society. Though every culture has at least two gender categories, some have more. Even where there are only two gender categories, assignment of gender is not necessarily congruent with biological sex. In an account such as this, it is often difficult to maintain the distinction between these two concepts. When I use the term "sex" or "gender" here, I am usually referring to some aspects of both concepts. In this chapter, the use of either of these terms should be understood as a shorthand through which I avoid repeated use of the awkward construct "sex/gender."

With Schlegel, I assume power to mean the ability to exert control, *by whatever means*, over the behavior of others (and I would add, over their access to valued resources). Authority and influence I view as subcategories of power, though I do not see these concepts as exhausting the range of forms power may take. This usage is clearly derived from that of Weber, as are definitions of power used by other authors discussed here (e.g., Schlegel, Sanday, Begler), but is not identical with it. In Weber's terms: "Power (*Macht*) is the probability that one actor within a social relationship will be in a position to carry out his own will despite resistance, regardless of the basis on which this probability rests" (Weber 1947:152). Authority is legitimated power: a person exercises control over certain areas because he or she is recognized by others as having the right to do so. Influence is rooted in persuasion: a person is able to exert control over another by convincing him or her that a particular course of action is best (from whatever viewpoint—practical, expressive, moral, etc.). Weber's discussion implies that he understood power as always ultimately backed up by the possibility of the use of force. In the case of authority, threat of the use of force is not the primary motivation for compliance: "A criterion of every true relationship of imperative control [*Herrschaft*, sometimes translated "authority"] is a certain minimum of voluntary submission" (Weber 1947: 324). This submission is based in legitimacy (Weber 1947:325). My usage of "authority" thus very closely follows that of Weber.

My usage of "influence" differs from Weber's. Influence is based in persuasion, and is not necessarily backed up by force. But the need to persuade implies at least initial resistance. Influence thus is subsumed by power as Weber initially defined it, though not as he ultimately developed the terms "power" and "political" (Weber 1947:155–56). Rather than distinguish influence from power, I prefer to view it as a form of power, one means by which a social actor may gain compliance with his or her will. I find this approach particularly useful in discussing the distribution of power between the sexes, because though ethnographic examples of women using or threatening to use physical force against men are rare, women frequently have other means, influence being but one of them, of gaining male compliance. Thus, influence is one form of power, and threat or use of force is another. The ability to withhold valued goods or services is another, and there are undoubtedly still others.

Autonomy is, as Schlegel has put it, freedom from control by others. Deference is discussed at length by Stephens, who defines it as "the general posture of respect, submissiveness and obedience . . . a sort of ritual expression of social inequality" (Stephens 1963:291). Deference customs include obedience, walking behind the deferred-to person, "bowing, kneeling, hand-kissing; speech etiquette, such as speaking in a low voice, not joking, not arguing or contradicting; mealtime etiquette, such as giving the deferred-to person the seat of honor, giving him the best food, letting him eat first; and body-elevation rules" (Stephens 1963:85).

It is clear that judgments of differential power depend partly on authority and influence. It may often be more instructive not to ask which sex has *more* power (though I think this extremely important when it can be clearly determined) but rather which sex has access to what forms of power. What is important, when power is looked at this way, is the realization that the fact that only men hold formal authority positions does not logically imply that women are cut off from all sources of power. There are probably no societies in the world where women are utterly powerless. It is common to read in ethnographic accounts that women lack authority but have a great deal of influence over important decisions in certain arenas. The degree of control that can be achieved through influence undoubtedly varies from one cultural context to another. When we have clearly separated this concept analytically from other related concepts, we can proceed to ask what other factors are related to this variation. This is equally true for such concepts as autonomy and deference.

It is logically possible for women in a particular society to have very little power and yet have a great deal of autonomy. If women are highly autonomous, this necessarily implies that men's power over them is restricted. Yet it does not necessarily mean that male power over women is absent. Total autonomy of individuals is an assumption Leacock (1978) apparently makes for band-level, egalitarian societies, and this assumption leads her to treat autonomy as theoretically equivalent to absence of

power. Where autonomy is less than total, this will not necessarily hold. It is possible that even with a high level of female
autonomy, there is still a residue of male power over women
that is not counterbalanced by a similar residue of female control
over men. It is also logically possible for a society to exist in
which, though each sex may have the same amount of power
over the other, one sex has far less autonomy than the other because its autonomy is restricted in patterned relationships with
members of the same sex (e.g., elders and juniors, mothers-in-
law and daughters-in-law). It is therefore important to separate
autonomy analytically from power, while recognizing that these
two concepts are nevertheless intimately connected.

Deference behavior is easy to see and document, and though
in some sense it certainly appears to be a statement about power
relations, it would be very misleading to assume that it is always
a simple index of them. Ethnographic instances abound in which
relatively extreme forms of public deference behavior coexist
with relatively egalitarian behind-the-scenes behavior. It is even
possible, in some cases, for deference to be given to the subordi-
nate party in a power relationship—witness the code of chivalry
in Euro-American culture. This, of course, is relevant to the question of whether it makes sense to measure prestige by deference, as Schlegel does. No simple, intrinsic connection between
prestige, or power, and deference can be assumed a priori.

If these power-related concepts are easy to distinguish analytically, this cannot be said for the extremely conceptually and
emotionally loaded term "male dominance." The best developed
definitions of the term dominance come from the field of ethol-
ogy, where it means "priorities accorded to different animals"
and "the ability of an animal to control or influence the behavior
of animals around him or her" (Dolhinow 1972:378) and has to
do further with preferential access to "high-priority objects"
(Dolhinow 1972:381). Dictionary definitions echo this usage—
dominance means "rule" or "control." However, there is another common-sense connotation of dominance that has to do
with degree of importance. "Universal male dominance" is thus
sometimes equated with a universal ascription of greater cultural importance to male activities by members of both sexes.
An argument then made against the ubiquity of male domi-

nance relies on showing that the assumption that male activities are everywhere accorded foremost prestige by all members of all societies is an error resulting from Western and/or male ethnographic bias.

The trouble with the term "male dominance" is that we want it to mean too much, and try to make it include everything that we deem significant about male-female relations. My position is that at the very least this term should be restricted to the power dimension of inequality and dropped from the discussion of differential prestige. Even then, there is still room for many confusing alternate usages. For example, does "male dominance" mean a situation of nearly absolute control of women by men, or simply one in which men have a slight edge in a sexual balance of power?

Once, not so long ago, we were told even by feminist anthropologists that male dominance is cross-culturally ubiquitous if not universal (Rosaldo 1974; Gough 1975; Lamphere 1977). Now we are being told that male dominance is not only not universal, it is not even cross-culturally very common (Rogers 1978; Poewe 1980; Sanday 1981). Sanday (1981:165) writes that "the relationship between the sexes is classified as equal in 32% of the societies in this study and unequal in 28%. . . . The remaining 40% of the societies either fit the criteria expressive of 'mythical' male dominance or represent cases in which women exercise economic but no political power." The difference between these two points of view about the cross-cultural incidence of male dominance lies in the criteria for deciding what counts as a case of a society that is marked by male dominance. Sanday accepts as an unequivocal case of male dominance only a situation in which female input into economic decisions or control over any produce is absent (and presumably, since economic power and political participation form a Guttman scale, female political participation is also absent) (Sanday 1981:254–55). Cases in which women have *any* economic or political power, even in the presence of an ideology of male superiority or a high level of male aggression against women, are counted as examples of "mythical male dominance" (Sanday 1981:255).

Scholars who believe that the data support the interpretation that male dominance is widespread are working with a much broader (though sometimes not as explicitly defined) idea of what this concept means. Many who consider male dominance the usual state of affairs cross-culturally, I am sure, would also have no difficulty in accepting the proposition that societies in which women are powerless, both economically and politically, are rare in the world. Note that Sanday counts as egalitarian the cases in which "women have political and economic power and/or authority and male aggression in the form of rape or raiding other groups for wives is absent" (Sanday 1981:254). In other words, if women have *any* political power, even if it is less extended or significant than that of men, and even though there may be moderate or frequent wife beating (a point lower on her male aggression scale than rape or raiding for wives), we are dealing with a society in which the sexes are equal.

Sanday's work is admirable in that it focuses attention on the degree to which the balance of power between the sexes varies cross-culturally, and on the very real sources of power that women frequently have. Her suggestions about the other cultural and ecological factors that correlate with high or low levels of male dominance (or as she would put it, the presence or absence of male dominance) are also extremely important. However, the way in which she defines male dominance obscures more than it illuminates. The denial of male dominance as a common cross-cultural phenomenon means that anthropologists who view the societies they work in as male-dominated can be labeled as either male-brainwashed or trapped within Western models of "reality," or both. In the late 1960's and early 1970's, feminist anthropologists were faced with the problem of explaining why, if sex roles are not biologically preordained, male dominance is so cross-culturally common. One school of feminist anthropologists has chosen to explain this phenomenon by explaining it away.

I have contended throughout this work that male dominance is a fact of life in Nandi. I have also taken pains to define the limits of Nandi male dominance. Still, the fact that women have some degree of access to and control over resources and are not totally powerless in relations with men does not make the sexes equal. There is a balance of power in Nandi, it is true, but the scale is heavily tipped in favor of men.

It is possible that someone could read my ethnographic description without all the caveats I have imposed on it and get the impression that Nandi women are far more powerful than in fact they are. Following Sanday's stated criteria for placement in her categories, I myself would have to assign Nandi to the "mythical male dominance" category. Since this category as defined by Sanday does account for the majority of cases in her sample, and since I do not believe Nandi intergender relations are extremely ethnographically atypical, there is some logic to this. If the *njoget ab chebiosok* (punishment of women) institution were still intact, it is even possible that Nandi would have to be placed in the category of sexually egalitarian societies on the basis of women having a form of political power. Either of these terms as a description for Nandi, as it is conventionally used and with the connotations it implies in ordinary language, does violence to the ethnographic data. Male dominance is not merely "mythical" in Nandi, it is very real. Moreover, I doubt that the description I have given of the general outline of sex and gender relations in Nandi is valid only for the Nandi. Rather, similar sex role patterns are probably quite common cross-culturally.

Some of Sanday's theoretical framework is taken from the work of Susan Carol Rogers. Rogers believes that sexual dominance has to do with "the distribution of power between men and women" (Rogers 1978:154). Power, she continues, "may be measured in terms of control over significant resources. 'Resources' is here broadly defined to include not only economic resources (e.g., land, labor, food, money), but also such resources as ritual knowledge, specialist skills, formal political rights, and information" (Rogers 1978:155). Rogers is also concerned with ideological differentiation by sex, a situation in which men and women hold "separate ideological systems and . . . two contrasting evaluations of the importance and attractiveness of each sex group and its activities" (Rogers 1978:145), and behavioral differentiation, in which men and women perform distinctly different social and productive roles. According to Rogers,

where both ideological and behavioral differentiation exist, a balance of power is most likely to occur. . . . Assuming that each sex group in this case controls essential resources, one cannot dominate the other because they are equally interdependent and complementary. Furthermore, because differentiation is stressed on the ideological level, the two groups may not be related hierarchically, because they are perceived as two different things. . . . I would suggest that the first pattern (ideological and behavioral differentiation) is the most common cross-culturally, and the one in which a dominant/subordinate relationship between the sexes is least likely to occur. [Rogers 1978:155–56.]

Ideological differentiation is an important consideration. Probably this does often lead to a situation in which it is difficult to compare men and women in terms of relative prestige; but this does not necessarily eliminate the possibility of sexual stratification in the power dimension. The fact that two categories of persons are seen as fundamentally different does not mean that one cannot hold power over the other. In fact, such an ideology is frequently attached to situations of social inequality. Masters can avoid any psychological discomfort they may feel in oppressing slaves because "after all, they're different, they don't feel things in the same way as we do." That it doesn't matter if women are denied access to male rituals that they don't give a hoot about anyway is a more important point. This still does not mean that power is necessarily absent from relations between the sexes—only that the matter of which resources are important is so difficult to judge in some cases that perhaps control of important nonmaterial resources is not a good definition of power.

Rogers is right to see male dominance as an aspect of the distribution of power between the sexes. The problem is that her definition of power is so broad that it lumps together practically everything. I do not deny the importance of the nonmaterial resources that she wants to include in the definition, or that many of these resources may in some cases be sources of power. Nevertheless, I do not think that such potential sources of power should be analytically confused with power per se. The ability to control the behavior of others is a definition of power that is perfectly clear, though it may not always be simple to apply. Ritual knowledge may help one gain control over others' behavior in a particular cultural context—or it may not. The relationship between ritual knowledge and power (in the sense of control of others' behavior) cannot be investigated if these two items are definitionally lumped.

Another problem is that it is surely too simple to record that one sex "controls" a particular resource. It is doubtful, for most societies, that rights in most resources reside exclusively with members of one sex. We must examine the structure of various parties' rights in resources, taking into account, where members of one sex have greater rights than members of the other in a particular resource, how great the differential is as well as the fact that it exists.

For these reasons, I wish to define sexual dominance independently of control of resources. Tentatively, I propose that in order to decide which sex (if either) exercises dominance, we should investigate situations in which conflicts of will occur between members of different sex or gender categories—in which a woman desires one outcome and a man desires another, and these outcomes are mutually exclusive. We should ask, for such situations, which party has the ability (through whatever means) to gain the other's compliance with his/her will more frequently, on average. There are two possible situations that could be considered sexually egalitarian: (1) members of both sexes never comply with the will of members of the other sex or social contexts in which desired outcomes conflict never arise (the kind of total autonomy that logically follows from some of Leacock's statements); (2) women succeed in getting men to comply in about the same percentage of cases as men succeed in getting women to comply. With this type of definition the relationship between the structure of control of resources and the matter of ideological differentiation, and the presence, absence, or degree of male dominance becomes a problem for investigation rather than a tautology.

An approach to the problem of male dominance that I find appealing is that taken by Begler (1978) in an article I feel has received less attention than it deserves. The major point Begler makes is that not all "egalitarian" or band-organized societies are sexually egalitarian: some are (e.g., the Mbuti pygmies of the Congo basin) and some aren't (e.g., the Walbiri of central Australia). Begler analyzes these two cases in detail. For the Walbiri, she relies heavily on the ethnography of Mervyn Meggitt (1962). This ethnography is subject to criticism as a representation of sex roles in "egalitarian" society on two counts: that it accepts male evaluations of the relations between the sexes at face value, and that it reflects a historical period in which the people under study were already extremely dependent for survival on European ranches and missions and women's former sources of authority and power had decayed. Meggitt places much emphasis on the ways in which male power over women is asserted and acted out among the Walbiri. Bell (1980) presents a different interpretation of relations between the sexes in traditional Warlpiri (Walbiri) society, one that focuses on women's traditional power and autonomy.

Whether or not Begler has drawn the correct conclusion by regarding the modern Walbiri as described by Meggitt as a case of a band-level society marked by male dominance, her approach to the problem of defining this concept is a useful one. Begler is cognizant of the argument that in some societies women have a great deal of autonomy and that women and men may lead largely independent lives, that women may control important resources, and that insofar as men and women may occupy different cognitive worlds it becomes impossible to judge which sex is the more significant. However, she views these issues as important but irrelevant to the question of whether one sex can dominate the other: "The issue at hand when considering the relative statuses of the sexes, just as when considering the relative statuses of different ethnic or racial groups in a society, is not what happens while the groups are separated, but rather, what happens when they come together . . . the type of data most useful to our analysis derives from the actual occurrence of disputes" (Begler 1978:574–75). In other words, which sex (other things being equal) is able to get members of the other sex to go along with its wishes if there is a disagreement? Who gives in?

If dominance is defined in this way, autonomy does matter in determining the degree to which one sex dominates the other. As Begler says, male dominance has to do with what happens when males and females interact. Autonomy has to do with whether or not they interact very much. It is possible to imagine two similar societies in which interaction between men and women in conflict situations takes the same form when it occurs—men tend to control the outcome. However, in one society such interactions occur frequently whereas in the other they occur very infrequently. In the latter case, women have a high level of autonomy. Male dominance is clearly more signifi-cant in the society in which women have less autonomy. Auton-omy and dominance thus are very closely connected concepts, but they are not merely two sides of the same coin. It is impor-tant to keep them analytically distinct.

The definition of male dominance I have outlined above is the one I am using when I contend that men are dominant in Nandi.

Sexual Stratification in Nandi: General and Economic

Whether stratification is defined in terms of differential access to power and prestige (Schlegel 1976) or unequal access to basic (economic) resources (Fried 1967), Nandi is a sexually stratified society.

Sexual stratification in Nandi is evidenced by the following facts: that men, in their roles as elders in local courts and com-munity meetings, make political decisions but women do not; that men, but not women, occupy ritual positions with authority over both sexes (though this appears formerly not to have been the case); that men are culturally defined as superior to women; that men ideally control the means of production; that though wives have rights in cattle, husbands can abrogate these rights and exercise unilateral control, and the reverse is not true; that women normally do not disagree with their husbands' decisions unless they hold very strong opposing opinions; that husbands can, in the final analysis, compel their wives' compliance with their wishes by beating them; and that traditionally a woman who attempted to reverse any of the prerogatives of men could be cursed to die. Though there are roles in which men can con-trol the behavior of women—husbands have power over wives, and as community elders men as a group have power over women as a group—there are no complementary roles in which women control the behavior of men in similar ways. The closest approximation to such a situation is the case of widows and their sons, in which the widows can make demands on sons for deference behavior and for assistance in cultivation through la-bor and/or money with no reciprocal obligation. However, par-ents of both sexes can make demands for deference on children of both sexes. They can make economic demands also, especially if children and parents coreside. The case of widows and their adult sons is simply a case where the importance of sex in defining the direction of inequality in a relationship is overridden by age and kinship status.

In terms of the economic definition of stratification, the analysis of the foregoing chapters makes it quite clear that men have far greater control of the means of production than do women. Several indices of sexually based economic stratification may be cited: traditionally "male" property is of greater economic importance than traditionally "female" property; men, in general, have greater autonomy in the control of "male" property than women have in the control of "female" property, particularly if a significant cash-generating potential is involved; greater income-generating opportunities are available to men than to women; men have independent control of their own incomes, but women do not unless the amounts involved are petty; husbands have greater rights than wives over the alienation of family property; a wife's ability to prevent her husband from alienating family property is very limited.

Even though, in historic times, Nandi has always been a sexually stratified society, it may be argued that it once was less so than it is now. Institutions such as "the punishment of women" and the essential role of female experts in community-wide rituals are indications of female authority now lost.

Economic dimensions are perhaps more important in showing how sexual stratification has increased. Nandi men have always had greater control than Nandi women over the means of production, but as long as land was not privately held women were not cut off from access to the means to support themselves. Today a Nandi woman gains access to land only through her relationship to a man (except for the case of woman-woman marriage), and some women can be cut off from access to land altogether. Though Fried's definition of stratification is not intended to apply to gender categories, this is precisely the type of situation he would call stratification if the categories of persons involved were landed male patrons and landless male client-tenants. Thus, in terms of the ownership of land, relations between the sexes in Nandi today (as well as in many other modern African societies) must be considered an example of stratification even in the narrower sense of the term.

The fact that Nandi society must be viewed as sexually stratified does not, however, mean that male dominance is absolute or that women are powerless. Women do have important rights in the most important forms of property, land and livestock. Under certain circumstances, wives can block their husbands' decisions to alienate property by appealing to a community council of elders. Women have the right to control certain forms of produce, even to the point of having, in some cases, control of the residual portion of the wife's share of the staple crop. In practice, wives enjoy a high degree of autonomy owing to men's belief that being closely concerned with their wives' activities is beneath their dignity. Wives' public deference to their husbands is at least in part a façade that masks more nearly egalitarian private relations in which wives often have significant input into household decisions. Most women reach a stage in their life cycle (widowhood) in which they have access to economic resources and a level of personal autonomy that approaches that of men. Women are important actors in some extradomestic settings such as arranging marriages, acting as protectors of wives' rights in case of marital discord, and effecting reconciliations.

Thus in spite of sexual stratification, both social and economic, certain factors in Nandi society attenuate the power of men over women, giving the situation of women both negative and positive aspects. How the status of women in Nandi compares with that of women in other societies is another matter. It is not difficult to answer the question of whether Nandi women or Nandi men have the more favorable economic position, but it is not so easy to conclude that Nandi women occupy a higher or lower status than women in other societies, or even than women in other East African societies.

The "Status" of "Women"

The term "the status of women" has a long history in social science theory. Recently some attempts have been made to define this concept in a way that is cross-culturally viable and can be used to make comparisons between societies, whether societies that are relatively similar to one another or societies which diverge widely.

One of the most definitive works on the status of women is that of Whyte (1978). Using every other case in Murdock and White's Standard Cross-Cultural Sample, Whyte and his colleagues analyzed data on a total of 52 variables that have been taken as indicative of high or low status of women in theoretical writings speculating on the genesis of relatively high or low female status. One of Whyte's goals was to determine whether these various indices are highly intercorrelated. Though this attempt to find correlations between possible indices of female status was not notably successful, it was not a total failure. Thirty-three of the initial list of 52 variables were found to form ten clusters, each with five or fewer variables. Whyte categorized these ten clusters as property control by women, power of women in kinship contexts, value placed on women's lives (which includes the absence of physical abuse of women), value placed on women's labor, domestic authority of women, ritualized separation of the sexes, control over women's marital and sexual lives, ritualized fear of women, male-female joint participation (in labor, social settings, and public meetings), and informal influence (Whyte 1978:98–100). He found positive correlations among the following clusters of variables: ritual female solidarity correlated positively with lack of control of women's sex lives, domestic authority of women, power of women in kinship contexts, and value of women's lives. Domestic authority of women also was found to correlate with female control of property and value of women's lives (Whyte 1978:106). Only three clusters—value of women's labor, ritual fear of women, and women's informal influence—did not correlate with any other clusters of variables (Whyte 1978:107).

On the other hand, though certain clusters of variables correlated with one another, there were very few correlations between any of them and other independent variables. As might be expected, there was an association between matriliny and matrilocal residence and strong property rights for women. Another intriguing correlation (which Whyte did not explore) was between female ritual solidarity and female domestic authority on the one hand and reliance for subsistence on hunting and frequent warfare on the other (Whyte 1978:171). The only very strong constellation of variables that Whyte explored in great detail was a correlation of low female domestic authority, lack of female solidarity, strong restrictions on sexuality, somewhat fewer property rights for women, high informal influence for women, and high joint participation of the sexes with certain measures of societal complexity, particularly plow agriculture, the presence of settled towns and cities, irrigation, weaving, and social stratification (Whyte 1978:138, 172). I shall discuss this constellation of variables at greater length below.

That a certain amount of intercorrelation did occur among Whyte's variables seems to suggest that certain regularities exist in the data that might be revealed more clearly with more refined definitions of variables. Whyte himself, however, was more impressed by the lack of intercorrelation between the various presumed indices of women's status:

While small groups of discrete measures of aspects of the status of women can be formed into coherent scales, and while a few of these have consistent patterns of association with some others, the thrust of our results is that there is a large amount of independent variation in what we have been considering the general status of women . . . the degree of independent variation (or lack of association) is quite striking. We find that knowing how much of the subsistence in a particular culture is produced by women will not help us to predict what sort of property rights women will have, or whether they will have their sexual and marital lives severely restricted. Likewise, the fact that men monopolize the property in a particular culture does not allow us to predict how women's lives will be valued or how much informal influence women will have . . . we are dealing with very complex phenomena. [Whyte 1978:107–8.]

The major conclusion that Whyte arrives at, therefore, is that the status of women is an essentially nonunitary phenomenon and attempts to compare the "status of women" in a broad sense in different societies or types of societies are fruitless endeavors.

Other studies have been somewhat more successful in finding a certain type of patterned relationship between some aspects of what we may call "female status" and others. In a pilot study of twelve societies, Sanday (1974) found that women's participation in political life, and women's solidarity groups devoted to political or economic interests, seem to occur only where women's control over material goods in relations going beyond the household and extradomestic demand for women's produce are present as preconditions (Sanday 1974:192). These phenomena formed a Guttman scale with female control of produce as its lowest point and female political and economic solidarity groups as its highest. Since Whyte found no such series of correlations, he was highly critical of Sanday for "building theories about the place of women in social life on the basis of limited and noncomprehensive samples of cultures" (Whyte 1978:147). The presence of preconditions, or lower points on a Guttman scale, does not necessarily imply a simple correlation with higher points, however. The former are necessary but not sufficient conditions for the latter, and may occur as frequently alone as in association with them. If such a relationship as that proposed by Sanday existed, it would not necessarily show up in a cluster analysis such as that performed by Whyte. Further, Whyte may not have discovered such a relationship though Sanday did because of definitional differences. Sanday is discussing only female solidarity groups that have political and economic functions; her definition specifically excludes those with ritual functions only, and it apparently also excludes productive groups. Whyte's definition of female solidarity is an amalgam of several social phenomena that are intercorrelated, but quite different from Sanday's female solidarity groups: single-sex work groups, menstrual taboos, and female initiation ceremonies (Whyte 1978:99).

More recently, as part of a larger study, Sanday recreated the same Guttman scale of female economic and political power using a larger sample of societies. She used Murdock and White's Standard Cross-Cultural Sample, and eliminated 30 cases for insufficient information, resulting in a sample of 156 cases for her total study (Sanday 1981:232). Of these, enough information was available on 96 for inclusion in the female economic and political power scale. The scale itself differs slightly from that of the pilot study. It now includes: (1) no indicator, (2) flexible marriage mores (easy divorce or mild punishment for adultery), (3) female production of goods with wider than domestic distribution, (4) demand for such female produce, (5) female control of the allocation of products of their own labor, (6) female political participation, and (7) female solidarity groups that discuss matters of extradomestic importance or are official and consolidate female power (Sanday 1981:250–51). These points form a Guttman scale with reproducibility coefficient of 0.91. This scale correlates with certain other social and ecological phenomena: symbolism that portrays a female or a couple as originators of the world, in nonforaging societies (Sanday 1981:132); a long history of settlement in the same place (Sanday 1981:133); ethnographic description having occurred prior to 1925, which suggests that colonization contributed to a decline in female status in many societies (Sanday 1981:158); and a constant food supply or storage facilities to prevent periodic famine (Sanday 1981:159).

Sanday also creates a Guttman scale of male aggression, with the following points: (1) an ideology of machismo or male toughness, (2) separate places for men to gather away from women, (3) moderate or frequent interpersonal violence (including wife beating), (4) rape institutionalized or reported as more than occasional, and (5) wives taken from hostile groups (Sanday 1981:254). Sanday combines these two Guttman scales to form a measure that she calls male dominance (Sanday 1981:254–55). The sexes are considered equal "when women have political and economic power" (presumably point 6 on the female power scale) and male aggression is below point 4. Cases of "mythical male dominance" appear to be those where point 5 or above on the female power scale is combined with points 4 or 5 on the male aggression scale. (I have already pointed out that I consider "equal" or "mythical male dominance" to be unfortunate designations for many of these cases.) Lumped with "mythical" cases are those that are characterized by "some" male dominance, in which the female power scale is located at exactly point 5 and the male aggression scale is below point 4. Sexually inegalitarian societies are those in which women have no economic or political power. It is not clear to me exactly what point on the female power scale this means (Sanday 1981:254–55). Male dominance thus defined correlates with most of the same phenomena as the female power scale, but with opposite values. In addition, it correlates positively with endemic warfare (Sanday 1981:174). Correlations between the male dominance measure and rules of descent and residence are not clear cut. "Sexual equality" characterizes 52 percent of matrilineal societies, 41 percent of bilateral societies, and only 19 percent of patrilineal societies. Sexual inequality (or high male dominance) is found in 33 percent of matrilineal cases, and is only slightly more common in patrilineal cases. It is least likely in societies with bilateral descent rules (13 percent). Mythical or some male dominance is very rare in matrilineal societies (14 percent) but is the most common pattern in both patrilineal and bilateral societies (42 percent and 46 percent, respectively).

There are few strong associations between Sanday's male dominance measure and residence patterns, except that neolocal cases are rarely sexually inegalitarian (6 percent). Sanday lumps matrilocal and avunculocal cases, whereas a priori I would expect sexual inequality to be rare in cases of matrilocal residence but not necessarily so in cases of avunculocal residence (it is present in 29 percent of the two types taken together). Strong male dominance is more common with patrilocal than with any of the other types of residence rules, but not startlingly so (Sanday 1981:178). Sanday also finds some relationship between the male dominance measure and at least one measure of societal complexity—advanced agriculture. Only 27 percent of societies with advanced agriculture are sexually egalitarian (Sanday 1981: 170). This is in keeping with the findings of others. Sanday sums up the association between "male dominance" and other phenomena: "Male dominance is associated with increasing technological complexity, an animal economy, sexual segregation in work, a symbolic orientation to the male creative principle, and stress" (Sanday 1981:171).

Sanday's connection of technological complexity with male dominance recalls the constellation of variables relating to "female status" that Whyte found associated with societal complexity measures. The interconnectedness of many of these phenomena was noted by Goody (1976). Goody found an association between stratified state polities, intensive agriculture, the predominance of male labor, land shortage and individualized land tenure, "diverging devolution" (bilateral inheritance of property and/or dowry), monogamy, and strong control over women's sexuality on the one hand, and nonstratified polities (including "ranking" societies, e.g., African kingdoms), extensive cultivation, the predominance of female labor, plentiful land and nonindividualized land tenure, "homogeneous devolution" (property inheritance from men by men and from women by women), bridewealth, polygyny, and weak control over women's sexuality on the other. He shows further how these possibly disparate phenomena are functionally connected to one another in each of these two configurations, which he refers to by the shorthand labels "Eurasian" and "African" systems (Goody 1976:36):

The scarcer productive resources become and the more intensively they are used, then the greater the tendency toward the retention of these resources within the basic productive and reproductive unit, which in the large majority of cases is the nuclear family. . . . Greater volume of production can maintain an elaborate division of labour and a stratification based upon different "styles of life." An important means of maintaining one's style of life, and that of one's progeny, is by marriage with persons of the same or higher qualifications. . . . This system . . . tends to make provision for women as well as men. The position of women in the world has to be maintained by means of property, either in dowry or inheritance—otherwise the honour of the family suffers a setback. . . . Advanced agriculture is virtually a condition of the extensive differentiation by styles of life that in turn encourages the concentration of property by inheritance and marriage. . . . The positive control of marriage arrangements . . . is stricter where property is transmitted to women. It is a commentary upon their lot that where they are more propertied they are initially less free as far as marital arrangements go. [Goody 1976:20–21.]

The direct transmission of significant property from parents to children also creates a concern about filiation, reflected in strict norms of marital sexual fidelity for women. Women's chastity as well as the social quality of the marriages they make reflects on the honor of the family, and virginity becomes a prerequisite for a "good" match. Whyte interprets the set of relationships he has found between some of his "female status" variables and societal complexity as fully congruent with Goody's theory (Whyte 1978:162). Whyte further links low female domestic authority with monogamy, as women in polygynous societies may have autonomy associated with the fact that their husbands are not constantly present.

Thus, in one area at least, the correlation of certain disadvantages for women (low domestic authority, lack of female solidarity, and strong restrictions on women's sexuality) with societal or technological complexity and stratification, there is a convergence among a number of theorists of "women's status."

There is at least one other point of agreement. Whyte's findings confirm Bacdayan's "mechanistic cooperation" hypothesis. Absence of work segregation by sex correlates with participation of both sexes in community meetings (Whyte 1978:100). These two items go together (along with participation of both sexes in warfare) in the scale Whyte calls "joint participation." The general correlation of lack of task segregation with lack of segregation in other aspects of social life is also noted by Sanday (1981:83).

In what ways can the points I have been making about Nandi be located within this general context of theory about female status? The theory proposed by Goody may give clues to the direction in which Nandi and many other societies in the world are now moving, under conditions of increasing land scarcity, individualized tenure, and the emergence of stratification. If Goody is right, these changes should give rise to monogamy, "diverging devolution," dowry rather than bridewealth, and ultimately to strict control of women's sexuality and lowered female domestic authority. No changes are as yet observable in any of the latter areas. Control of female sexuality has lessened, if anything, and bridewealth is still almost invariably transferred and is higher than formerly. It is commonly said, however (though as yet it cannot be demonstrated statistically), that polygyny is on the decline, and at least one sign of incipient "diverging devolution"—the assertion of several informants that daughters as well as sons should have the right to inherit family property—has been observed. New relations to property have been in place for a very short time, and the social system cannot be expected to adjust itself completely overnight. It will be interesting to see whether with time Nandi and other similar societies will show the changes Goody's theory would predict.

Whyte's work certainly points up the difficulty of ascribing supposed indices of "the status of women" to any one crucial variable. Various phenomena relating to sex roles are very complexly interrelated. Whyte demonstrates that there are various kinds of "female status"—that it is not a simple unitary phenomenon. The data I have presented for Nandi bear out this point.

Further, if "status" is not a unitary phenomenon, neither are women a monolithic category. The Nandi case shows how thoroughly a woman's situation can vary over her life cycle. This leads to the conclusion that scales that ask coders to judge whether "women" can alienate economic resources (for example) have an inherent flaw. In Nandi, the rating would have to be quite different depending on whether one has in mind young wives or widows. Thus, in a society like Nandi it may be possible to evaluate the "status," or rather "statuses," of various categories of women, but not of "women."

Despite Whyte's failure to find many interrelationships between aspects of "female status" and his general caveat, Sanday's work shows that the further refinement of concepts of female status of particular types or in particular realms can lead to the discovery of relationships not immediately apparent. The quest to find measures that will enable us to compare the position of women cross-culturally is not necessarily futile. It is possible that Sanday's two major scales (female economic and political power and male aggression) provide a framework that enables us to make such comparisons. Though I am dissatisfied with the labels the placement entails, I am able to locate the Nandi on these two scales. Nandi belongs somewhere between points 4 and 5 on the female power scale. I base this judgment on the facts that strong sanctions for adultery are rare, that there was a traditional trade in grain and livestock conducted by women both within and outside Nandi, and that women to some extent controlled this trade. I am hesitant about giving a clear-cut rating of 5, because I think that to some extent this control may have been limited by the rights of husbands in livestock being traded. Because of the fairly common occurrence of rape and the relative nonchalance with which it is viewed, together with frequent wife beating, the institution of *kok* (the neighborhood shade tree) as a male gathering place, and an ideology of male toughness, Nandi would rate a 4 on the male aggression scale. This puts Nandi in the 65th percentile for male aggression and somewhere around the 50th percentile for female power—rankings I find myself intuitively able to accept.

It would seem to be particularly possible to compare women's position in different societies where comparisons are made between societies existing in geographical proximity to one another, having similar basic economic and social patterns and sharing, to some extent, a common history. In the next section I undertake this type of comparison between the Nandi and some of their neighbors.

Women's Place: The Nandi and Their Neighbors

Two societies that neighbor the Nandi—the Luo and the Maasai—are particularly good ground for cross-cultural comparisons of the situation of women because they have been the subject of recent field studies that specifically focus on women's roles and intergender relations.* Both these societies, as well as neighboring the Nandi, share with them a common Nilotic cultural heritage. The Luo belong to the "River-Lakes" branch of the Nilotes, the Maasai to the "Plains" branch (see Chapter 2). Among East African peoples, only other Kalenjin, and Tatoga-speakers such as the Barabaig, are more closely related to the Nandi. The Nandi have historically absorbed migrants from both Luo and Maasai. All these people keep cattle, but form a continuum in the relative importance of horticulture. The Luo are most dependent on cultivating, the Nandi less so, and the Maasai are often considered "purely pastoral" (though the question of how much they have ever been grain-dependent and/or by what means they obtained grain is not at all settled—see Schneider 1974; Conant 1974). All three societies are patrilineal and virilocal, and in all, marriage involves the transfer of cattle bridewealth.

Luo communities are composed of agnatic lineages that have traditionally in some senses jointly held the land they occupy, though specific plots of land are also held individually. A Luo woman, according to Potash, has no rights in land except through her husband. Moreover, should she leave her husband,

---

*See the work of Margaret Jean Hay, Betty Potash, and Achola Pala Okeyo on the Luo, and that of Melissa Llewelyn-Davies on the Maasai.

she has "no automatic rights in her natal home and cannot acquire land there from which to support herself" (Potash 1978:390). Pala Okeyo says that "females have usufructuary rights to land by virtue of being a daughter or a wife" (Pala Okeyo 1980:188). There may have been regional variation in this regard, or perhaps the key is Potash's use of the term "automatic"—that is, it may have been possible for a daughter to acquire land rights, but not inevitable. Or, which seems most likely and is important to Pala Okeyo's argument about the impact of colonization, women's lack of land rights in their natal lineage lands is the result of recent individualization of land tenure combined with increasing land scarcity. Though women's rights in their natal homes were perhaps not "automatic," so long as land was plentiful, they were effective. Pala Okeyo agrees with Potash that "for a woman, marriage carried more security of tenure than being unmarried" (Pala Okeyo 1980:195). It seems probable that traditionally Nandi women had somewhat more secure access to land than did Luo women. Currently, land tenure reform has affected women's land rights similarly: land titles have been given to men, and it is possible for women to be cut off from access to land. It is possible now, in both societies, for men to alienate land upon which women depend (Pala Okeyo 1980:206). Whether Luo women have any effective means to block the sale of land by their husbands, such as Nandi women's right of appeal to the *kokwet* (neighborhood or community) elders, is not clear.

Luo women seem to have fairly unrestricted rights in their own produce. Traditionally, they alone decided how much of their crop would be kept for home consumption and what portion they would use for trade (Hay 1976:92). Today women grow their own cash crops. A woman is also obliged to cultivate cash crops for her husband, which he alone controls.

Traditionally, Luo women could apparently own livestock in their own right. "Each wife was responsible for producing enough grain to feed her family through the year. It was her right, however, to dispose of the surplus from her own fields as she saw fit, and a number of women accumulated livestock through trade. A woman regarded these cattle as her own" (Hay 1976:95). Luo women used cattle they acquired in this way for their sons' bridewealth. Such accumulation of cattle was impossible for Nandi women, except as widows. It is still possible for Luo wives to own livestock, including cattle, whereas Nandi wives do not legitimately own cattle independently of their husbands, but only have rights in cattle as part of the family estate. It must be remembered, however, that large-scale ownership of cattle was not common among Luo women. Though Nandi wives' rights to own cattle independently were restricted (and still are), Nandi men do not have the same kinds of unrestricted rights in their cattle that Luo men have. Nandi wives share rights in most cattle with their husbands, Nandi husbands normally respect these rights particularly where the cattle concerned are their wives' wedding cattle and the cattle's offspring, and though it is not common, it is possible for a Nandi wife to block the sale of a cow by her husband. Perhaps these rights are not as significant as independent cattle ownership. But it must be recalled that *most* Nandi women hold such rights, whereas Luo female cattle owners are surely a minority.

Potash (1978:388) views the economic situation of Luo women as tenuous. It is possible for Luo husbands to divorce their wives and disinherit them. For this reason, the burden of adjusting to a marital situation falls primarily upon the wife. "Women say they must please their husbands, avoid complaining too much, and not be 'too stubborn' . . . a woman is constrained to comply outwardly with her husband's wishes . . . women say they can do little to affect a man's behavior" (Potash 1978:388). Nandi wives do not experience the same tenuousness of rights in a husband's property. A Nandi wife cannot initiate a divorce in order to seek a better marriage, but neither can she be divorced. In traditional Nandi society there was virtually no divorce, and a wife's rights in the family estate could never be abrogated. In the modern setting, a wife can desert her husband for many years at a time and ultimately return and reactivate her claim to her house's share of her husband's estate. The Luo situation offers women greater theoretical autonomy, though few women are in a position to take advantage of it. The Nandi situation assures women of greater economic security.

A Luo woman can be divorced, and if bridewealth is returned, remarry. Nandi marriage is irrevocable. Yet because of situational constraints, separation and divorce are only slightly more common in Potash's Luo community than they are in Nandi (Potash 1978:386). Are Luo women "freer"? It has been argued that the impossibility of divorce is a mark of low female status. In the Nandi case, however, it serves to protect women's economic position. The fact that there is no divorce is intrinsically connected to women's inalienable rights in property under the house-property system. The fact that a woman once married cannot divorce and remarry does not seriously restrict her personal autonomy, for she can live apart from her husband without losing her property rights. It is thus questionable whether Luo women's greater divorce "rights" indicate any sort of status differential between Luo and Nandi women. Specifically as divorce relates to property rights, it is precisely Nandi women's lack of divorce rights that keeps their position relative to property from being tenuous, like that of most Luo women who are not themselves property owners.

Maasai women, unlike Nandi and Luo women, do not cultivate. Their work in basic production is milking and the care of young calves (Llewelyn-Davies 1978:211). They are also responsible for all domestic labor, including house construction, and child care. Llewelyn-Davies maintains that the only decision about production into which women have input is how much milk to take for human consumption and how much to leave for calves. Jacobs adds to this that "the decision to let calves graze with the main herd is made jointly by a husband and his wife" (Jacobs 1965:183). Women apparently also make most decisions relating to the care of calves. The allocation of the product (milk), however, is entirely at a woman's individual discretion, provided milk is available for her husband when he wants it (though it is not clear whether she would be free to sell it). Jacobs (1965: 184) makes even clearer the right of women to distribute milk. A man cannot ask a woman for milk but must wait to be offered it. It is shameful for a man to himself go into his wife's milk calabashes. Jacobs does not say whether a woman could withhold milk in case of a marital dispute, but he does note that a man can get milk direct from his wife's cow by milking himself, and to do so publicly is shameful to his wife.

Like a Nandi woman, a Maasai woman is allocated animals

from her husband's herd at marriage. These animals cannot be reallocated. Women have a right to keep the hides of animals in their herds, or money gained from the sale of hides (Llewelyn-Davies 1978:228). The herd of a woman's house also includes some animals she receives as gifts from her own kin, but her rights in such animals appear to be less inviolable than those of a Nandi woman. Llewelyn-Davies says (1978:213): "A husband may give away or slaughter any of his wife's allocated animals, including those that she has been given by her own kin. However, a wife has the right to complain to her father or brother if her husband tries to reallocate any of her stock to another wife. Unless there is a very compelling reason for doing so, such as the death of most of the co-wife's herd, this action will be taken as grounds for divorce."

Maasai women do have the right to allocate specific animals to their sons. A woman "can decide to give nothing at all to a particular son. At her death, any unallocated animals pass directly to her youngest son" (Llewelyn-Davies 1978:212). The point that women allocate the progeny of their herds to their sons is also made by Jacobs (1965:191).

Nandi and Maasai women, then, both have limited rights in livestock, but the nature of these rights is different. Maasai women have greater control of the inheritance of their house property than Nandi women do, but Nandi women have greater control over the management of animals not acquired from their husbands.

Maasai women, as widows, do not have the right to hold their own cattle. If a woman has no sons, her husband's cattle are inherited by sons of her co-wife or other male agnates of her husband, and she is effectively dependent on charity. One strategy by which this fate can be avoided by a woman with a daughter is similar to Nandi "marriage to the center post": a daughter can be kept at home to bear heirs for her mother's house (Llewelyn-Davies 1978:213).

Though Llewelyn-Davies takes the position that women have no control of livestock, she also says that a bride will not enter her husband's village until she has been promised gifts of livestock by some of the women (Llewelyn-Davies 1978:223). It therefore seems possible that her original absolute statement about women's lack of rights in stock is an oversimplification. She goes on to say, however (p. 223), that the women who usually promise gifts are co-wives or husband's brothers' wives: "No woman can alienate an animal from her husband's herd without his approval, but women who belong to the household of the same man (and are, therefore, supported by the same herd) are expected to give to each other. Full brothers, for example, consider it appropriate for their women to give gifts to each other, especially if their herds have not yet been completely separated."

Rigby finds Llewelyn-Davies's statements about the degree of control Maasai women have over the herd and her assertion that Maasai men own cattle, the means of production, contradictory. He resolves the contradiction by demonstrating that control of the herd exists at various levels, and that there is really no such thing as individual "ownership." The most significant wealth is counted in social relationships rather than economic resources. Rigby says (1980:55): "as an elder pursues this goal of notability and 'wealth' (*enkarsisiho*), his control over the primary means of production is progressively weakened and diluted, since wives, sons, affines and matrilateral kinsmen increasingly claim their rights to, and control of, certain portions of the herd. We see, therefore, that the so-called 'owner' of a herd at no time has exclusive, individual control of the means of production nor over the product." If individual women do not have full rights of control over cattle, neither do individual men. Rigby further stresses the fact that women have virtually total control of the distribution and consumption of products of the herd, as well as an essential role in the transfer of control of and access to the means of production (Rigby 1980:56, 63). Rigby's position, then, is that by concentrating attention on the jural assertion that men "control" or "own" (in Maasai, *aitore*) the means of production, Llewelyn-Davies seriously underestimates the strength of Maasai women's economic position.

As in the case of the precolonial Nandi, there is an institution whereby Maasai women punish men for inappropriate sexual activity, primarily sex with women in the wrong age category (Llewelyn-Davies 1978:226). The form of the "punishment" is very similar to that described for the Nandi "punishment of the women." This does not seem to be conceptualized as a matter of punishment for "crimes against women" in the same way that the Nandi women's sanction was, however. There is also a ritual context in which women are free to demand money (to be used for the ritual) from men on threat of a curse, or to attack men who beat their wives (Llewelyn-Davies 1978:225).

Unlike Nandi women, Maasai women do not have an important voice in arranging marriages. Llewelyn-Davies stresses the degree to which this right resides with a girl's father (Llewelyn-Davies 1978:213). As in Nandi, marriage is permanent if the ceremony has been properly conducted and the bridewealth has been paid. Women do assertively maintain control of their own sexuality. Adultery is frequent and expected, and women choose their own lovers (Llewelyn-Davies 1978:232). As in Nandi, the help provided by sons to their mothers is phrased as an obligation (Llewelyn-Davies 1978:214). There is, therefore, at least one relationship in which it is possible for women to dominate men.

It is possible to ask whether the situation of Nandi, Luo, or Maasai women is the most favorable, but it is futile to expect a clear-cut answer. Nandi and Luo women both reach point 5 on Sanday's scale of female power (female control of extradomestic allocation of their product); Maasai women (at least from knowledge available to me) apparently have to be placed at point 2, because their product is not distributed extradomestically. That women have complete control of their own product is somewhat clearer for Luo than for Nandi. Do Luo women, then, have the most power? I believe that Nandi and Maasai would rank similarly on Sanday's male aggression scale, and both would place higher than the Luo. Is male dominance less marked in Luo? Not if it has to do with which sex can control the behavior of the other. Potash shows clearly that the tenuousness of Luo women's economic position makes it extremely difficult for them to confront their husbands or hold out in disagreeing with them on any issue. In this regard, I believe Nandi women fare better; what the situation is for Maasai women I do not know. Divorce is possible for Luo but not for Nandi or Maasai women, but as has been argued above, it is not clear that there is any benefit for them in this. Both Nandi and Maasai women, but not, apparently, Luo women, traditionally had an institution through which they sanctioned men. One should probably not put too much emphasis on this as an example of female political participation, however, because the contexts in which such sanctions could be applied were highly ritualized and infrequent. The respective situations of Nandi, Luo, and Maasai women can also be compared in terms of workloads. Luo are more dependent than either of the other two societies on cultivation, and the most time-consuming parts of this process are and were performed by women with very little help from men. Luo women, by all accounts, work very hard. Maasai women, of the three, probably have the most leisure time.

By Sanday's scale, the Luo seem to come out slightly ahead of Nandi and Maasai women in female power and even further behind in male dominance. To my mind, however, even this brief comparison shows that it is far from clear that Luo women are "better off" than Nandi women in a general sense, or that either group of women is better off than Maasai women. This is true even if we limit our interest to economic rights and responsibilities. Undertaking comparisons of this sort is a fruitful exercise not because it leads to a clear-cut definition of "women's status" that allows us to say definitively that the economic or social position of Nandi women is more favorable, or less favorable, than that of Luo or Maasai women, but because it leads to a sense of the variety of positive and negative consequences for women's position that result from quite different configurations of economic, social, and property relations. Even within a small geographical and cultural area, it is difficult to define a construct such as "the economic position of women" or "women's property rights" in a way that makes it possible to rank-order cases. Rather, there are several different configurations of the sexual stratification package, and it is difficult to choose one or the other as representing a more or less favorable situation for women. It is extremely difficult to say which of these three neighboring societies is the least sexually stratified.

If this is true even for peoples with basic cultural similarities and some degree of common history, does this mean that broad cross-cultural comparisons are useless and that the comparative study of sex and gender stratification should be abandoned? Not at all. Broad interrelationships between certain phenomena that have been thought to be related to the "status of women" can be discerned, as is shown by the work of Sanday, Goody, and even Whyte, though he appears to feel that he has largely failed in this endeavor. The effort breaks down when we try to establish fine ranking-criteria that will distinguish individual cases. This is not to say that it will never be possible to discover such a set of criteria—only that we are still extremely far away from doing so.

Colonialism, Capitalism, and the Status of Women

I have shown in Chapters 5, 6, and 7 how Nandi women's economic status has been undermined as the result of colonization, incorporation into a cash economy, and commoditization of virtually all economic resources. Some of the phenomena that have been described for Nandi have occurred so frequently throughout the world that they form an almost standard colonialist–capitalist package. Others—particularly the specific forms taken by normative changes—are more special to limited cultural settings.

Colonization brought with it everywhere the introduction or intensification of cash economies and ultimate integration into the world capitalist system. Broadly speaking, the implicit effect of colonialist expansion was the incorporation and exploitation of labor within the capitalist sector, either directly as wage labor or indirectly through the promotion of the production of a surplus that can be expropriated. Colonial rule was usually introduced, as it was in Nandi, with taxation imposed only upon men. Such a policy had the conscious intent of inducing men to seek cash—either through wage labor or through producing cash crops—and this was its usual effect.

Boserup (1970) argues that this policy, particularly as it promoted cash-cropping, had its origins in pervasive European prejudices combined with an essentially benevolent desire to promote "economic development." The European colonialist model was that men were the stronger sex and by rights should do the hard physical labor to support their families. By "forcing" agricultural labor on women, lazy men were oppressing them. Further, truly efficient modern farming could be promoted only when the stronger sex did most of the work: "virtually all Europeans shared the opinion that men are superior to women in the art of farming, and it then seemed to follow that for the development of agriculture male farming ought to be promoted to replace female farming" (Boserup 1970:54).

Meillassoux (1975) concentrates attention on the direct labor-generating effects of colonial policies rather than attempts to introduce cash cropping. The incorporation of an ever greater number of laborers into capitalist exploitation is in his view the driving force behind colonialist expansion: taxation, forced labor, and other colonial government policies are means of driving labor out of the villages and "served to establish an irreversible rural dependence" (Meillassoux 1975:127). The replacement of craft products by manufactured goods and of craft activities by wage labor is a means of "making the domestic sector dependent for the supply of essential goods on the colonial sector" (Meillassoux 1975:127). A need for commodities and therefore a need for cash is gradually built up so that ultimately this itself is enough to recruit labor: "because its means of production are much more efficient, the capitalist sector is able to offer a wage whose purchasing power is superior to the market value of goods produced in the domestic sector in the same length of time" (Meillassoux 1975:128). Domestic production, in this case, is a part of the reproduction of the labor force—and is left in the hands of women.

Boserup and Meillassoux are looking at two different aspects of colonial exploitation—the direct exploitation of labor and the expropriation of surplus product. In some areas, one of these aspects or the other was clearly dominant in the colonial setting. In many areas, including Nandi, both phenomena occurred together, their relative importance shifting throughout the course of colonial history. Whichever aspect of colonialism took on greater significance, the consequences for women vis-à-vis men were usually negative.

Taxation of males, then, is accompanied by the opening up of wage labor opportunities for men but not for women or by the development of male cash-cropping. There are at least two ways in which the promotion of male cash-cropping takes place. There may be a conscious program of development of the cash-generating potential of resources traditionally controlled by men but not those traditionally controlled by women (Boserup 1970:56). The abandonment of significant attempts at poultry upgrading in Nandi is an example of lack of support for the development of female-controlled resources. Alternatively, entirely new cash crops with high income-producing potential may be introduced to men only (Boserup 1970:56; Guyer 1980:364). Such crops in Nandi were maize (originally) and tea. The development of male cash-cropping gives rise to a concentration of agricultural extension services on men. Boserup (1970:55–56) documents this tendency with many examples, and it has been the subject of study by Staudt (1975, 1978) and Pala Okeyo (1980).

Colonial economic planners (e.g., the 1954 Swynnerton Plan) often came to the conclusion that truly efficient and economically rational modern farming systems could only be developed if farmers owned their own land and were individually responsible for its development and conservation. Accordingly, European colonial governments frequently introduced land tenure reforms in which land was surveyed and individual titles to particular plots were distributed. In such circumstances, land titles were usually given to men but not to women (Boserup 1970:60). Nandi was not a rarity in this regard. It might be argued that in areas like Nandi this was merely an inadvertent mistake that happened because administrators did not fully realize the significance of women's former use-rights in land. In parts of Southeast Asia, however, such as Malaya, the British administration forced changes in matrilineal inheritance of land (Boserup 1970:61). In Sri Lanka, forced change was even more extreme. Though women traditionally inherited and held land, under colonial laws married women were forced to register their land in their husbands' names (Samarakkody 1979:137). In central Africa, propaganda against matrilineal inheritance was also rife (Boserup 1970:60). Where women's rights in land were absolutely clear-cut, colonial land reform policies that denied them cannot be viewed as simply an error. Through the forcible imposition of legal norms external to most societies, male private ownership of land has within a brief historical period become institutionalized throughout the world.

Boserup (1970:58–59) points out that even in those cases

where land title was not automatically distributed to men only, commoditization of land coupled with male wage labor or cash-cropping means that men still end up owning most of the land because only men have sources of cash sufficient to purchase it. She cites a 1960 study by R. E. S. Tanner of three villages in the coastal area of Tanzania. In these villages, men and women inherited almost equal numbers of plots, but plots acquired by purchase were all owned by men. In the village in which land was the most commoditized, women owned only 26 percent of the plots, as opposed to 46 percent in the village with least land commoditization. Further, the distribution of land title to men only has an even more severe effect on women in societies where divorce is frequent, because divorced women lose access to land (Boserup 1970:61). Indeed, it is this possibility that Potash (1978) sees as contributing to the stability of Luo marriage. Also, the fact that only men hold land titles means that only men have access to credit with which to develop their agricultural enterprises (Pala Okeyo 1980:204).

This whole constellation of conditions results in a situation in which, as I have shown for Nandi in Chapter 6, men typically control far greater sums of cash than women do. Guyer (1980:370) has documented this development for the Yoruba and Beti, two West African societies with very different traditional economic systems and divisions of labor by sex, but in both of which cocoa has become an important cash crop. Another typical outcome is that women's workload is increased by the male pursuit of cash, as women take on tasks in the subsistence economy or the household that were formerly performed by men. This has been documented for extremely diverse societies, from the Bari Indians of Colombia (Buenaventura-Posso & Brown 1980:127) to East African cases (LeVine 1966; Hay 1976). The situation for the Gusii (western Kenya), among whom male migrant labor is common, is summarized as follows:

Many tasks in which men formerly participated are now relegated exclusively to their wives and children. The men have retained their rights in land and livestock, and they also control the cash income derived from their employment and the sale of cash crops. While the absence of the men unquestionably loosens the control they once had over their wives' activities, the women who remain behind cannot be said to have gained status relative to men. [LeVine 1966:188.]

LeVine further argues that women's heavier workload is reflected in physiological stress indicators (such as high blood pressure) and aggression toward their children (LeVine 1966: 188–89). As I have shown in Chapter 6, this phenomenon is exacerbated by the economic differentiation that is brought about by commoditization and individualized land tenure. Land-poor men must spend more time than others in working for wages, so the extra demands on their wives' labor are greater. These women, in many areas, are already working especially hard to manage subsistence through intensive cultivation of small holdings (Winans 1972).

It is all too clear that many of the factors I have been describing for Nandi occurred repeatedly in different parts of the world during colonial history. Occasionally, forces such as the commoditization of resources have worked in women's favor. Phoebe Ottenberg's article on Afikpo Ibo women's gains in autonomy through participation in the cash economy has become a classic (Ottenberg 1959; also quoted at length in LeVine 1966). Cassava was introduced to the Afikpo early in the colonial era. Men, who were primarily responsible for the cultivation of the ritually important yam crop, rejected cassava as beneath their dignity, but women planted it between yam mounds. Because cassava prevented annual famines and shortages, it became an important crop—one controlled by women. Ottenberg quotes an informant: "Nowadays women do not care if the husband doesn't give them any food, for they can go to the farm and get cassava. If a woman has any money, she buys (rents) land and plants cassava. The year after she does this, she can have a crop for cassava meal, which she can sell and have her own money. Then she can say, 'What is a man? I have my own money!'" (Ottenberg 1959:215).

It was possible for Afikpo women to gain economic autonomy through this crop because they were already trading on a small scale, and cultural norms were accepting of their autonomous control of small quantities of cash. Ottenberg portrays Afikpo society prior to colonial rule and the cash economy as extremely male dominated. However, the Igbo peoples as a group are very diverse, and the more recent research has not shown their history everywhere as one that should be held up as a shining example of the benefits of colonialism for women's status. Romalis (1979) and Okigbo (1965) have described the effects of changes in the palm-oil industry among the Igbo of Calabar, Onitsha, and Owerri provinces. Originally, the palm nuts were collected by men, but women extracted the oil. The profits from the oil belonged to a man, but his wife got to keep the kernels, which could be sold to commercial trading firms for export. In the 1940's, oil factories were established and men began to sell to them direct, thus eliminating women from any income from the palm-oil industry. The formerly important political institutions of Igbo women, and their decay under colonial rule, have been described by Van Allen (1972, 1976) and Okonjo (1976). It is Igbo women who have become the best-known example of women's active resistance to colonization through the famous "Aba Riots" or "Women's War."

Thus, though there have been cases in which women have gained through colonial policies or entry into a cash economy, evidence is mounting that the effects of colonialism and the penetration of capitalism have most frequently been detrimental to the position of women. As Sanday says:

Though in some cases Westernization opened opportunities for women, in most instances contact with the male-dominated European society had a deleterious effect. It is no accident that most (63%) of the societies in this study in which females enjoy political power are societies which were described before 1925, whereas most (60%) of the societies in which there is no female economic or political power are societies that were described later. . . . Time of description is not a wholly reliable measure of Westernization, but one can expect that, by and large, societies described in the mid-twentieth century have been the most affected by contact with Europeans. [Sanday 1981:157–58.]

Sanday speaks in terms of "Westernization" and "contact with European culture." I think we must be careful not to place too much emphasis on the impact of the European cultural ideology of male dominance in changing the ideas about sex roles held by people in other cultures. This ideology was important, but its

primary importance lies in its impact on colonial economic policy—for example, the promotion of male farming and the distribution of land titles to men. Most of the forces that contributed
to the decline of women's position in the Third World are at-
tributable to the specific economic and social conditions that
were part of the historical experience of colonization. My intensive examination of the Nandi case shows in detail the way in
which many of the processes of colonization and commoditization that have undermined the position of women operate.

Nandi Women's World

I have been arguing that many of the changes that have taken
place in Nandi as the result of colonial policy and integration
into the cash economy have had unfavorable consequences for
the position of women relative to men, particularly in the economic dimension. I must make it clear that this is an analytical
position that I have worked out through careful consideration of
the impact of various socioeconomic changes individually and
as a group. It does not necessarily reflect the way the world
looks to Nandi women.

The women I interviewed could sometimes take note of the
kinds of changes I have been discussing on an individual basis,
but they did not attempt to put them all together and express
anything resembling the position I have taken: that women's
economic position has eroded. Some women I talked to felt that
the distribution of land titles to men was unfair, but it was difficult for them to say just why it was unfair. Saying women
should own land would be placing ownership of the means of
production in female hands, and they could not go that far. Nor
did they actually declare that women had more secure rights in
land when it was not owned by anyone. Mainly, when I pursued
the subject, they concluded that since men inherit cattle, they
are the ones who own things—therefore it is to be expected that
they will own land. Some women, particularly older ones, spoke
against young men's invasion of the vegetable-growing line.
They said it was "impolite."

In other words, although my analysis of the various Nandi
categories of property (particularly livestock) and the different

patterns of various parties' rights in them is based on the statements of informants, the informants themselves did not systematize things in this way. In fact, when Nandi women talk specifically about how the changes of the past eighty years have affected the position of women relative to men, they underestimate many of the changes I have discussed by overstating the degree to which past behavior conformed to their abstract stereotypes. In the past, they say, men owned everything and held all the power. They usually contend, when speaking in broad terms, that this is also true in the present. When one gets down to cases, women admit that in the present, male power is not absolute and unambiguous. It is, of course, sometimes possible to get beyond the sweeping generalization of absolute male power with old women, but this is not the version of things they present spontaneously, and mostly the ambiguities of the past are lost sight of and ignored. The women only rarely note how their condition as compared with men's has changed for the worse.

Nandi women are much more impressed with certain positive changes for them in the present age. First and foremost of these is improved material well-being. As one informant put it: "Compared with long ago, people today are swimming in a sea of wealth." As I have said before, compared with many areas in Kenya, Nandi is rich in land and resources. Near-universal cash cropping has converted this land wealth into money wealth. Most people in Nandi control some cash without working terribly long hours for it. This is true for women as well as men, though the amounts they control are much smaller. General affluence distracts attention from the fact that men have gained more than women. It is ironic, perhaps, to study the negative consequences of socioeconomic change in a society that has not fared so badly under changed conditions as numerous other societies have.

Further, at least two things that women view as most difficult about their former condition have changed for the better. The first is the reduction in infant mortality. Old women often talked to me, and to younger Nandi women, about how hard it was to keep on bearing children and losing many of them. I think that living in a society in which infant mortality has been low for a relatively long time, we may frequently lose sight of its tremendous impact on the lives of women in traditional societies. It does not seem surprising to me that a total context of change in which one of the changes has been that one's children can now be expected to live rather than die would be viewed positively by the majority of women.

The second important positive change that Nandi women frequently mention is the abandonment of the system of restrictions placed on women by beliefs in feminine-child pollution. Old women, who used to have to go daily to the nearest river when they were nursing a child to scrub themselves with water and cow dung, speak of the old customs as a form of extreme oppression of women. They view the cessation of this practice, and of the beatings they say they had to endure if they were thought careless, as a mark of liberation; and they praise the fact that young men are now willing to have contact with children.

The data presented in the foregoing chapters demonstrate that the economic position of Nandi women has worsened in many ways. The fact that the women themselves do not emphasize these negative changes but focus their attention elsewhere is not merely false consciousness: certain important things about their lives *have* improved, from any point of view. But the general affluence masks the basic deterioration of their economic position relative to that of men. As long as resources the women see as important are not in short supply, they do not view this deterioration with alarm. On the other hand, the expansion of population and shrinking land for each household will mean a growing scarcity of resources over time. It is already clear that poor Nandi women suffer more from the economic differential between the sexes than women in elite households (see Chapter 6). If affluence declines, will Nandi women continue to be indifferent to their eroded economic position?

An interesting parallel is found in the case of the Mundurucú of Brazil, described by Yolanda and Robert Murphy (1974). Prior to European penetration, the Mundurucú occupied a savannah environment, depending on the cultivation of bitter manioc and other garden produce, and hunting. They lived in matrilocal households of several nuclear families each. Both sexes participated in various stages of cultivation. Men hunted, often in groups. Women's most time-consuming task was the processing of bitter manioc into farinha, which was done in cooperative work groups. They controlled the distribution of both this product and meat from the animals killed by the men. The men spent most of their time in a village men's house, considered women both inferior and threatening, and had an elaborate male secret cult. The women failed to concur in the men's evaluation of them as inferior, and the Murphys were very impressed with their solidarity, autonomy, and economic power. European penetration brought rubber tapping. Everywhere, Mundurucú men spend some part of the year collecting rubber, which is sold as a source of cash, but some have moved from the savannah to river locales to be closer to sources of rubber and thus tap it year-round. In the riverine communities, men spend more time collecting rubber, a solitary task, or fishing. When they hunt, it is often alone, with rifles. Further, the Catholic mission preaches against men's houses and in favor of the nuclear family, which has largely replaced matrilocal households in riverine communities. This breaks down the sexual division of labor. With no other women available to help a wife form a household manioc-processing work group, she depends on her husband to participate. Fathers also care for children when their wives are busy. The change that the Murphys view as fundamental, however, is that the riverine Mundurucú have come to depend very heavily on cash gained from the rubber trade, which is thoroughly controlled by men. Wives depend on their husbands to buy them things. Moreover, "the attenuation of cooperative work patterns has radically diminished the cohesion of the women, and it has also undercut the leadership of the senior women of households. Men have emerged as clear heads of the dwellings, and on the Cururú it is rare to hear a person refer to a house as being that of a woman" (Murphy & Murphy 1974:200).

In many ways, Mundurucú women's position has declined, but they prefer life in the nuclear families of the riverine settlements. They like having their husbands present to help with child care and share their most burdensome task. They are glad to be rid of the men's house and its "ritual and mythic apparatus of male dominance" (Murphy & Murphy 1974:199). And they enjoy the material goods they gain through the rubber trade. The Murphys conclude, however: "When the men discover the implications of their control over property and the commerce in rubber, the women may well discover that they have traded the symbolic domination of men, as a group, over the women, as a group, for the very real domination of husbands over wives" (Murphy & Murphy 1974:212). If these words are prophetic for the Mundurucú, I think they may be equally so for the Nandi.

In summary, this study demonstrates that though Nandi society has probably always been economically stratified on the basis of sex, changes stemming from colonial policy, entry into the cash economy, and commoditization of virtually all resources have widened the gap between men and women.

In spite of this clear economic stratification on the basis of sex, however, Nandi women's property rights are not inconsiderable, nor are women powerless in other aspects of life. An important aim of this study has been to describe and analyze the complex network of rights held by various parties in the family estate. When such information is considered, it becomes clear that it is a gross oversimplification to talk about male "ownership" of any part of the family estate—even cattle, the form of property that is most consistently identified with men. Wives have rights in definite categories of cattle that husbands do not even attempt to breach. Wives also have rights in family land, which they actively defend if they are threatened. Some categories of women, such as widows, are extremely economically autonomous.

One view of East African patrilineal societies is that they are societies in which women are particularly oppressed. Schneider (1974:274) says that "in the vast majority of cases in East Africa women are in important respects the instruments of men." More recently, he has referred to East African wives as "chattels" of their husbands (1979:116), and has written "it is clear from my discussion of these societies that women are extremely servile to men" (Schneider 1979:255).

I agree with Schneider that most East African patrilineal societies are marked by male dominance in that men hold the edge over women in the system of sexual stratification. However, an image of such societies as simple, absolute, and unambiguous patriarchies is distorted.

This study demonstrates that Nandi women, though less powerful than men, are not powerless. A good marriage in Nandi is an active give and take between husband and wife. In a bad marriage, a wife has strategies by which she can have her grievances aired before the community. Women have a high level of autonomy in their day-to-day lives. Older women, especially widows, may be extremely assertive in their dealings with men. It is probably common cross-culturally that what appears superficially to be relatively total male dominance is revealed upon further analysis to be rather a (perhaps unequal) balance of power between the sexes.

In Nandi, much of the weight on the female side of the scale is the result of women's very definite rights in property. The traditional system had built into it both security in the form of house property, and institutions that allowed women significant access to and control of economic resources. In Nandi, as elsewhere, new socioeconomic conditions have undermined women's rights in and access to property in many ways. This process is tipping the sexual balance of power still further toward the side of the men.

Reference Matter

Nandi Kin Terms

Korge or *mama* (high tone). Term of address for mother. The term of reference is *kamet*. Also used for MZ, FW, and FBW.

Aba or *baba*. Term of address for father. The term of reference is *kwanit*. Includes FB, MZH, and FFBS.

Mama (low tone) (Reference = *imamet*). This term is distinguished from that for "mother" by tonality. Its primary referent is "mother's brother," but it is also used for the following kin-types: MBS, MFBS, or MMZS, and to some extent MBW, MBD, MFBD, and MMZD. It is also used reciprocally by mother's brother, etc., to address sister's child, etc.

Senge. Father's sister. The term of reference is *senget*.

Kogo. MM, FM, MMZ, FMZ, MFZ, FFZ, and in general any female relative of the grandparental generation. Used reciprocally for child's child of either sex and any relative of the grandchild's generation. The term of reference is *ingoget*.

Agui. The term of reference, *inguget*, is derived from *kugo*, which means "great-grandfather/ancestor." *Agui* includes MF, FF, MFB, FFB, MMB, FMB, or any male relative of the same generation. Like *kogo*, it is used reciprocally for the grandchild generation.

Tupchet. This is a term of reference. Siblings when addressing each other normally use personal names. Includes B, Z, FBS, FBD, MZS, MZD.

Lakwet. Means "child." (*Lakwani* = "this child," direct address; *lakwen-nyu* = "my child.") Used for one's own children of both sexes, a man's brother's children, a woman's sister's children, and by extension the children of other relatives referred to as *tupchet*. Sometimes extended by a man to his sister's children and by a woman to her brother's children.

Kwonda. Term of reference for wife. There is no particular term of direct address in general use. A man may address his wife as *chebiosoni*, "this woman."

Boiyot. This is a term of extremely broad application. It is derived from the verb *bou*, to rule or control, and means effectively "ruler," though "elder" may be a better gloss. English speakers usually translate it as "old man." It can be used for any elder, father, or father-in-law (woman speaking), but a woman may also refer to her husband as *boiyonnyu*, "my elder," or address him as *boiyondonni*, "this elder."

Siyet. Term of reference for co-wife. Co-wives would ordinarily address each other as "Mother of So-and-so," using a child's personal name.

Sandana. A broad term used by a woman's family for the husband of their daughter/sister. *Kapsandana* (*sandana's* family), *saan*, and *kapsaan* are broad terms used for all members of a family into which a girl of one's own family has married. The term of reference, *sandet*, also means "boy friend" in popular parlance.

Kapyugoi. A broad term used by a man in referring to the family of his wife. The only specific term subsumed by it is *karucho*—wife's mother.

Bamuru. Woman speaking: HB, ZH. Man speaking: BW, WZ. The term of reference is *bamurto*.

Kamati. Used only by women. HZ, BW. The term of reference is *kamatet*.

Bamwai. A reciprocal term used between people whose children are married, i.e., the respective parents of a pair of spouses. It is also used by other kinds of affines who do not call each other by any particular term (e.g., for the father- or mother-in-law of one's brother, though a man might use *kapyugoi* for these people). It may also be used between the families of children who have been initiated together. Its etymological derivation is for the word *mwaita* (oil), and thus in its broadest sense it means "people who have together undergone a ceremony involving anointing with oil." The term of reference is *bamwait*.

Lemenyi. A reciprocal term used between men married to sisters. WZH.

References Cited

Bacdayan, Albert S. 1977. "Mechanistic Cooperation and Sexual Equality among the Western Bontoc." In Alice Schlegel, ed., *Sexual Stratification*. New York: Columbia University Press.

Barker, R. G., and H. F. Wright. 1955. *Midwest and Its Children: The Psychological Ecology of an American Town*. New York: Harper & Row.

Begler, Elsie. 1978. "Sex, Status, and Authority in Egalitarian Society." *American Anthropologist* 80:571–88.

Bell, Diane. 1980. "Desert Politics: Choices in the 'Marriage Market.'" In Mona Etienne and Eleanor Burke Leacock, eds., *Women and Colonization: Anthropological Perspectives*. New York: Praeger.

Bennett, George. 1965. "Settlers and Politics in Kenya up to 1945." In Vincent T. Harlow and E. M. Chilver, eds., *History of East Africa, Vol. II*. Oxford: Clarendon Press.

Boserup, Esther. 1970. *Women's Role in Economic Development*. New York: St. Martin's Press.

Brett, E. A. 1973. *Colonialism and Underdevelopment in East Africa: The Politics of Economic Change, 1919–1939*. London: Heinemann.

Brown, L. H. 1968. *Agricultural Change in Kenya, 1945–1960*. Studies in Tropical Development: Food Research Institute, Stanford University.

Buchler, Ira R., and Henry A. Selby. 1968. *Kinship and Social Organization: An Introduction to Theory and Method*. New York: Macmillan.

Buenaventura-Posso, Elisa, and Susan E. Brown. 1980. "Forced Transition from Egalitarianism to Male Dominance: The Bari of Colombia." In Mona Etienne and Eleanor Burke Leacock, eds., *Women and Colonization: Anthropological Perspectives*. New York: Praeger.

Chiñas, Beverly. 1973. *The Isthmus Zapotecs: Women's Roles in Cultural Context*. New York: Holt, Rinehart & Winston.

Conant, Francis P. 1974. Comment on Harold K. Schneider, "Economic Development and Economic Change: The Case of East African Cattle." *Current Anthropology* 15:259–76.

Daniels, Robert E. 1982. "The Extent of Age-Set Coordination among the Kalenjin." Paper presented at the annual meeting of the African Studies Association, Washington, D.C.

Dolhinow, Phyllis Jay. 1972. "Primate Patterns." In Phyllis Jay Dolhinow, ed., *Primate Patterns.* New York: Holt, Rinehart & Winston.

Ehret, Christopher. 1968. "Cushites and Highland Nilotes." In Bethwell A. Ogot and J. A. Kieran, eds., *Zamani: A Survey of East African History.* Nairobi: East African Publishing House.

———. 1971. *Southern Nilotic History: Linguistic Approaches to the Study of the Past.* Evanston, Ill.: Northwestern University Press.

Elam, Yitzchak. 1973. *The Social and Sexual Roles of Hima Women.* Manchester: Manchester University Press.

Ellis, Diana. 1976. "The Nandi Protest of 1923 in the Context of African Resistance to Colonial Rule in Kenya." *Journal of African History* 17:555–75.

Ember, Carol R. 1973. "Feminine Task Assignment and the Social Behavior of Boys." *Ethos* 1:424–39.

Etienne, Mona, and Eleanor Burke Leacock, eds. 1980. *Women and Colonization: Anthropological Perspectives.* New York: Praeger.

Fried, Morton H. 1967. *The Evolution of Political Society: An Essay in Political Anthropology.* New York: Random House.

Garretson, Lucy. 1972. "The Nature of the American Woman: A Cultural Account." Ph.D. dissertation, University of Texas.

Gluckman, Max. 1950. "Kinship and Marriage among the Lozi of Northern Rhodesia and the Zulu of Natal." In A. R. Radcliffe Brown and D. Forde, eds., *African Systems of Kinship and Marriage.* London: Oxford University Press, for the International African Institute.

Gold, Alice. 1977. "Cultivation vs. Herding in Southern Nandi, ca. 1840–1914." Staff seminar paper, Department of History, University of Nairobi.

———. 1978. "Women in Agricultural Change: The Nandi (Kenya) in the Nineteenth Century." Paper presented at the annual meeting of the African Studies Association, Baltimore.

Goldberg, Susan, and Michael Lewis. 1969. "Play Behavior in the Year-Old Infant: Early Sex Differences." *Child Development* 40:21–31.

Goldschmidt, Walter. 1976. *The Culture and Behavior of the Sebei.* Berkeley: University of California Press.

Goody, Jack. 1976. *Production and Reproduction: A Comparative Study of the Domestic Domain.* Cambridge: Cambridge University Press.

———, ed. 1958. *The Developmental Cycle of Domestic Groups.* Cambridge: Cambridge University Press.

Gough, Kathleen. 1975. "The Origin of the Family." In Rayna R. Reiter, ed., *Toward an Anthropology of Women.* New York: Monthly Review Press. (Originally published 1971.)

Gray, Robert F., and Philip H. Gulliver, eds. 1964. *The Family Estate in Africa*. Boston: Boston University Press.

Greenberg, Joseph H. 1963. *The Languages of Africa*. The Hague: Mouton, for Indiana University Press.

Greenstein, Lewis J. 1975. "Africans in a European War: The First World War in East Africa, with Special Reference to the Nandi of Kenya." Ph.D. dissertation, Indiana University.

Gulliver, Philip H. 1955. *The Family Herds*. London: Routledge & Kegan Paul.

Guyer, Jane. 1978. "Women's Work in the Food Economy of the Cocoa Belt: A Comparison." Working Paper no. 7, African Studies Center, Boston University.

——. 1980. "Food, Cocoa, and the Division of Labor by Sex in Two West African Societies." *Comparative Studies in Society and History* 22:355–73.

Hafkin, Nancy J., and Edna G. Bay, eds. 1976. *Women in Africa: Studies in Social and Economic Change*. Stanford: Stanford University Press.

Hay, Margaret Jean. 1976. "Luo Women and Economic Change during the Colonial Period." In Nancy J. Hafkin and Edna G. Bay, eds., *Women in Africa: Studies in Social and Economic Change*. Stanford: Stanford University Press.

Heyer, J. 1974. "A Survey of Agricultural Development in the Small Farm Areas of Kenya since the 1920's." Working Paper no. 194, Institute for Development Studies, University of Nairobi.

Hollis, A. C. 1909. *The Nandi: Their Language and Folk-lore*. Oxford: Clarendon Press.

Huntingford, G. W. B. 1950. *Nandi Work and Culture*. London: H.M.S.O. for the Colonial Office.

——. 1953a. *The Nandi of Kenya: Tribal Control in a Pastoral Society*. London: Routledge & Kegan Paul.

——. 1953b. *The Southern Nilo-Hamites*. London: International African Institute.

Institute for Development Studies. 1975. "Second Overall Evaluation of the Special Rural Development Programme." Occasional Paper no. 12, Institute for Development Studies, University of Nairobi.

Jacobs, Alan H. 1965. "The Traditional Political Organization of the Pastoral Maasai." D.Phil. thesis, Oxford University.

Johnson, Allen. 1975. "The Allocation of Time in a Machiguenga Community." *Ethnology* 14:301–10.

Kenya, Republic of. 1969. *Kenya Population Census, Vol. III*. Nairobi: Statistics Division, Ministry of Finance and Economic Planning.

——. 1980. *Kenya Statistical Abstract*. Nairobi: Government Printer.

Kenya National Archives. 1930–58. District Commissioner for Nandi, Annual Reports. (File DC/NDI/1/4.)

———. 1934a. Acting Provincial Commissioner's Report to the Director of Agriculture. (File PC/RVP/6A/11/28/3.)

———. 1934b. District Commissioner's Report: Nandi Reserve Development Programme. (File PC/RVP/6A/11/28/1.)

———. 1934–49. Nandi Local Native Council Minutes. (File PC/RVP/6A/11D/2.)

———. 1934–57. General Documents. (File PC/RVP/6A/11/28.)

———. 1942. District Commissioner for Nandi, Report to the Information Officer on the Governor's Visit to Kapsabet. (File PC/RVP/6A/1/11D/2.)

———. 1944–50. Documents—Education. (File PC/RVP/6A/12/3.)

———. 1950. District Commissioner for Nandi, Confidential Report, January 13. (File DC/NDI/10/5.)

———. 1955. District Commissioner for Uasin Gishu, Confidential Report, September 19. (File DC/NDI/10/2/9.)

———. 1958. District Commissioner for Nandi, Confidential Handing-Over Notes. (File DC/NDI/2/2.)

Kettel, Bonnie Lee. 1980. "Time Is Money: The Social Consequences of Economic Change in Seretunin, Kenya." Ph.D. dissertation, University of Illinois.

———. 1981. "Gender and Class in Tugen-Kalenjin Social Organization." Paper presented at the annual meeting of the African Studies Association, Bloomington.

Kipkorir, B. E., with F. B. Welbourn. 1973. *The Marakwet of Kenya: A Preliminary Study*. Nairobi: East African Literature Bureau.

Klima, George. 1970. *The Barabaig: East African Cattle Herders*. New York: Holt, Rinehart & Winston.

Lamphere, Louise. 1977. "Review Essay: Anthropology." *Signs* 2: 612–27.

Langley, Myrtle. 1979. *The Nandi of Kenya: Life Crisis Rituals in a Period of Change*. New York: St. Martin's Press.

Leacock, Eleanor Burke. 1978. "Women's Status in Egalitarian Society: Implications for Social Evolution." *Current Anthropology* 19:247–75.

Legesse, Asmarom. 1975. *Gada: Three Approaches to the Study of African Society*. New York: Free Press.

LeVine, Robert A. 1966. "Sex Roles and Economic Change in Africa." *Ethnology* 5:186–93.

Leys, Colin. 1974. *Underdevelopment in Kenya: The Political Economy of Neo-Colonialism, 1964–1971*. London: Heinemann.

Llewelyn-Davies, Melissa. 1978. "Two Contexts of Solidarity among Pastoral Maasai Women." In Patricia Caplan and Janet M. Bujra, eds., *Women United, Women Divided: Comparative Studies of Ten Contemporary Cultures*. Bloomington and London: Indiana University Press and Tavistock.

Maccoby, Eleanor Emmons, and Carol Nagy Jacklin. 1974. *The Psychology of Sex Differences*. Stanford: Stanford University Press.

McElroy, Ann, and Carolyn Mathiasson, eds. 1979. *Sex Roles in Changing Cultures*. Occasional Papers in Anthropology, no. 1: Department of Anthropology, State University of New York at Buffalo.

Magut, P. K. 1969. "The Rise and Fall of the Nandi Orkoiyot, c. 1850–1957." In B. G. McIntosh, ed., *Ngano: Studies in Traditional and Modern East African History*. Nairobi Historical Studies, no. 1: East African Publishing House.

Manners, Robert A. 1967. "The Kipsigis of Kenya: Culture Change in a 'Model' East African Tribe." In Julian H. Steward, ed., *Three African Tribes in Transition*. Urbana: University of Illinois Press.

Marsh, Zoe, and G. W. Kingsnorth. 1972. *A History of East Africa: An Introductory Survey*. Cambridge: Cambridge University Press.

Matson, A. T. 1972. *Nandi Resistance to British Rule, 1890–1906*. Nairobi: East African Publishing House.

Meggitt, Mervyn. 1962. *Desert People*. Chicago: University of Chicago Press.

Meillassoux, Claude. 1975. *Maidens, Meal, and Money: Capitalism and the Domestic Community*. Cambridge: Cambridge University Press.

Middleton, John. 1965. "Kenya: Changes in African Life, 1912–1945." In Vincent T. Harlow and E. M. Chilver, eds., *History of East Africa, Vol. II*. Oxford: Clarendon Press.

Miracle, Marvin P. 1966. *Maize in Tropical Africa*. Madison: University of Wisconsin Press.

Mungeam, G. H. 1966. *British Rule in Kenya, 1895–1912*. Oxford: Clarendon Press.

Murphy, Yolanda, and Robert F. Murphy. 1974. *Women of the Forest*. New York: Columbia University Press.

Ng'eny, Samuel K. 1970. "Nandi Resistance to the Establishment of British Administration, 1883–1906." In Bethwell A. Ogot, ed., *Hadith 2: Proceedings of the 1968 Conference of the Historical Association of Kenya*. Nairobi: East African Publishing House.

Obbo, Christine. 1976. "Dominant Male Ideology and Female Options: Three East African Case Studies." *Africa* 46:371–84.

Oboler, Regina Smith. 1977a. "Work and Leisure in Modern Nandi: Preliminary Results of a Study of Time Allocation." Working Paper no. 324, Institute for Development Studies, University of Nairobi.

———. 1977b. "The Economic Rights of Nandi Women." Working Paper no. 328, Institute for Development Studies, University of Nairobi.

————. 1980. "Is the Female Husband a Man?: Woman/Woman Marriage among the Nandi of Kenya." *Ethnology* 19:69–88.

————. 1982. "Women, Men, Property, and Change in Nandi District, Kenya." Ph.D. dissertation, Temple University.

Okigbo, Pius. 1965. "Social Consequences of Economic Development in West Africa." In Pierre Van Den Berghe, ed., *Africa: Social Problems of Change and Conflict*. San Francisco: Chandler.

Okonjo, Kamene. 1976. "The Dual-Sex Political System in Operation: Igbo Women and Community Politics in Midwestern Nigeria." In Nancy J. Hafkin and Edna G. Bay, eds., *Women in Africa: Studies in Social and Economic Change*. Stanford: Stanford University Press.

Ominde, Simeon. 1975. *The Population of Kenya, Tanzania, and Uganda*. Nairobi: Heinemann.

Ortner, Sherry B. 1974. "Is Female to Male as Nature Is to Culture?" In Michelle Zimbalist Rosaldo and Louise Lamphere, eds., *Woman, Culture, and Society*. Stanford: Stanford University Press.

Ottenberg, Phoebe V. 1959. "The Changing Economic Position of Women among the Afikpo Ibo." In William R. Bascom and Melville J. Herskovits, eds., *Continuity and Change in African Cultures*. Chicago: University of Chicago Press.

Pala (Okeyo), Achola. 1975a. "The Role of African Women in Rural Development: Research Priorities." Discussion Paper no. 203, Institute for Development Studies, University of Nairobi.

————. 1975b. "A Preliminary Survey of the Avenues for and Constraints on Women in the Development Process in Kenya." Discussion Paper no. 218, Institute for Development Studies, University of Nairobi.

————. 1976. "Definitions of Women and Development: An African Perspective." In Wellesley Editorial Committee, *Women and National Development: The Complexities of Change*. Chicago: University of Chicago Press.

————. 1980. "Daughters of the Lakes and Rivers: Colonization and the Land Rights of Luo Women." In Mona Etienne and Eleanor Burke Leacock, eds., *Women and Colonization: Anthropological Perspectives*. New York: Praeger.

Peristiany, J. G. 1939. *The Social Institutions of the Kipsigis*. London: Routledge & Kegan Paul.

Poewe, Karla. 1980. "Universal Male Dominance: An Ethnological Illusion." *Dialectical Anthropology* 5:111–25.

Potash, Betty. 1978. "Marital Stability in a Rural Luo Community." *Africa* 48:380–96.

Rigby, Peter. 1980. "Pastoralist Production and Socialist Transformation in Tanzania." In A. O. Anacleti, ed., *Jipemoyo—Development and Culture Research*, vol. 2. Uppsala: Tanzania Department of Research and Planning, Academy of Finland Research Council for the Humanities, and the Scandanavian Institute of African Studies.

Rogers, Susan Carol. 1978. "Woman's Place: A Critical Review of Anthropological Theory." *Comparative Studies in Society and History* 20: 123–62.

Romalis, Shelly. 1979. "Sexual Politics and Technological Change in Colonial Africa." In Ann McElroy and Carolyn Mathiasson, eds., *Sex Roles in Changing Cultures*. Occasional Papers in Anthropology, no. 1: Department of Anthropology, State University of New York at Buffalo.

Rosaldo, Michelle Zimbalist. 1974. "Woman, Culture, and Society: A Theoretical Overview." In Michelle Zimbalist Rosaldo and Louise Lamphere, eds., *Woman, Culture, and Society*. Stanford: Stanford University Press.

Sacks, Karen. 1976. "State Bias and Women's Status." *American Anthropologist* 78:565–69.

Samarakkody, Amara. 1979. "The Impact of European Laws on the Status of Women in Sri Lanka." In Ann McElroy and Carolyn Matthiason, eds., *Sex Roles in Changing Cultures*. Occasional Papers in Anthropology, no. 1: Department of Anthropology, State University of New York at Buffalo.

Sanday, Peggy Reeves. 1974. "Female Status in the Public Domain." In Michelle Zimbalist Rosaldo and Louise Lamphere, eds., *Woman, Culture, and Society*. Stanford: Stanford University Press.

———. 1981. *Female Power and Male Dominance: On the Origins of Sexual Inequality*. Cambridge: Cambridge University Press.

Sanderson, P. 1955. *Primary School Atlas for Nandi and the Rift Valley Province*. Nairobi: Eagle Press.

Schlegel, Alice, ed. 1977. *Sexual Stratification*. New York: Columbia University Press.

Schneider, Harold K. 1957. "The Subsistence Role of Cattle among the Pokot and in East Africa." *American Anthropologist* 59:278–300.

———. 1974. "Economic Development and Economic Change: The Case of East African Cattle." *Current Anthropology* 15:259–76.

———. 1979. *Livestock and Equality in East Africa: The Economic Basis for Social Structure*. Bloomington: Indiana University Press.

Sexton, Lorraine Dusak. 1980. "From Pigs and Pearlshells to Coffee and Cash: Socioeconomic Change and Sex Roles in the Daulo Region, Papua New Guinea." Ph.D. dissertation, Temple University.

Singer, Alice. 1973. "Marriage Payments and the Exchange of People." *Man* n.s. 8:80–92.

Smock, Audrey. 1977. "Women's Education and Roles in Kenya." Working Paper no. 316, Institute for Development Studies, University of Nairobi.

Snell, G. S. 1954. *Nandi Customary Law*. London: Macmillan.

Staudt, Kathleen. 1975. "The Effects of Government Agricultural Policy on Women Farmers: Preliminary Findings from Idakho Location, Kakamega District." Working Paper no. 225, Institute for Development Studies, University of Nairobi.

———. 1978. "Agricultural Productivity Gaps: A Case Study in Male Preference in Government Policy Implementation." *Development and Change* 9:398–414.

Stephens, William N. 1963. *The Family in Cross-Cultural Perspective*. New York: Holt, Rinehart & Winston.

Sutton, J. E. G. 1968. "The Settlement of East Africa." In Bethwell A. Ogot and J. A. Kieran, eds., *Zamani: A Survey of East African History*. Nairobi: East African Publishing House.

———. 1970. "Some Reflections on the Early History of Western Kenya." In Bethwell A. Ogot, ed., *Hadith 2: Proceedings of the 1968 Conference of the Historical Association of Kenya*. Nairobi: East African Publishing House.

Thompson, Warren S., and David T. Lewis. 1965. *Population Problems*. New York: McGraw-Hill.

Van Allen, Judith. 1972. "'Sitting on a Man': Colonialism and the Lost Political Institutions of Igbo Women." *Canadian Journal of African Studies* 6:165–81.

———. 1976. "'Aba Riots' or Igbo 'Women's War'?: Ideology, Stratification, and the Invisibility of Women." In Nancy J. Hafkin and Edna G. Bay, eds., *Women in Africa: Studies in Social and Economic Change*. Stanford: Stanford University Press.

Van Baal, J. 1971. "The Part of Women in the Marriage Trade: Objects or Behaving as Objects?" *Bijdragen tot de Taal-, Land-, en Volkenkunde* 126: 289–308.

Van Zwannenberg, R. M. A., with Anne King. 1975. *An Economic History of Kenya and Uganda, 1800–1970*. Atlantic Highlands, N.J.: Humanities Press.

Walter, B. J. 1970. "The Territorial Expansion of the Nandi of Kenya, 1500–1905." Papers in International Studies, African Series no. 9, Athens, Ohio.

Weber, Max. 1947. *The Theory of Social and Economic Organization* (English translation of *Wirtschaft und Gesellschaft*, Part I, originally published ca. 1920.) Ed. Talcott Parsons, trans. A. M. Henderson and Talcott Parsons. New York: Oxford University Press.

Weisner, Thomas S., and Ronald Gallimore. 1977. "My Brother's Keeper: Child and Sibling Caretaking." *Current Anthropology* 18:169–90.

Whyte, Martin King. 1978. *The Status of Women in Preindustrial Societies*. Princeton: Princeton University Press.

Winans, Edgar V. 1972. "Migration and the Structure of Participation: An Investigation of the Effects of Migration on Small Farms and the Role of Women." Provisional draft prepared for the ILO mission to Kenya, April 1972.

Wrigley, C. C. 1965. "Kenya: The Patterns of Economic Life." In Vincent T. Harlow and E. M. Chilver, eds., *History of East Africa, Vol. II*. Oxford: Clarendon Press.

Index

Library of Congress Cataloging in Publication Data

Oboler, Regina Smith, 1947–
    Women, power, and economic change.

    Bibliography: p.
    Includes index.
    1. Nandi (African people)—Economic conditions.
2. Sex role—Kenya.   I. Title.
DT433.545.N34026   1985   305.4'8893   83-45345
ISBN 0-8047-1224-7